Focus
on
the
Learner

Focus on the Learner:
Pragmatic Perspectives
for the Language Teacher

Edited by:

JOHN W. OLLER, JR.

University of New Mexico

JACK C. RICHARDS

Regional English Language Center, Singapore

NEWBURY HOUSE PUBLISHERS, INC.

NEWBURY HOUSE PUBLISHERS, Inc.

Language Science
Language Teaching
Language Learning

ROWLEY, MASSACHUSETTS 01969

ISBN: 912066-67-9

First printing: September 1973
Second printing: October 1975
Third printing: October 1976
Fourth printing: March 1977
Fifth printing: June 1978

Printed in the U.S.A.   10   9   8   7   6   5

ABOUT THIS BOOK

This book of readings has been prepared primarily for language teachers. It should also be useful for linguists, psycholinguists, sociolinguists, and other theoreticians who are inclined toward practical theories of language and learning. The articles are mostly self-contained and do not generally presuppose prior background reading of a technical sort.

The focus is on language learners—their capacities, attitudes, learning strategies, and, of course, what it is that they learn. All of these considerations are of paramount importance to language teaching. We have aimed for maximum coherence among the papers included, in spite of the fact that they come from a wide variety of sources and deal with a great diversity of topics. We believe that an important thread of commonality can be characterized under the rubric of pragmatics. Throughout the book—from content-level linguistic coding operations, and the debate about the applicability of various linguistic theories that have been proposed to explain them, to relationship-level attitudinal factors which have recently come into the spotlight—the pragmatic theme appears and reappears.

As in all books of this kind, there is considerable diversity of viewpoint. In many cases, however, the various authors do converge on topics, and occasionally they agree on conclusions. Wherever possible we have attempted to cross-reference these meeting points in order to evaluate instances of agreement and disagreement. The cross-references occur in the Discussion Questions at the end of each Part of the book, and the reader may wish to look through these questions before reading the separate articles to which they refer. We believe that the reader will benefit most by taking the articles in each section in the order in which they appear. The Discussion Questions are ordered on this basis. The questions are not intended to be exhaustive of possible topics by any means. However, it is hoped that they will serve to stimulate fruitful exchanges of ideas. No doubt the instructor will want to delete some and, hopefully, will add others of his own.

Part I is devoted to some theoretical issues concerning theories of language and language learning and their relevance to language teaching. A variety of viewpoints, including significant controversies, are presented. Part II deals somewhat more specifically with language learning processes. Especially it explores relationships between theories and data from studies of first and second language learning. In Part III, attention is centered on the unique problems of the second language learner. Theories of second language learning are discussed. Part IV takes up some of the psycholinguistic and sociolinguistic considerations relevant to language testing. Significant contrasts between approaches based on different theoretical assumptions are illustrated. Part V enters the all-important but little-understood domain of sociocultural and motivational factors, and Part VI concludes with a discussion of some possible alternatives to formal language classes.

It is hoped that this book will stimulate teachers and researchers alike, not only to a greater awareness of theories and research in second language learning, but also to a greater appreciation of the fact that the ordinary classroom teacher is daily performing experimental research in second language learning. We will be gratified if, even in a small way, the book lessens credulity concerning theories of language and learning, and if it increases interest in theoretical issues which can and will have a practical impact on classroom teaching.

John W. Oller, Jr.
University of New Mexico

Jack C. Richards
Regional English Language Center, Singapore

ACKNOWLEDGEMENTS AND COPYRIGHTS

The editors are grateful to the co-authors of this volume—the many contributors who agreed to let us reprint material or who provided us with previously unpublished material. We are especially indebted to Graeme D. Kennedy and H. H. Stern who wrote papers particularly for this volume. Similar thanks are due to contributors who offered previously unpublished material—John Macnamara, Bernard Spolsky, and Eugène J. Brière.

We also wish to express our gratitude to the various publishers of the journals and volumes listed below for their permission to reprint the articles indicated (they are listed here in the order in which they appear in the text). Lois Oller, Judy Benedetti, and Joan Ruiz helped with the typing of some of the manuscripts and other materials. Our special thanks to them.

Mackey, W. F. "Language Didactics and Applied Linguistics." *Uuoskidirja 4: Suomen Uusien Kielten Opettajien Liitto.* Revised version appeared in *English Language Teaching*, 20 (1966), 197-206.

Stern, H. H. "Psycholinguistics and Second Language Teaching." *Perspectives on Second Language Teaching*. H. H. Stern (ed.). Toronto: Ontario Institute for Studies in Education, 1971. Pp. 47-56.

Chomsky, Noam. "Linguistic Theory." *Northeast Conference on the Teaching of Foreign Languages.* R. G. Mead (ed.). Menasha, Wis.: George Banta, 1966. Pp. 43-49.

Oller, J. W., Jr. "Some Psycholinguistic Controversies." Prepared for this volume.

Macnamara, J. "The Cognitive Strategies of Language Learning." Paper presented at the Conference on Child Language sponsored by the International Association of Applied Linguistics and its Commission on Child Language (Stockholm), Center for Applied Linguistics (Washington D. C.), and American Council on the Teaching of Foreign Languages (New York), held in Chicago, November, 1971. (Also submitted to *IRAL*.)

Kennedy, G. D. "Conditions for Language Learning." Prepared for this volume.

Hocking, B. D. W. "Types of Interference." *Language and Education in Eastern Africa.* T. Gorman (ed.). Nairobi: Oxford University Press, 1969.

Richards, J. C. "A Noncontrastive Approach to Error Analysis." Paper presented at the TESOL Convention in San Francisco, March, 1970. Appeared in *English Language Teaching*, 25 (1971), 204-19.

———. "Error Analysis and Second Language Strategies." Revised version of a paper which appeared in *Language Sciences*, 17 (1971), 12-22.

Ravem, R. "Language Acquisition in a Second Language Environment." *International Review of Applied Linguistics*, 6 (1968), 175-85.

George, H. V. "Two Practical Experiments with Teachers-in-Training, and Some Conclusions." *Bulletin of the Central Institute of English*, (Hyderabad, India), 3 (1963), 20-30.

Spolsky, B. "What Does It Mean to Know a Language, or How Do You Get Someone to Perform His Competence?" Paper presented at the Second Conference on Problems in Foreign Language Testing, held at the University of Southern California, November, 1968.

Upshur, J. A. "Productive Communication Testing: Progress Report." Paper presented at the Second International Congress of Applied Linguistics, Cambridge, England, September, 1969. *Applications of Linguistics*. G. Perren and J. L. M. Trim (eds.). Cambridge, England: Cambridge University Press, 1971. Pp. 435-42.

Oller, J. W., Jr. "Discrete-Point Tests Versus Tests of Integrative Skills." Prepared for this volume.

Upshur, J. A. "Context for Language Testing." *English Language Testing: Report of the RELC Fifth Regional Seminar.* Bangkok: in press.

Brière, E. J. "Cross-Cultural Biases in Language Testing." Paper presented at the Third International Congress of Applied Linguistics, Copenhagen, August, 1972.

Gardner, R. C. "Attitudes and Motivation: Their Role in Second Language Acquisition." *TESOL Quarterly*, 2 (1968), 141-50.

Tucker, G. R., and W. E. Lambert. "Sociocultural Aspects of Language Study." A modified version appeared in *Northeast Conference on the Teaching of Foreign Languages.* Menasha, Wis.: George Banta, 1972.

O'Doherty, E. F. "Social Factors and Second Language Policies." *Languages and the Young School Child*. H. H. Stern (ed.). London: Oxford University and Hamburg: UNESCO Institute for Education, 1969. Pp. 47-55.

Spolsky, B. "The Limits of Language Education." *Linguistic Reporter*, 13 (1971), 1-5. Also published in *The Language Education of Minority Children*. B. Spolsky (ed.). Rowley, Massachusetts: Newbury House Publishers, 1972. Pp. 193-200.

Stern, H. H. "Bilingual Schooling and Second Language Teaching: A Review of Recent North American Experience." Prepared for this volume.

Dykstra, G., and S. S. Nunes. "The Language Skills Program of the English Project." *Educational Perspectives*, 9 (1970), Pp. 31-36.

Hale, T. M., and E. C. Budar. "Are TESOL Classes the Only Answer?" *Modern Language Journal*, 54 (1970), 487-92.

LIST OF CONTRIBUTORS

WILLIAM F. MACKEY
Laval University, Quebec

H. H. STERN
Modern Language Center
Ontario Institute for Studies of Education
Toronto

NOAM CHOMSKY
Massachusetts Institute of Technology
Cambridge, Massachusetts

JOHN W. OLLER, JR.
University of New Mexico
Albuquerque

JOHN MACNAMARA
McGill University
Montreal

GRAEME D. KENNEDY
Victoria University, Wellington

B. D. W. HOCKING
Linguistic Advisor
Eastern Africa

JACK C. RICHARDS
Regional English Language Center
Singapore

ROAR RAVEM
University College for Teachers
Norway

LIST OF CONTRIBUTORS (continued)

BERNARD SPOLSKY
University of New Mexico
Albuquerque

JOHN A. UPSHUR
University of Michigan
Ann Arbor

EUGÈNE J. BRIÈRE
University of Southern California
Los Angeles

R. C. GARDNER
University of Western Ontario
London (Canada)

G. RICHARD TUCKER
McGill University
Montreal

WALLACE E. LAMBERT
McGill University
Montreal

E. F. O'DOHERTY
St. Patrick's College
Dublin

GERALD DYKSTRA and SHIHO S. NUNES
University of Hawaii
Honolulu

THOMAS M. HALE and EVA C. BUDAR
State of Hawaii Department of Education
Honolulu

CONTENTS

PART I

THE RELEVANCE OF LINGUISTICS AND PSYCHOLOGY TO LANGUAGE TEACHING

INTRODUCTION

The four papers in this section introduce the central focus of the entire volume: how does the second language learner acquire a target language, and how can this process be facilitated by teaching? Second language teaching has often been viewed from rather narrow perspectives. Sometimes it has been seen as little more than an application of the findings of theoretical linguistics and psychology. The first paper in this section, by Mackey, suggests that this view is inappropriate. He argues that language teaching may use ideas from linguistics and psychology, but that it should be regarded as a discipline in itself. Mackey's paper, and the one which follows it, by Stern, provide useful information concerning the history of psychological and linguistic theories in relation to second language teaching. Since Mackey speaks primarily as a *linguist* and language teacher, while Stern discusses some of the same issues from the viewpoint of a *psychologist* and language teacher, the two papers complement each other. Stern's paper also provides some useful background information for Chomsky's address to the Northeast Conference on the Teaching of Foreign Languages.

No doubt Chomsky's paper was one of the most shocking ever presented to an audience in the language teaching profession. The shock comes from its thesis that many of the widely accepted principles of psychology and linguistics are themselves questionable and of dubious importance for language teaching. It is hoped that the papers assembled in this volume will confirm Chomsky's skepticism about the utility of directly applying to language teaching linguistic or other theories which were originally conceived for other purposes. We also hope these papers will reinforce the need for focusing on the learner and his capacities as the crucial variables in second language teaching.

In the last paper in this section, Oller discusses what he believes are some of the important controversies in present-day theories of language use and language learning. He attempts to show that the different viewpoints considered have had, and continue to have, both desirable and undesirable effects in the classroom. All four papers suggest a need for detailed observation of the process of second language learning as the ultimate basis for anything that may usefully be said about second language teaching. This is a point reiterated by many of the contributors to this volume.

LANGUAGE DIDACTICS AND APPLIED LINGUISTICS

William F. Mackey

> Nor did Pnin, as a teacher, ever presume to approach
> the lofty halls of modern scientific linguistics, that
> ascetic fraternity of phonemes, that temple wherein
> earnest young people are taught not the language
> itself, but the method of teaching others to teach that
> method.
>
> Vladimir Nabokov, *Pnin*

In the past few years, language teachers have been hearing a great
deal about "applied linguistics." In some quarters, language teaching
is considered to be the exclusive province of this new science. And in
certain countries national agencies have been convinced that no one
not trained in the technique of applied linguistics can successfully
teach a language.

What is applied linguistics? What does one apply when one applies
linguistics? How does it relate to language learning? How does it
concern language teaching? Of what use is it to the teacher? What is
new about it? These are some of the questions which language
teachers have been asking; it is the purpose of this article to supply
some of the answers, without necessarily trying, as many such efforts
often do, to sell the product at the same time. Let us take the above
questions in the order in which they appear:

1. What is applied linguistics?

The term "applied linguistics" seems to have originated in the
United States in the 1940's. It was first used by persons with an
obvious desire to be identified as scientists rather than as humanists;
the association with "applied science" can hardly have been
accidental. Yet, although linguistics is a science, "applied science"
does not necessarily include linguistics.

The creation of applied linguistics as a discipline represents an
effort to find practical applications for "modern scientific
linguistics." While assuming that linguistics can be an applied science,
it brings together such diverse activities as the making of alphabets
by missionaries and the making of translations by machines. The use
of the term is now becoming crystalized in the names of at least two
language centers, three reviews, half a dozen books, and a score of
articles.[1]

---

[1]See *References*, p. 14-15.

2. What does one apply?

What does one apply when one applies linguistics? What is applied may be a theory of language and/or a description of one.

If it is a theory of language, what is applied depends of course on the sort of theory being used. If the theory is based on the existence of units of meaning, for example, the results will be different from what they would be if the theory ignored the existence of such units.

There are dozens of ways in which one theory may differ from another; and there are dozens of different theories of language, several of which are mutually contradictory. Some of these constitute schools of language theory, like the Saussurian School, the Psychomechanic School, the Glossematic School, the Bloomfieldian School, the Prague School, the Firthian School, and others. When we examine the many theories of different schools and individuals we note that very few indeed have ever been applied to anything. We also notice that those which have been applied are not necessarily the most applicable. On the other hand, the fact that a language theory has never been applied to language teaching does not mean that it cannot be. Some of the more ambitious and inclusive theories, which seem to be the most relevant, have in fact never been applied.

Secondly, if it is a description of a language that is being applied, it might include any or all of its phonetics, grammar, or vocabulary. And since descriptions based on the same theory often differ, there are more varieties of description than there are types of theory.

Descriptions differ in their purpose, extent and presentation. Some descriptions aim at being concise; others, at being extensive. Some analyze the language by breaking it down; others, by building it up. Some are made as if the language described is unknown to the linguist; others, as if it is already known to the reader. Some will present the language in two levels (grammar and phonology); others, in as many as fourteen. Yet the number of levels of a description is no indication of its linguistic range; a three-level description may have a wider scope than an eight-level one, which excludes vocabulary, meaning, or context. Some descriptions are based on written works; others, on speech. Some may cover all areas in which the language is spoken; others may be limited to a single city. Some may be compiled from the speech of a single person over a period of a few weeks; others may be based on the writings of many authors covering a few centuries.

It is obvious, therefore, that the problem of the language teacher is not only whether or not to apply linguistics, but whose linguistics to apply, and what sort.

3. How does it relate to language learning?

In order to exist, a language must have been learned; but in order to be learned, a language does not have to have been analyzed. For the process of learning a language is quite different from the process of analyzing one. Persons who have never gone to school find it difficult to divide their language into such classes as the parts of speech, despite the fact that they may speak their native language with a great deal of fluency and elegance. Foreign languages have also been successfully mastered throughout the ages without benefit of analysis.

It is the production of methods of *analysis* that is the business of the linguist. But if the linguist claims that such and such a method is the best way to *learn* the language, he is speaking outside his competence. For it is not learning, but language, that is the object of linguistics. Language learning cannot therefore be the purpose of linguistics—pure or applied. Linguistics is not language learning.

Therefore the units used for analyzing a language are not necessarily those needed for learning it. As an illustration, let us take a sample of an analysis of English done by a representative of one of the schools of linguistics which has done the most applied linguistics in language teaching. As a case in point, let us take the description of the English pronouns. The pronouns are arranged into seven sets, which include 23 units. To explain these, 34 other units (called *morphs*) are brought into the picture, although they have no further function than to explain the first 23. Rules are then given to "convert the abstract forms into those actually found." For example, after having learned that the abstract form for the first person plural object is *{w-i-m}, we get the form actually found, the form *us*, by applying the following rule:

1. *we*: {w-i-y}
2. *us*: *{w-i-m}; {-m} after {w-i-} becomes {-s}; *{w-i-} before resulting {-s} becomes {-ə-}, a portmanteau
3. *our*: *{w-i-r}; before {-r} and {r-z}, intitial consonant and vowel are transposed, giving *{i-w-}; initial *{i-} becomes {a-} before {-w-}
4. *ours*: *{w-i-r-z} (See rules given for 3.) [2]

If this is to be applied linguistics, it should justify the definition of philology sometimes attributed to Voltaire, "la science où les

---

[2] A. A. Hill, *Introduction to Linguistic Structures: From Sound to Sentence in English* (New York: Harcourt, 1958), p. 150.

voyelles ne comptent pour rien, et les consonnes pour peu de chose."
One can imagine what happens when two languages are contrasted on
this basis.

It is true, however, that some linguists have pointed out the
disparity between language learning and language description. For
example, the former head of the department of linguistics of Harvard
University has written: "A linguistic description of a language is of
little help in learning the language; recently published structural
accounts of European languages rebut any disclaimer to this
judgment.[3]" For two descriptions of the same language can be so
different that a learner may not be blamed for wondering whether
the units and categories alleged to form the essential elements of the
language exist only in the minds of those who have attempted to
describe it.

4. How does it concern language teaching?

Although the linguistic descriptions of the same language are not
identical, it is now widely admitted that the linguist is the competent
person to write our grammars, phonetic manuals, and dictionaries. In
some quarters it is assumed that the very fact he can do this makes
him qualified to form language teaching policy and prepare language
teaching texts. In the use of "applied linguistics" in language
teaching, it has been further assumed that if one is able to do a
thorough description of the forms of a language, one is by that very
fact able to teach it.

These assumptions are obviously ill-founded, for there have been
outstanding language teachers with no knowledge of linguistics. And
it has been demonstrated that "the methods of the linguistic scientist
as a teacher are not necessarily the most effective.[4]" This can be
explained by the different preoccupations of the two disciplines.
Much of the present state of applied linguistics in language teaching
is due to the fact that some linguists have been more interested in
finding an application for their science than in solving the problems
of language teaching. Some of the unhappy results have been due to
a desire to apply to language teaching a one-sided technique of

---

[3]J. Whatmough, *Language: A Modern Synthesis* (New York: St. Martin's Press, 1956), p.
145.

[4]J. B. Carroll, *The Study of Language: A Survey of Linguistics and Related Disciplines in
America* (Cambridge, Mass.: Harvard University Press, 1953), p. 192.

formal description with no universal validity, even in the field of linguistic analysis.

Much is made of the ability of the linguist to predict mistakes by comparing the native language of the learner with the language he is being taught. This differential description is sometimes confusingly called "contrastive linguistics," a term which also means the analysis of a single language based essentially on the contrast of its units one with the other. What is the use of predicting mistakes already heard? Since anyone who has taught a language can predict from experience the sort of mistakes his students are likely to make *a posteriori*, is he any the wiser for the *a priori* and less reliable prediction which the linguist makes on the basis of a differential analysis?

It has been stated as a principle of "applied linguistics" that all the mistakes of the language learner are due to the makeup of his native language. This is demonstrably false. Many mistakes actually made have no parallel in the native language; they are simply extensions of the foreign language patterns into areas in which they do not apply, e.g., *I said him so* on the analogy of *I told him so*. Other mistakes are due to a confusion of new material with parts of the language not deeply enough ingrained; this inhibition is a matter of order and rate of intake. Still other mistakes are due to the habit, which language learners soon acquire, of avoiding the similarities with their native language. This may result in either blind guessing or the systematic avoidance of native patterns, even though these exist in the foreign language, e.g., words like *attack* (a cognate of the French *attaque*) are stressed on the first syllable by French learners of English, despite the fact that both French and English versions have the stress on the final syllable. Texts for language teaching based only on the differences between the two languages cannot take these important tendencies into account.

Even for the many mistakes due directly to interference from the native language the practicing teacher is in a better position than the descriptive linguist. For although a differential description, of English and French for example, may indeed point out the fact that a French learner of English may have difficulty pronouncing the interdental sounds of *thin* and *then* because of their absence from the French phoneme inventory, it cannot predict as well as can an experienced teacher which way a given learner or group of learners will handle the difficulty. In point of fact, different learners with the same native language do make different mistakes; the above interdental sounds, for example, are rendered sometimes as /s, z/, sometimes as /t, d/. But this information is supplied, not by an *a priori* comparison of English and French, but by the observations of language teachers.

Actual applications of differential descriptions do not produce the same type of teaching. For some teachers will start drilling the differences because they are difficult, while others wills start using the similarities because they are easy (e.g., the "cognate method".)

Most of the available differential descriptions are so superficial and incomplete as to be misleading. This is because they are at best based on a unit-by-unit and structure-by-structure comparison of two languages. They fail to show all the units of the first language which are equivalent to structures in the second, and the structures in the first, equivalent to units in the second. They also ignore the units and structures of one level that are equivalent to structures and units of another. And even with this, they are still dealing only with the makeup of the languages, not with the multiple differences in contextual usage, with the fact that in such and such a circumstance a learner must say one thing in his native language but something entirely different in the foreign language. Since we do not have such complete differential descriptions of any two languages—even of the most widely known—we are likely to get better results by collecting and classifying the mistakes which the learners make than by trying to predict those we should expect him to make.

5. Of what use is it to the teacher?

It is the business of the language teacher to know the foreign language, to know how to teach it, and to know something about it. It is in relation to this latter need that linguistics might be expected to be useful. But even when he does master the technicalities of linguistics, the language teacher soon encounters conflicting theories and contradictory methods. Should he believe in one and not try even to understand the others? Or should he study all of them?

What is the language teacher to do when faced with the multiplicity of approaches to the analysis of a language and the different trends in descriptive linguistics? What should be his attitude when asked to give up his grammars on the grounds that they are unscientific—that they give recipes rather than formulas?

Above all, the language teacher must be interested in results; and tested recipes are often better than untested and sometimes unformulated formulas. Until more complete and definitive analyses are available, language teaching will have to rely for its description of a language on those abundant and serviceable grammars of the past. For a language teacher, the completeness of a grammar is more relevant than its scientific consistency; clarity is more important than conciseness; examples, more useful than definitions. For the language teacher to wait until more scientific grammars are produced is to put himself in the position of the tanner of hides who stops tanning until the chemists find the chemical formula describing exactly what is done. The formula, once discovered, might eventually improve the tanning operation; but until it is formulated and tested and proven more effective, the only sensible thing to do is to continue tanning hides in a way that has given the best results.

The fact is that most of the new, "linguistically approved" grammars being applied to language teaching are more difficult to use and far less complete than are the older works. Some are no more than undigested research essays on the making of a grammar. Others represent a sort of do-it-yourself grammar-making kit allegedly designed to "crack the code" of any language in the world.

Although the ability to analyze a language may not be the most important qualification of a language teacher, some training in practical linguistics can enable him to establish with more precision than he otherwise might what is the same and what is different in the languages in which he has to deal. It can also help him understand, evaluate, and perhaps use some of the descriptions of the language he is teaching. And if the training is neither too one-sided nor doctrinaire it may prevent him from becoming the prisoner of a single school of thought and encourage him to surmount the great terminological barriers which have prevented any mutual understanding in linguistics, obliging each school to be responsible for its own glossary of linguistic terms (e.g., the Prague School,[5] the American descriptivists,[6] and the school of Ascoli.[7]).

Ideally, such training could put the teacher in a position to analyze each linguistic contribution or application to language teaching, from the small details of analysis to the hidden theoretical assumptions on which the analysis is based. Such training would

---

[5] J. Vachek and J. Dubsky, *Dictionnaire de linguistique de l'école de Prague* (Utrecht: Spectrum, 1960).

[6] E. P. Hamp, *A Glossary of American Technical Linguistic Usage: 1925-1950* (Utrecht: Sprectrum, 1957).

[7] E. de Felice, *La terminologia linguistica de G. I. Ascoli e della sua scuola* (Utrecht: Spectrum, 1957).

make it unnecessary for the language teacher to swallow a man's philosophy along with his linguistics. For the main attraction of some analyses is their consistency with certain philosophical beliefs. Is it then any advantage to deny the beliefs and admit the consistency, for consistency's sake? Or is it better to seek an analysis which is philosophically more palatable but perhaps less consistent?

Finally, the proper sort of training could enable the teacher to distinguish between the scientific status of linguistics and the scientific pretensions of linguists. For some linguists seem to be so eager to appear "scientific" that they state or restate the most banal facts about a language in a pseudo-scientific notation and a collection of technical terms borrowed indifferently from several disciplines and heavy with scientific associations. Old ideas about language do not become better when couched in an unfamiliar jargon. This leads us to our final question.

6. What is new about it?

As far as language teaching is concerned, there are very few ideas proposed as applied linguistics which were not familiar to teachers at one time or another. What, for example, is essentially different in practice between the "phonemic transcription" being proposed today and the "broad transcription" used by language teachers in the past century?

Throughout the history of formal language teaching there has always been some sort of applied linguistics, as it is known today. For language teachers have always tended to apply language analysis to the teaching of a language; in fact some of the first descriptions of a language were made for the purpose of teaching it. Yet the sorts of descriptions actually produced have varied with the needs and contingencies of the epoch. And some of the oldest are still some of the best. Such ancient classics as the grammars of Panini, Dionysius, Priscian and Donatus are not outclassed by those of today. Yet the blind application of the categories of these grammars to the description of modern European and even to non-European languages was obviously so unsuitable as to create a series of reactions which resulted in the attitude of scientific superiority which afflicts contemporary linguistics.

One is the reaction against the linguistic analysis of exotic languages made in the past century—a type of analysis which superimposed the structure of European languages on the facts of the native language being described. As a reaction against this, techniques of description were developed by Boas, Sapir, and, especially, by Bloomfield and his associates. These techniques were apparently so successful that they were later applied to languages, like English, with a long tradition of linguistic analysis. This in turn was a reaction against the current English school grammars which still propagated the traditional definitions of the eighteenth century. But in the process the best linguistic traditions were ignored, including the works of such linguists as Sweet and Jespersen, so that the language might be handled as if the person describing its elements were unable to understand them. And the movement, which started as an effort to prevent the analysis of exotic languages as if they were English, found itself analyzing English as if it were an exotic language.

Against this trend, other reactions are beginning to take shape. These are appearing as a reformulation of the traditional approach to grammar, a compromise with the older grammatical categories, a return to the study of ancient grammatical theory. It is now being admitted that the old universal grammatical theories were more in need of revision than of repudiation. And some linguists are beginning to consider the descriptions of "modern scientific linguistics" as nothing more than another arrangement of the grammatical data, according to a less traditional outline, but nevertheless according to a completely arbitrary set of labels which has become fossilized within its own short linguistic tradition.[8]

If linguistics has been applied to the language part of "language learning," psychology has been applied to the learning part of it. The history of the application of the principles of psychology to the learning of languages is analogous to that of the applications of linguistic analysis. So is the situation today. There are almost as many different theories of learning as there are theories of language. Most of them are still based on the observations of animal learning. Although there is a promising branch of psychology devoted to verbal learning and verbal behavior, it is still involved in solving problems related to the learning of isolated words.

In one form or another, both language analysis and psychology have always been applied to the teaching of foreign languages. In fact, the history of language teaching could be represented as a cyclic shift in prominence from the one to the other, a swing from the strict application of principles of language analysis to the single-minded insistence on principles of psychology. The history

---

[8]R. B. Lees, review of Noam Chomsky's *Syntactic Structures*, in *Language*, 33, 377.

zig-zags, with many minor oscillations in between, from the Mediaeval grammarians to Comenius, from Plötz to Gouin. And today's interest in applied linguistics represents another swing toward the primacy of language analysis in language teaching.

Is is likely that language teaching will continue to be a child of fashion in linguistics and psychology until the time it becomes an autonomous discipline which uses these related sciences instead of being used by them. To become autonomous it will, like any science, have to weave its own net, so as to fish out from the oceans of human experience and natural phenomena only the elements it needs, and ignoring the rest, be able to say with the ichthyologist of Sir Arthur Eddington, "What my net can't catch isn't fish."

Contemporary claims that applied linguistics can solve all the problems of language teaching are as unfounded as the claims that applied psychology can solve them. For the problems of language teaching are central neither to psychology nor linguistics. Neither science is equipped to solve the problems of language teaching. Nor are teams of linguists and psychologists, since the smallest question in language teaching involves a detailed knowledge of certain highly specialized aspects of both psychology and linguistics.

The only sensible solution is the elaboration of the science of language didactics starting from a synthesis of the relevant findings in the appropriate fields. It would probably be no more of an exact science than is medicine; but just as medicine makes use of chemistry, physics, physiology and other sciences, language didactics could make use of such disciplines as phonetics, descriptive linguistics, semantics, pedagogy, comparative stylistics, psycholinguistics, mathematical linguistics, psychometry, and any other science or technology which may help solve its basic problems. But these would never be more than tools at the service of the theories and techniques elaborated by an autonomous discipline.

REFERENCES

Reviews

1. *Etudes de linguistique appliquée.* Publication du Centre de Linguistique Appliquée de la Faculté des Lettres de Basançon. Paris: Didier (France).
2. *International Review of Applied Linguistics in Language Teaching.* Heidelberg: Dolmetscher-Institut (Germany).
3. *Language Learning. A Journal of Applied Linguistics.* Ann Arbor: University of Michigan (U.S.A.)

Books

1. Allen, H. B. *Readings in Applied English Linguistics.* New York: Appleton, 1958.
2. Bellasco, S. (ed.). *Anthology for Use with a Guide for Teachers in NDEA Language Institutes.* Boston: Heath, 1961.
3. Cardenas, D. N. *Applied Linguistics: Spanish. A Guide for Teachers.* Boston: Heath, 1961.
4. Politzer, R. N., and C. N. Stauback. *Teaching Spanish: A Linguistic Orientation.* Boston: Ginn, 1961.
5. Pulgram, E. (ed.). *Applied Linguistics in Language Teaching.* Washington: Georgetown University Press, 1954.
6. Sainte-Marie, P. *De la nécessité d'une linguistique appliquée.* Paris: Coulouma, 1953.
7. Wähmer, K. *Sprachlernung und Sprachwissenschaft.* Leipzig: Teubner, 1914.

Articles

1. Andreev, N. D., and L. R. Zinder. "Osnovnye problemy prikladnoj linguistiki" (Fundamental Problems of Applied Linguistics). Voprosy jazykoznanija, 4, 1-9.
2. Cardenas, D. N. "The Application of Linguistics in the Teaching of Spanish." *Hispania,* 455-60.
3. Fries, C. C. "American Linguistics and the Teaching of English." *Revue des langues vivantes,* 21, 294-310.
4. ———. "Structural Linguistics and Language Teaching." *Classical Journal,* 52, 265-8.
5. Glaksch, K. H. "Zur Frage der theoretischen Grundlagen des Grammatikunterrichts und ihrer methodischen Bedeutung für den Unterricht in den modernen Fremdsprachen." *Wissenschaft. Z. der U. Greifswald,* 4, 139.
6. Haas, R. "The Application of Linguistics to Language Teaching." *Anthropology Today.* A. L. Kroeber (ed.). Chicago: Chicago University Press, 1953.

7. Haden, E. F. "Descriptive Linguistics and the Teaching of a FL." *Modern Language Journal*, 38, 170-6.
8. Halliday, M. A. K. "Linguistique générale et linguistique appliquée." *Etudes de linguistique appliquée,* 1, 5-42.
9. Haugen, E. "Linguistics and the Wartime Program of Language Teaching." *Modern Language Journal*, 34, 243-5.
10. Hill, A. A. "Language Analysis and Language Teaching." *Modern Language Journal*, 40, 335-45.
11. Kandler, G. "Zum Aufbau der angewandten Sprachwissenschaft." *Sprachforum*, 1, 3-9.
12. Lee, W. R. "Linguistics and the Practical Teacher." *English Language Teaching* 13, 159-70.
13. Long, R. B. "Linguistics and Language Teaching: Caveats from English." *Modern Language Journal*, 45, 149-55.
14. MacAllister, A. T. "The Princeton Language Program." *PMLA*, 70, 15-22.
15. Métais, C. "Quelques problèmes immédiats de la linguistique appliquée." *Les langues modernes*, 56, 235-7.
16. Molès, A. "Acoustique, phonétique et enseignement des langues vivantes." *Les langues modernes*, 46, 33-41.
17. Moulton, W. G. "Linguistics and Language Teaching in the United States: 1940-1960." *Trends in European and American Linguistics: 1930-1960*, Utrecht: Spectrum, 1961.
18. Mues, W. "Kernfagen des modernen englischen Sprachunterrichts." *Die neuren Sprachen*, 4, 14, 66, 117.
19. Perkins, M. L. "General Language Study and the Teaching of Languages." *Modern Language Journal*, 40, 113-19.
20. Perrenoud, A. "Linguistique et pédagogie." *Mélanges Niedermann*, 179-84. Neuchâtel; Université de Neuchâtel, 1944.
21. Prensler, W. "Sprachwissenschaft und Schulunterricht." *Die neuren Sprachen*, 3, 392-400.
22. Pulgram, E. "Linguistics for More Language Teachers." *The French Review*, 32, 147-55.
23. Real, W. "Linguistique et pédagogie." *Mélanges Bally*, 63-71. Geneva: Georg, 1939.
24. St. Clair-Sobell, S. "Phonology and Language Teaching." *Journal of the Canadian Linguistic Association*, 2, 14-18.
25. Siertsema, B. "Language Learning and Language Analysis." *Lingua*, 10, 128-47.
26. Valdman, A. "Vers l'application de la linguistique à l'enseignement du français parlé.' *Le français dans le monde*, 7, 10-15.
27. Waterman, J. T. "Linguistics for the Language Teacher." *Modern Language Forum*, 41, 9-16.

PSYCHOLINGUISTICS AND SECOND LANGUAGE TEACHING

H. H. Stern

I have been asked to write on the relationship between psycholinguistics and second language teaching. There are attempts on record, which have been made by distinguished psychologists and linguists, to relate psychology to language teaching and learning. Among recent ones, for example, are those by Carroll, Anisfeld, Broadbent, and Jakobovits.[1] All of these show how problematical it can be to attempt to bring the psychology of language and language acquisition to bear on second language learning, so much so that one can quite sympathize with Chomsky who, perhaps in a more radical fashion than those I have named, very coolly stated: "I am, frankly, rather skeptical about the significance, for the teaching of languages, of such insights and understanding as have been attained in linguistics and psychology."[2]

In spite of the obvious difficulties I believe that from contact with psycholinguistics one can derive certain ideas and attitudes that can set the keynote for a day in which the practical concerns of how to teach English better to speakers of other languages must predominate. Linguistics, psychology, or the borderline discipline of psycholinguistics can hardly provide detailed tips or techniques, but they can influence both the overall methodology of teaching and the teacher's outlook on language use and language learning.

Let me begin by drawing your attention to three basic ideas in psycholinguistics which I believe have bearing on language teaching. I should then like to briefly sketch the development of psycho-linguistics, outline a few major language models and themes of psycholinguistics, and suggest what, in my view, they have to do with language teaching.

1. Language is complex

The first observation I wish to make may seem obvious and trite, yet it is often disregarded: *second language learning is an exceedingly complex process*. The wish to make it simple, palatable, and attractive is entirely justifiable just because it is so complex.

---

[1] See *References* p. 27.

[2] See p. 29, Chomsky's article, this volume.

Nevertheless, if second language learning is not always as successful as we would like it to be, the blame must admittedly sometimes lie with the teacher, the materials, the facilities, or other external factors. But failures in second language teaching or learning are due, more than to anything else, to the complexity of language itself and of the second language learning process. A study of language by whatever discipline—linguistics, psychology, or psycholinguistics—reveals this complexity in an interesting and exciting way. It makes one feel humble and undogmatic about the methods of language teaching. Even if it does not give one new techniques and new tricks, it may well make one look at the old tricks with greater understanding and less naiveté and make one less facile about languages and language learning. In short, a study of psycholinguistics can counteract primitivism in language teaching.

2. Language is not jibberish: it is always ordered

Any language to the native user, speaker, or listener, forms an ordered kind of network, structure, or system, or even several layers of interconnected systems. This ordered character of language is often overlooked when we learn a second language higgledy-piggledy, running hither and thither, picking up bits here and there. The native speaker may not be conscious of this ordered system with its rules and regularities, but if you disregard it he knows there is something wrong. As you, as native speakers, read this paper the networks or systems are in action. Your knowledge of the language, the network in each person's mind, and indeed the totality of your linguistic background and experience, are activated.

Talking and listening to talk demand a strange interplay of the novel and the familiar, the inventive and the expected. If my paper were full of words and sentences you had already heard in *exactly* that form or manner before, it would be completely expected or redundant, and you would say, "There he is off again on his old tack." On the other hand, if my paper is too unfamiliar, or too novel, or if I liberties with the syntax take, for example, as I have just done, I may be accused of being incomprehensible, being above the heads of my audience, or of producing nonsense. The writer who hits the right measure of familiarity and novelty is regarded as "interesting" or "original." But he must remain within the framework of the rules of the language that the native listener expects. Having this kind of network is an important part of what we call "knowing a language." As we shall see shortly, this is now often referred to as "linguistic competence."

As English teachers, our ambition is to bring to the learner of English as a second language the same sense of English that enables us to use and understand English discourse. If we knew the secret of how to impart to the learner of a second language this intuitive grasp that everyone of us has of his native language, we could say that the problem of second language learning would be solved.

3. Language in use is always language in a meaningful context.

We have seen that language to the user is an ordered system, a structure, a frame of reference, and indeed, this is recognized by many language teachers and many linguists. Teachers are often so preoccupied with the forms of language, the patterns of sentences, points of pronunciation, and so on, that they quite forget that the language is used by people for communication. Newcomers to Canada especially, whether they are young or old, need language for use all the time—to inquire, to understand directions and explanations, to explain themselves, and so forth.

Psycholinguistics emphasizes the *human being as a user of language* and thus can serve as a healthy antidote when we, as teachers, get too caught up in the formal aspects of the language, which I have just discussed, and fall into the snares, of drill for drill's sake. A language comes to reality in contexts, situations, actual speech events, in wanting to say something, and in wanting to listen; it fits into a social setting, and it arouses feelings in the speaker and listener. In language teaching it is easy to forget how closely linked language is with thinking and emotions, and how much it forms part of social life and culture, in short the uses of language. And yet language learning without paying attention to use, especially when it is so desperately needed, as English is by new Canadians, can be disheartening because it is so literally useless.

PSYCHOLINGUISTICS

Let me now briefly substantiate these ideas by saying a few words about the psychology of language.

Psycholinguistics as a term and as a defined area of study is of fairly recent origin. Not yet twenty years old, and as the name leads one to expect, it is a fusion of psychology and linguistics, a study of the area common to both. The two parent disciplines have a history of thought about language and the psychology related to language going back at least one hundred years, but with roots reaching into antiquity. Thus psycholinguistics may appear novel and modern, but the problems it studies have interested many thinkers of the past.

Nearly one hundred years ago, and for many decades following, the growing study of child psychology included penetrating observations on the development of language in the child. Around the turn of the century, one of the most fascinating approaches to the emotional dynamics of speech was Freud's treatment of slips of the tongue and pen; another approach was Jung's experimentation on word associations. The behaviorists consistently displayed an interest in language, starting with Watson in the twenties, Dollard and Miller in the forties, to Skinner's much debated *Verbal Behavior* in the fifties.

Language, however, was not in the center of the psychological stage in the interwar years. But, with the growth of linguistics during that same period and with the ingenious work on information theory by physicists, mathematicians, and communication engineers, the three groups, linguists, psychologists, and engineers, came together in the early fifties to look at each others' work, to coordinate it and to develop a dialog, a common theory, and a joint program of inquiry. And it is thus that psycholinguistics in the modern sense was created.

One surprising feature of this development is that throughout the whole period and even into the present, only relatively little interest has been shown in the puzzling psychology of second language learning. Yet, here is one of the most challenging theoretical questions, which at the same time has great practical significance: *why is it that first language acquisition is foolproof, whereas second language learning so frequently fails?*[3]

Nevertheless, second language teaching theory in the fifties and the early sixties was in tune with the prevailing psycholinguistic climate of thought. It talked in similar terms of "conditioning," "stimulus and response," "habit formation," "reinforcement," and "generalization;" and course materials and methods often (although sometimes rather crudely) claimed to be based on psycholinguistic thought.

Such views were strengthened by Skinner's ingenious book *Verbal Behavior*. The thesis of this book, an avowedly bold speculation, is that language is nothing special. To use language even in poetry or philosophical thought requires no new principle of explanation. All behavior, even of the lowliest organisms, as well as man, is very much alike. There is no fundamental difference between a pigeon learning a skill and using it to get at food and a human learning and using language. The implication of this view for language teaching and

---

[3]This problem is discussed in "First and Second Language Acquisition." See Stern (1971).

learning (although Skinner himself has not said so) is that all language learning is alike and that it is really no different from any other form of training including animal training. First language learning appears here to be the result of a highly ingenious and extremely successful form of parental training that second language teachers might well emulate.

Recent developments

It is now nearly ten years since Chomsky, in one of the most celebrated reviews of all times, attacked the thesis of Skinner's *Verbal Behavior*, but beyond that, the whole behaviorist position in the psychology of language. Psycholinguistics in the last ten years has been completely under the impact of this attack and has attempted to work out its implications. We have turned full circle: instead of attempting to interpret language in terms of other forms of behavior, Chomsky argues that language provides "a remarkably favorable perspective for the study of human mental processes" and that we should look afresh at human psychology in the light of what is revealed about it through language.[4]

Psycholinguistics of the fifties seemed to say: Look at behavior anywhere in biological organisms and you will know what language is like. In the sixties, largely as a result of the work of Chomsky, Lenneberg, and Miller, we have increasingly come to say: Look at language and it will tell you a lot about the human mind.

What is this new view of language? To characterize it briefly, I should like to give you a few quotations which are all taken from Chomsky's 1966 paper in which he questions the applicability of findings of psychology and linguistics to language teaching.[5] Here are a few examples:

Language is not a "habit structure."

Repetition of fixed phrases is a rarity.

The notion that linguistic behavior consists of "responses" to "stimuli" is as much a myth as the idea that it is a matter of habit and generalization.

Ordinary linguistic behavior characteristically involves innovation, formation of new sentences and new patterns in accordance with rules of great abstractness and intricacy.

There are no known principles of association or reinforcement, and no known sense of "generalization" that can begin to account for this characteristic "creative" aspect of normal language use.

---

[4]N. Chomsky, *Language and Mind* (New York: Harcourt, Brace & World, 1968), p. 84.

[5]See pp. 29-35.

What is meant by this "creative aspect of normal language use"? "The native speaker of a language has internalized a 'generative grammar'—a system of rules that can be used in new and untried combinations." The native speaker, e.g., a child, is of course not aware of this grammar which constitutes "an unconscious, latent knowledge" which Chomsky calls the speaker's "intrinsic 'linguistic competence.' "

It is quite clear that the dominant modern theory of language teaching today is still very much a child of the fifties. If we are told by the new school of thought that stimulus and response, habit formation, conditioning, overlearning, and reinforcement are inadequate for the acquisition and use of language, this must indeed be disturbing to us as teachers because many of the techniques that have been developed have made use of these ideas. The new view of language offered today is indeed quite different. I am personally not worried about the fact that we have to look at our theoretical assumptions again and again, and I can well believe that there might be a place in second language learning for the linguistic creativeness and inventiveness that the modern school of linguistics emphasizes.

Language teaching, as I said before, suffers from oversimplification and primitivism, and anything that shakes us and helps us to rethink, in the light of what we actually see and experience as we teach, can only be to the good. And the theoretical jolt we have received can do no harm provided we do not now join a kind of antibehavioristic witch hunt. For even if all the theoretical assumptions of the so-called audio-lingual method may not be beyond question, pedagogically the techniques that this method has brought into language teaching have great merit.

I now want to talk about *three different models of language* and *three different themes of psycholinguistics*. All of them in my view are relevant to language teaching.

LANGUAGE MODELS

Language like a chain or string

The three different models one meets again and again in psycholinguistics reveal different aspects of language. The first is the *linear* or *sequential model*. It looks upon the utterances as "sequences" or as links in a chain that we produce or receive. If I say, "Chickens cackle and ducks—" you can easily complete this sentence.[6]

---

[6]Adapted from Osgood and Sebeok, *Psycholinguistics*, p. 111. See *References*.

When a person speaks you can rapidly make forward guesses of what sounds will come next, what word or grammatical part of the sentence is likely to follow, and what meaning should come next. These are the more or less familiar, the more or less repetitive, the more or less redundant aspects; here we find varying degrees of probability. All these form part of the native speaker's linguistic expectancies. Although much of this is habitual and repetitive it is not mechanical or automatic. The user's forward guess and confirmation and new guess form a sequence which is roughly paralleled in language teaching by the pattern drill.

The "Oh, à propos" approach

This is the *associationist model*. Association is a very old concept and has been used in psychological research for many years. The idea of association is also widely used by language teachers. But language teachers, I suggest, use it somewhat differently from the way it is employed in psychology, and this difference is important, The idea of association is simple. If I say a word to you this word is likely to make you think of another word, to give you a thought, or to call up an image. Words, thoughts, images, like the animals in the Ark, tend to come two by two, or perhaps even in threes or larger groups. To put it another way, we can never think of just a word alone; mentally, words relate to something else. Psychologists have tried to understand what associations occur and why.

When language teachers make use of this idea, they tend to say something like this, "I want to avoid creating associations between the second language and the first language," or "I am creating associations between an object and a word, between a picture and a sentence, between actions and language. The teacher is right of course; the right associations are important for proper language use. But we, as language users, find that we just *have* associations, they just *happen.* No one can or does *create* them for us. The fact that any one of us as human beings has associations does not imply that a teacher can create in our minds the associations he would like us to have. What might happen in second language learning is that the teacher would like to create a particular association, but in fact the learner has quite a different one. These are the realities of language from which we cannot escape.

The "That-doesn't-sound-like-English-and-I-can't-tell-you-why-but-I-know-what-you-mean" approach[7]

This model, which, after Chomsky, can be called the *competence model*, lays emphasis on the inherently structured and ordered relationships in native language uses. The "competence" shows itself, for example, in the fact that the native speaker can make up sentences which conform to the pattern of his own language and can avoid making up nonconforming sentences. It also helps him to distinguish well-formed sentences from nonsense sentences, or to reinterpret in terms of his own system the semi-sentences which we often casually produce, or the nonconforming sentences of children or foreign speakers. When we say to a learner of English, "Yes you can say this," or "No you can't say that," we are providing a kind of standard of right and wrong or of appropriateness against which to match utterances, and this is an important aspect of the competence model.

PSYCHOLINGUISTIC THEMES

The three models of language have been used to study three major themes of psycholinguistics, from various points of view.

How does a baby come to speak his language?

The first theme is *language acquisition.* Any mother or father has of course witnessed his or her child's language learning. How does the child do it? A language is so intricate. How can he possibly manage it? Ingenious studies have been made to show how early a child obeys the rules of his language. In the past, some psychologists, although by no means all, tended to say, "It is all a matter of association, conditioning, habit, or repetition." But today—and here Lenneberg's work has been of particular importance—language acquisition is treated much more as a matter of biological growth. It is argued that because language is so complex and is used also in an inventive way, mere repetition and conditioning cannot account for the flexible competence that every child seems to acquire in his native tongue. But if language acquisition is purely a matter of innate growth in infancy, does it mean simply that language cannot be

---

[7]Please note that our "internalized grammar" enables us to create and understand this unusual "innovative" adjectival construction.

learned? Does it mean also that we as language teachers are perhaps now out of business? Or is it that these theories are not beyond dispute and are not completely applicable to the second language situation.[8] In any case, the study of language acquisition has led to the most radical rethinking of beliefs and assumptions held about the mind for at least two centuries.

What happens when we speak and understand speech?

Another major theme can be described as *language use*. Here psycholinguistics has tried to study what happens when we speak and listen, i.e., either transmit or receive a communication. To most language users these activities are so much a part of living that one is hardly aware of a problem when it does arise. But when things go wrong, say in aphasia, or stammering, or when we use a foreign language, or when we design communication systems, such as the telephone, radio, etc., we realize there is much to be learned about speaking and listening. The psycholinguistic experiments have taken these processes, so to speak, under the microscope.

Among general findings, it seems to me, the following is of particular importance to us. In language use, one's whole background enters into the process of speaking and listening. I described this earlier as an internal network. This means that even in listening the mind is extremely active, matching, classifying, coding, and decoding. Unless one possesses that network one can neither speak nor understand. The second language learner instinctively uses his existing mother-tongue network as a frame of reference for his new language experiences, although this is patently wrong and out of place. He behaves like someone entering a room with distorting mirrors or false perspectives. He uses his existing frame of reference, in spite of the fact that it blocks him and cannot help him in perception. In learning a second language we have to build up a totally fresh frame of reference or network. We can see, if that is so, that even listening to a language is an extremely active process. The idea that speaking is an active skill and listening a passive one is not tenable. Both are active skills, and they have much in common. Both must be based on the operation of the inner networks of language one has built up.

What does language really mean and do to us?

A third major theme—too vast to receive more than a mention here—is the *intricate relationship between language and meaning*,

---

[8]See "First and Second Language Acquisition," pp. 59-63, Stern (1971).

between language and thought and emotion, between language and culture. The questions that have puzzled the scholars here are whether language is shaped by these various factors, or merely reflects them, or, whether language, in turn, exercises a shaping influence on them. The general tenor of the discussion suggests the close interaction between language and many other factors. In language teaching, we tend to make similar assumptions and to stress that language becomes meaningful in situational and personal contexts, but time and again, as I have pointed out already, we teachers tend to restrict ourselves too much to the purely formal aspects and to overlook motivated use, social and cultural context, and meaningful situations.

Unfortunately, I must confine myself to these few remarks about the models and themes which psycholinguistics has developed, and I have said next to nothing about the ingenious experimentation and research that substantiate these ideas.

CONCLUSIONS FOR LANGUAGE TEACHING

In drawing a few specific conclusions for second language teaching I am making my points quite dogmatically for the sake of brevity, although I want to add that my personal view of language teaching methods is undogmatic, simply because I believe that the complexities of language make a narrow dogmatism quite unjustified.

This, in fact, leads me to my first point: *when the argument is raised about whether we should teach English as an experience or in graded structural progression, should we not remind ourselves that languages are sufficiently complex to require both approaches?*[9]

A second point I want to make is this: Take the word "this." You show your student, you implore him on your knees, to say simply "this," not "zzizz," or "zith," or "ssiss," or "thith;" or an adult German-speaking student in your class explains that his friend is not coming to the class because his wife "becomes a baby today." Don't fret or get annoyed at their absurdities or their obtuseness. *You must not and cannot ignore the student's mother tongue.* It constitutes his linguistic competence, or network, or frame of reference; it supplies him with a set of associations and a chaining of sounds and patterns that are different in many respects from English. You are helping him to construct a new and different framework, to acquire different sequences, to make new forward guesses. (I might add, language teaching contains far too little of this forward guessing, of training in

---

[9]This point in discussed briefly in "A Comparative View," p. 40.

active participant listening.) *You are helping him to acquire the associations that go with using English in an English-speaking context, so that gradually he gets that sense of right use that will constitute his new English competence.*

Third, *remember that your students, young and old, have heads.* Don't drive them to distraction with pattern practice acrobatics. You are not an animal trainer. They are not parrots or circus dogs. You do not have to condition them. They can cooperate in the language learning process. They can and want to understand the order and rules that govern the use of English; they don't want to grope in the dark. Aspects of language can be explained. Naturally students need practice, but we have no reason to believe that senseless practice is a real help. More than repetitive practice they need experience in using language as listeners or speakers, in real or simulated contexts that are meaningful to the individual learner or group.

When you give them the varied experiences they need, or *when you immerse them, make sure you don't drown them.* Through planned teaching and carefully guided experience we help a student to feel at home in the language, to experiment in his own way, and to come to the new language at his own rate. However much you as a teacher exert your energies, gesticulate or enunciate vigorously, eventually it is the pupil who has to organize the language for himself to develop his own internal network and thus make the language he learns his own.

To conclude, I am convinced there is much in psycholinguistics— and incidentally also in the psychology of learning, of which I have really said nothing—that is relevant to the teaching of a second language. If you are not convinced of this, you are, as I said at the beginning, in very good company.

May I end with one final remark which I address particularly to the sturdy skeptic. Psycholinguistics is an empirical study of language use and acquisition; it proceeds by methods of observation, experiment, and thought. In language teaching, too, it is possible to ask searching questions about language learning and use, to observe, and to think: What does the learner find hard? What does he find easy? What confuses him? What puzzles him? What helps him? What causes his success or failure? How does he learn? What does he find funny, or exciting, or boring? If you ask these and similar questions and seek answers by closely observing the learning of your students and by adapting your teaching to their specific needs, there is more real psycholinguistics in that than if you tried to read all the books and articles that have been written on this subject.

REFERENCES

Anisfield, M. "Psycholinguistic Perspectives on Language Learning." *Trends in Language Teaching.* A. Valdman (ed.). New York: McGraw-Hill, 1966.

Broadbent, D. E. "Notes on Current Knowledge Concerning the Psychology of Learning Modern Languages." Mimeographed. London: Committee on Research and Development in Modern Languages, Fundamental Research Sub-Committee, 1967.

Carroll, J. B. "The Contributions of Psychological Theory and Educational Research to the Teaching of Foreign Languages." *Trends in Language Teaching.* A. Valdman (ed.). New York: McGraw-Hill, 1966.

Chomsky, N. "Review of B. F. Skinner's *Verbal Behavior.*" *Language,* 35 (1959), 26-58.

Dollard, J., and N. E. Miller. *Personality and Psychotherapy: An Analysis in Terms of Learning, Thinking and Culture.* New York: McGraw-Hill, 1950.

Freud, S. *The Psychopathology of Everyday Life.* London: E. Benn, 1966. [Translation of *Zur Psychopathology des Allagslebens,* 1904].

Jakobovits, L. A. "Implications of Recent Psycholinguistic Developments for the Teaching of a Second Language." *Language Learning,* 18, Nos. 1/2 (1968), 89-109.

Jung, C. G. *Diagnostische Assoziationsstudien.* Leipzig, Vol I, 1906; Vol. II, 1910.

Lenneberg, E. H. *Biological Foundations of Language.* New York: Wiley, 1967.

———. "The Capacity for Language Acquisition." *The Structure of Language.* J. A. Fodor and J. J. Katz. (eds.). Englewood Cliffs, N.J.: Prentice-Hall, 1964.

Lewis, M. M. *Infant Speech: A Study of the Beginnings of Language.* London: Routledge and Kegan Paul, 1936.

Miller, G. A. "The Psycholinguists—On the New Scientists of Language." *Encounter* 23, No. I (1964), 29-37.

Miller, G. A., E. Galanter, and K. H. Pribram. *Plans and the Structure of Behavior.* New York: Henry Holt & Co., 1960.

Osgood, C. E., and T. A. Sebeok (eds.). *Psycholinguistics: A Survey of Theory and Research Problems.* Bloomington: Indiana University Press, 1965. [Includes "A Survey of Psycholinguistic Research 1954-1964." A. R. Diebold.]

Piaget, J. *Le Langage et la pensée chez l'enfant.* Paris: Delachaux et Niestle, 1923.

Skinner, B. F. *Verbal Behavior.* New York: Appleton-Century-Crofts, 1957.

Smith, F. B., and G. A. Miller (eds.). *The Genesis of Language.* Cambridge, Mass.: MIT Press, 1966.

Stern, H. H. (ed). *Perspectives on Second Language Teaching.* Toronto: Ontario Institute for Studies in Education, 1971. Pp. 47-56.

Stern, C. and W. Stern. *Die Kindersprache. Eine psychologische und sprachtheoretische Untersuchung.* Leipzig: Barth, 1907.

Watson, J. B. *Psychology from the Standpoint of a Behaviorist.* Philadelphia: J. B. Lippincott Co., 1919.

SUGGESTIONS FOR FURTHER READING

To my knowledge, there is no modern introduction to psycholinguistics specifically designed for second language teachers. In fact, although good books in psycholinguistics are available, especially excellent collections of readings, I know of no easy nontechnical introductory text. With this warning in mind the following works can be recommended:

Oldfield, R. C. and Marshall, J. C. (eds.), *Language: Selected Readings.* Penguin Modern Psychology Series. Harmondsworth, Middlesex, England: Penguin Books, 1968. [The readings are well introduced, and the book contains a useful classified annotated list of suggestions for further reading.]

Miller, G. A. *Language and Communication.* New York: McGraw-Hill, 1951. [The great classic of psycholinguistics. Although not up-to-date, it is still an excellent, informative, and well-written introductory text.]

Lenneberg, E. H. (ed.), *New Directions in the Study of Language*, Cambridge, Mass.: M.I.T. Press, 1964. [A brief set of conference papers discussing results and conclusions from different studies of language acquisition and verbal behavior.]

Hormann, H. *Psychologie der Sprache.* Berlin, Heidelberg, New York: Springer-Verlag, 1967. Translated into English by H. H. Stern as "Psycholinguistics—An Introduction to Research and Theory," same publisher, 1970. [A systematic introduction to psycholinguistic thought and research, seen against the background of psychology, philosophy, and linguistics, and based on a thorough and wide-ranging review of North American and European writings in this field.]

LINGUISTIC THEORY

Noam Chomsky

I should like to make it clear from the outset that I am participating in this conference not as an expert on any aspect of the teaching of languages, but rather as someone whose primary concern is with the structure of language and, more generally, the nature of cognitive processes. Furthermore, I am, frankly, rather skeptical about the significance, for the teaching of languages, of such insights and understanding as have been attained in linguistics and psychology. Surely the teacher of language would do well to keep informed of progress and discussion in these fields, and the efforts of linguists and psychologists to approach the problems of language teaching from a principled point of view are extremely worthwhile, from an intellectual as well as a social point of view. Still, it is difficult to believe that either linguistics or psychology has achieved a level of theoretical understanding that might enable it to support a "technology" of language teaching. Both fields have made significant progress in recent decades, and, furthermore, both draw on centuries of careful thought and study. These disciplines are, at present, in a state of flux and agitation. What seemed to be well-established doctrine a few years ago may now be the subject of extensive debate. Although it would be difficult to document this generalization, it seems to me that there has been a significant decline, over the past ten or fifteen years, in the degree of confidence in the scope and security of foundations in both psychology and linguistics. I personally feel that this decline in confidence is both healthy and realistic. But it should serve as a warning to teachers that suggestions from the "fundamental disciplines" must be viewed with caution and skepticism.

Within psychology, there are now many who would question the view that the basic principles of learning are well understood. Long accepted principles of association and reinforcement, gestalt principles, the theory of concept formation as it has emerged in modern investigation, all of these have been sharply challenged in theoretical as well as experimental work. To me it seems that these principles are not merely inadequate but probably misconceived—that they deal with marginal aspects of acquisition of knowledge and leave the central core of the problem untouched. In particular, it seems to me impossible to accept the view that linguistic behavior is a matter of habit, that it is slowly acquired by reinforcement, association, and generalization, or that linguistic concepts can be specified in terms of a space of elementary, physically defined criterial attributes." Language is not a "habit structure." Ordinary linguistic behavior characteristically involves innovation, formation of new sentences and new patterns in accordance with rules of great abstractness and intricacy. This is true both of the speaker, who constructs new utterances appropriate to the occasion, and of the hearer who must analyze and interpret these novel structures. There are no known principles of association or reinforcement, and no known sense of "generalization" that can begin to account for this characteristic "creative" aspect of normal language use. The new utterances that are produced and interpreted in the daily use of language are "similar" to those that constitute the past experience of speaker and hearer only in that they are determined, in their form and interpretation, by the same system of abstract underlying rules. There is no theory of association or generalization capable of accounting for this fact, and it would, I think, be a fundamental misunderstanding to seek such a theory, since the explanation very likely lies along different lines. The simple concepts of ordinary language (such concepts as "human being" or "knife" or "useful," etc., or, for that matter, the concept "grammatical sentence") cannot be specified in terms of a space of physical attributes, as in the concept formation paradigm. There is, correspondingly, no obvious analogy between the experimental results obtained in studies of concept formation and the actual processes that seem to underlie language learning.

Evidently, such an evaluation of the relevance of psychological theory to language acquisition requires justification, and it is far from uncontroversial. Nor will I attempt, within the framework of this paper, to supply any such justification. My point simply is that the relevance of psychological theory to acquisition of language is a highly dubious and questionable matter, subject to much controversy and plagued with uncertainties of all sorts. The applied psychologist and the teacher must certainly draw what suggestions and hints they can from psychological research, but they would be well advised to do so with the constant realization of how fragile and tentative are the principles of the underlying discipline.

Turning to linguistics, we find much the same situation. Linguists have had their share in perpetuating the myth that linguistic behavior is "habitual" and that a fixed stock of "patterns" is acquired through practice and used as the basis for "analogy." These views could be maintained only as long as grammatical description was sufficiently vague and imprecise. As soon as an attempt is made to give a careful and precise account of the rules of sentence formation, the rules of phonetic organization, or the rules of sound-meaning correspondence in a language, the inadequacy of such an approach becomes apparent. What is more, the fundamental concepts of linguistic description have been subjected to serious critique. The principles of phonemic analysis, for example, have recently been called into question, and the status of the concept "phoneme" is very much in doubt. For that matter, there are basic unsolved problems concerning even the phonetic representations used as a basis for analysis of form in structural linguistics. Whereas a decade ago it would have been almost universally assumed that a phonetic representation is simply a record of physical fact, there is now considerable evidence that what the linguist takes to be a phonetic transcription is determined, in nontrivial ways, by the syntactic structure of the language, and that it is, to this extent, independent of the physical signal. I think there are by now very few linguists who believe that it is possible to arrive at the phonological or syntactic structure of a language by systematic application of "analytic procedures" of segmentation and classifi- cation, although fifteen or twenty years ago such a view was not only widely accepted but was also supported by significant results and quite plausible argument.

I would like to emphasize again that this questioning of fundamental principles is a very healthy phenomenon that has led to important advances and will undoubtedly continue to do so. It is, in fact, characteristic of any living subject. But it must be recognized that well-established theory, in fields like psychology and linguistics, is extremely limited in scope. The applications of physics to engineering may not be seriously affected by even the most deep-seated revolution in the foundations of physics, but the applications of psychology or linguistics to language teaching, such as they are, may be gravely affected by changing conceptions in these fields, since the body of theory that resists substantial modification is fairly small.

In general, the willingness to rely on "experts" is a frightening aspect of contemporary political and social life. Teachers, in particular, have a responsibility to make sure that ideas and proposals are evaluated on their merits, and not passively accepted on grounds of authority, real or presumed. The field of language teaching is no exception. It is possible—even likely—that principles of psychology and linguistics, and research in these disciplines, may supply insights useful to the language teacher. But this must be demonstrated, and cannot be presumed. It is the language teacher himself who must validate or refute any specific proposal. There is very little in psychology or linguistics that he can accept on faith.

I will not try to develop any specific proposals relating to the teaching of languages—as I mentioned before, because I am not competent to do so. But there are certain tendencies and developments within linguistics and psychology that may have some potential impact on the teaching of language. I think these can be usefully summarized under four main headings; the "creative" aspect of language use; the abstractness of linguistic representation; the universality of underlying linguistic structure; the role of intrinsic organization in cognitive processes. I would like to say just a few words about each of these topics.

The most obvious and characteristic property of normal linguistic behavior is that it is stimulus-free and innovative. Repetition of fixed phrases is a rarity; it is only under exceptional and quite uninteresting circumstances that one can seriously consider how "situational context" determines what is said, even in probabilistic terms. The notion that linguistic behavior consists of "responses" to "stimuli" is as much a myth as the idea that it is a matter of habit and generalization. To maintain such assumptions in the face of the actual facts, we must deprive the terms "stimulus" and "response" (similarly "habit" and "generalization") of any technical or precise meaning. This property of being innovative and stimulus-free is what I refer to by the term "creative aspect of language use." It is a property of language that was described in the seventeenth century and that serves as one cornerstone for classical linguistic theory, but that has gradually been forgotten in the development of modern linguistics, much to its detriment. Any theory of language must come to grips with this fundamental property of normal language use. A necessary but not sufficient step towards dealing with this problem is to recognize that the native speaker of a language has internalized a "generative grammar"—a system of rules that can be used in new and untried combinations to form new sentences and to assign semantic interpretations to new sentences. Once this fact has become clear, the immediate task of the linguist is likewise clarified. He must try to discover the rules of the generative grammar and the underlying principles on the basis of which it is organized.

The native speaker of a language has internalized a generative grammar in the sense just described, but he obviously has no awareness of this fact or of the properties of this grammar. The problem facing the linguist is to discover what constitutes unconscious, latent knowledge—to bring to light what is now sometimes called the speaker's intrinsic "linguistic competence." A generative grammar of a language is a theory of the speaker's competence. If correct, it expresses the principles that determine the intrinsic correlation of sound and meaning in the language in question. It thus serves as one component of a theory that can accommodate the characteristic creative aspect of language use.

When we try to construct explicit, generative grammars and investigate their properties, we discover at once many inadequacies in traditional and modern linguistic descriptions. It is often said that no complete generative grammar has ever been written for any language, the implication being that this "new-fangled" approach suffers in comparison with older and well-established approaches to language description, in this respect. The statement concerning generative grammar is quite accurate; the conclusion, if intended, reveals a serious misunderstanding. Even the small fragments of generative grammars that now exist are incomparably greater in explicit coverage than traditional or structuralist descriptions, and it is important to be aware of this fact. A generative grammar is simply one that gives explicit rules that determine the structure of sentences, their phonetic form, and their semantic interpretation. The limitations of generative grammar are the limitations of our knowledge, in these areas. Where traditional or structuralist descriptions are correct, they can immediately be incorporated into generative grammars. Insofar as these descriptions merely list examples of various kinds and make remarks (which may be interesting and suggestive) about them, then they cannot be directly incorporated into generative grammars. In other words, a traditional or structuralist description can be immediately incorporated into a generative grammar to the extent that it is correct and does not rely on the "intelligence of the reader" and his "linguistic intuition." The limitations of generative grammar, then, are a direct reflection of the limitations of correctness and explicitness in earlier linguistic work.

A serious investigation of generative grammars quickly shows that the rules that determine the form of sentences and their interpretations are not only intricate but also quite abstract, in the sense that the structures they manipulate are related to physical fact only in a remote way, by a long chain of interpretative rules. This is as true on the level of phonology as it is on the level of syntax and semantics, and it is this fact that has led to the questioning both of structuralist principles and of the tacitly assumed psychological theory that underlies them. It is because of the abstractness of linguistic representations that one is forced, in my opinion, to reject not only the analytic procedures of modern linguistics, with their reliance on segmentation and classification, but also principles of association and generalization that have been discussed and studied in empiricist psychology. Although such phenomena as association and generalization, in the sense of psychological theory and philosophical speculation, may indeed exist, it is difficult to see how they have any bearing on the acquisition or use of language. If our current conceptions of generative grammar are at all accurate, then the structures manipulated and the principles operating in these grammars are not related to given sensory phenomena in any way describable in the terms that empiricist psychology offers, and what principles it suggests simply have no relation to the facts that demand explanation.

If it is correct that the underlying principles of generative grammars cannot be acquired through experience and training, then they must be part of the intellectual organization which is a prerequisite for language acquisition. They must, therefore, be universal properties, properties of any generative grammar. These are, then, two distinct ways of approaching what is clearly the most fundamental question of linguistic science, namely, the question of linguistic universals. One way is by an investigation of a wide range of languages. Any hypothesis as to the nature of linguistic universals must meet the empirical condition that it is not falsified by any natural language, any language acquired and used by humans in the normal way. But there is also another and, for the time being, somewhat more promising way of studying the problem of universals. This is by deep investigation of a particular language, investigation directed toward establishing underlying principles of organization of great abstractness in this language. Where such principles can be established, we must account for their existence. One plausible hypothesis is that they are innate, therefore, universal. Another plausible hypothesis is that they are acquired through experience and training. Either hypothesis can be made precise; each will then be meaningful and worthy of attention. We can refute the former by showing that other aspects of this language or properties of other languages are inconsistent with it. We can refute the latter by showing that it does not yield the structures that we must presuppose to account for linguistic competence. In general, it seems to me quite impossible to account for many deep-seated aspects of language on the basis of training or experience, and that therefore one must search for an explanation for them in terms of intrinsic intellectual organization. An almost superstitious refusal to consider this proposal seriously has, in my opinion, enormously set back both linguistics and psychology. For the present, it seems to me that there is no more reason for assuming that the basic principles of grammar are learned than there is for making a comparable assumption about, let us say, visual perception. There is, in short, no more reason to suppose that a person learns that English has a generative grammar of a very special and quite explicitly definable sort than there is to suppose that the same person learns to analyze the visual field in terms of line, angle, motion, solidity, persons with faces, etc.

Turning then to the last of the four topics mentioned above, I think that one of the most important current developments in psychology and neurophysiology is the investigation of intrinsic organization in cognition. In the particular case of language, there is good reason to believe that even the identification of the phonetic form of a sentence presupposes at least a partial syntactic analysis, so that the rules of the generative grammar may be brought into play even in identifying the signal. This view is opposed to the hypothesis that phonetic representation is determined by the signal completely, and that the perceptual analysis proceeds from formal signals to interpretation, a hypothesis which, I understand, has been widely quoted in discussions of language teaching. The role of the generative grammar in perception is paralleled by the role of the universal grammar—the system of invariant underlying principles of linguistic organization—in acquisition of language. In each case, it seems to me that the significance of the intrinsic organization is very great indeed, and that the primary goal of linguistic and psychological investigation of language must be to determine and characterize it.

I am not sure that this very brief discussion of some of the leading ideas of much current research has been sufficiently clear to be either informative or convincing. Once again, I would like to stress that the implications of these ideas for language teaching are far from clear to me. It is a rather dubious undertaking to try to predict the course of development of any field, but, for what it is worth, it seems to me likely that questions of this sort will dominate research in the coming years, and, to hazard a further guess, that this research will show that certain highly abstract structures and highly specific principles of organization are characteristic of all human languages, are intrinsic rather than acquired, play a central role in perception as well as in production of sentences, and provide the basis for the creative aspect of language use.

SOME PSYCHOLINGUISTIC CONTROVERSIES

John W. Oller, Jr.

> As long as the specialist guards his own results, they
> are vague in meaning and uncertain in content. That
> individuals in every branch of human endeavor be
> experimentalists engaged in testing the findings of
> theorists is the sole guarantee for the sanity of the
> theorist (John Dewey, *Essays in Experimental Logic*,
> 1916, p. 442).

There is an incestuous tendency among many of the so-called
"experts" in the academic disciplines, including linguists and
psychologists, to talk mainly to each other rather than to teachers or
other "lay" audiences. This inbreeding ultimately produces theories
expressed in jargons incomprehensible to all but a special breed of
expert. The intermarriage of theory exclusively with theory and not
with practice, if repeated over generations of theories results in at
least two types of deformed offspring: one is inapplicable theory,
and another is misapplied theory. The zealous exponents of the latter
type of theory adopt terms from a jargon without understanding
either the purpose or the mechanics of the theory which spawned it.
The former type of theory is the product of theoreticians who are
content to theorize in a way that is quite unconcerned with the
explanation, prediction, or understanding of the facts of language use
or language learning.

In the present discussion I wish to suggest: (1) that the currently
dominant theory of transformational grammar which has its roots in
American structural linguistics indulges in the error of asking *how
linguistic units are linked together* without giving sufficient attention
to questions concerning *what information is being coded*; (2) that
failure to give adequate attention to the use of language to convey
information has carried over into theories of second language
learning and methods of second language teaching; and (3) that the

---

*The material contained in this paper is drawn from the following articles:
"Transformational Theory and Pragmatics," *Modern Language Journal*, 54 (1970), 504-7;
"Language Communication and Second Language Learning," *Psychology of Second
Language Learning*, Pimsleur and Quinn (eds.), Cambridge, Mass.: Cambridge University
Press, 1971: "Language Use and Foreign Language Learning," *International Review of
Applied Linguistics*, 9 (1971) 161-8; "Controversies in Linguistics and the Teaching of
English as a Second Language," *UCLA TESL Workpapers* 6 (1972), 39-50. I want to thank
David Ewing for critical comments on the manuscript.

presupposition that language coding involves both complex linguistic forms and complex sets of extralinguistic information is essential to an adequate theory of second language learning.

1. Errors in Chomskian Thinking

To begin with, let us examine briefly some major tenets of transformational theory from 1957 through 1966. In *Syntactic Structures* (1957), Chomsky stated that his grammar was to be a completely formal description of language structure with "no explicit reference to the way this instrument is put to use" (p. 103). He argued that syntax and semantics were to be strictly separated, saying "grammar is best formulated as a self-contained study independent of semantics" (p. 106). Clearly, Chomsky's original thinking was that language was best understood apart from its instrumental use. This notion reflected the earlier theorizing of Leonard Bloomfield (1933) and Zellig Harris (1947).

In 1963, with the publication of Katz and Fodor's now famous paper on semantic theory, it finally became generally recognized by American linguists that an adequate theory of language would have to deal with meaning. However, Katz and Fodor assumed that the meanings of utterances could be described independently of the settings in which they might occur. They ruled out consideration of situational and linguistic contexts by arguing that "a sentence cannot have readings [i.e., meanings] in a context that it does not have in isolation" (p. 488). Again, they were attempting to treat language as a self-contained system apart from its actual use. Oller, Sales, and Harrington (1969) have argued to the contrary that an utterance cannot have any meaning in isolation that it does not have in some context. Sentences have meaning *because* they are used in communication. In order to understand their meaning and structure, it is necessary to study the relationships which hold between the units of language and the extralinguistic things talked about by speakers of the language. In addition to asking "How do linguistic units relate to linguistic units?", we must also ask "How do linguistic units relate to nonlinguistic settings?" In order to answer the latter question, it should be clear that the contexts of utterances are essential.

Katz and Postal (1964) followed Katz and Fodor (1963) in excluding the communicative contexts of utterances from consideration. Their semantic theory was largely adopted by Chomsky (1965) who continued to argue that it was fruitless to talk about "a semantic basis for syntax" (p. 78). In Chomsky (1966a), it is argued that the study of the relation between linguistic units and extralinguistic facts is not necessary to a theory of language.

More recent transformational theory still assumes that language is a self-contained system which is independent of its use. It continues to ignore the basic fact that "language is a tool for communicating *something to somebody*" (Schwarcz, 1970, p. 2). In response to earlier criticisms concerning this point, Chomsky (1968) still maintained that language is "free from the control of detectable stimuli, either external or internal" (p. 11). This assumption is the source of several erroneous conclusions which have had an impact on a broad spectrum of language theory and practice.

First, it leads to the rejection of the basic psychological principles of learning. Chomsky says, "It seems to me impossible to accept the view that linguistic behavior . . . is slowly acquired by reinforcement, association, and generalization" (this volume, p. 30). As an alternative to these principles he has proposed "innate ideas" which are defined as inborn knowledge of the structure of natural languages. A child is supposedly born with knowledge of language which is merely triggered and set in action by external stimulation (Chomsky, 1965, pp. 47-60). Katz and Postal (1964) have attempted to lend support to this view by proving that the phonetic form of utterances by itself is too "impoverished" to enable the child to acquire the capacity to speak and understand a language (p. 172-3). Katz (1966, pp. 250-2), presents a similar argument. To resolve the theoretical impasse Katz alleges that the child must possess innate ideas though he admits that no one has yet proposed what form they might take (p. 248).

I suggest that the need for "innate ideas" rests on the false premise that the phonetic form of utterances is the *only* information on which the child might base generalizations. The latter premise stems from the assumption that language is self-contained. When language use is taken into account, the phonetic form of utterances is obviously not the only information available to the child. The utterances which he observes occur in contexts that are rich in situational information. Words and sentences are observed to relate to persons, events, objects, and relations in a systematic way. The arguments of Katz and Postal are devoid of any practical consequence (Oller and Sales, 1969).

It seems to me that the very principles which transformational theory rejects undoubtedly constitute essential ingredients of the innate capacity that the child brings to the learning situation. Cognitive psychologists have long recognized the importance of man's ability to categorize the elements of his experience. This capacity is reflected in the principle of generalization and is a process involved in practically every aspect of human cognition (Bruner, Goodnow, and Austin, 1956; and Hunt, 1962). That it will continue to defy formalization in the future is improbable (for a preliminary attempt see Oller, 1972c). The fact that similar patterns are substitutable to the extent of their similarity is another likely candidate for status as a basic innate principle. In addition to these, there is the complex sensory apparatus and the abstract memory space that the child inherits.[1]

A second incorrect conclusion of transformational theory, which is based on the assumption that language is self-contained, is that "deep structure" is not related to sensory data in any way discoverable by the principles of generalization and association. There is, however, little agreement among leading transformationalists on just what deep structure is. In one of his more recent papers, Chomsky (1969) has challenged the various definitions suggested by Lakoff (1968), McCawley (1968), and Fillmore (1968).

Chomsky says, "a system of propositions expressing the meaning of a sentence is produced in the mind as the sentence is realized as a physical signal, the two being related by . . . *grammatical transformations* . . . . We can distinguish the *surface structure* of the sentence, the organization of categories and phrases that is directly associated with the physical signal, from the *deep structure*, also a system of categories and phrases with a more abstract character" (1968, p. 25). As an example he suggests the sentence "A wise man is honest" which in terms of surface structure is analyzed into the subject, "a wise man", and the predicate, "is honest". According to Chomsky, the deep structure consists of two propositions, "A man is wise" and "A man is honest". These are supposedly "interrelated in such a way as to express the meaning of the sentence 'A wise man is honest' " (pp. 25-6).

Notice that if we take "A man is wise" and "A man is honest" in their most obvious senses, their combined meanings are quite different from the assertion "A wise man is honest". Moreover, there is nothing in them to indicate that the sentence "A wise man is honest" means that wisdom requires honesty. Besides, if we relate the sentence "A wise man is honest" to men and the characteristics of men in the real world, the sentence can easily be understood

---

[1]Of course, Chomsky rejects the notion of an underlying memory space (1965, pp. 47-58; also, this volume, p. 3 0).

without the appeal to the so-called "deep-structure propositions". This is true for sentences in general.

Do we understand the sentence "Apple pie is delicious" on the basis of the abstract propositions "Pie is apple" and "Pie is delicious"? Or do we understand it because we know what apple pie is, and what delicious things are like? Do we comprehend the sentence "Pedantic scholarship is a lot of baloney" because we know the abstract propositions "Scholarship is pedantic" and "Scholarship is a lot of baloney"?

To suggest that one sentence is understood in terms of another, or others, leads us either into an infinite regress, or against a blank wall. Ultimately we must produce sentences which are either uninterpreted or are associated via transformational rules with other sentences which are uninterpreted. In addition to the fact that the process is circular, we will have confused sentences with meanings. This error is an identical twin to the one which leads to the semantic and logical paradoxes.[2] It stems from a failure to keep the symbol separate from what it stands for.

The third false conclusion of transformationalism which stems from the assumption that language is self-contained is that the primary source of information for theories of language is an "ideal speaker-listener . . . who knows its language perfectly" (Chomsky, 1965, p. 3). Since the knowledge of this hypothetical person is represented in a transformational grammar, the intuition of the linguist who conjured him up is the ultimate test of adequacy. Chomsky says that whenever an operational test is proposed for a grammar, the test must be subjected to linguistic intuition (1965, p. 19). Apparently, Chomsky means to say that if the test seems intuitively incorrect its results should be ignored. If language were a fully self-contained system, this argument would be impeccable.

The fourth erroneous conclusion derives directly from the third. The original distinction between "competence," the speaker's

---

[2]For example, if a man says, "I am lying" and if what he says is taken to refer to what he is saying at the time—that is, if we confuse the symbol with what is symbolized—we face a paradox. If the man is telling the truth, he must be lying because that is what he says he is doing. If he is lying, he must be telling the truth since he says he is lying. In either case he is both lying and telling the truth. The same sort of problem arises in set theory if a set is allowed to be a member of itself. Russell's solution to this in the theory of types is to require that a set be regarded as a higher logical type that its members. Otherwise the set violates the intuitive requirement that it be identical with itself—if it contains itself, it has to contain one member more than it actually contains. Moreover, if the set which contains itself—logically a different set from the set without itself as a member—is allowed to contain itself, we find ourselves in an absurd infinite regress. See Russell (1919).

capacity to use his language, and "performance," the actual instances of usage, has been obscured by equating competence with the knowledge of the ideal speaker, thus leaving real performance unaccounted for. While a transformational grammar may represent clearly the competence of a hypothetical construct, it cannot replicate even the simplest act of communication performed by real speakers of language. The fact that a woman in a commercial can say "My girdle is killing me" and that we can understand her is unexplained by the best of current transformational grammars. I believe that it is for this reason that Chomsky (1965, pp. 10-15) concluded that an additional "theory of performance" was needed.[3] Such a theory, however, could scarcely remedy the situation. The fact is that language communication is characterized by the same creativity as the generation of novel sentences. I may report having imagined a red-and-blue-spotted baboon swimming in purple dye, green-and-white-striped elephants floating around in the air, or orange-and-pink-speckled birds flying across the North Pole, and a speaker of English will have no difficulty in understanding me however odd he may think my imaginings. What we need is not an additional theory of performance, but an adequate theory of competence.

The fifth deduction of transformationalists is that their theory is not applicable to foreign language teaching in any definite way (Chomsky, 1966b, this volume). How could this conclusion possibly be wrong? As Santayana has said, "It is a great advantage for a system of philosophy to be substantially true."

2. Extensions to the Classroom

At this point, the reader may well ask how all of this relates to second language teaching and second language learning. I believe that the question of whether language is essentially a self-contained system or more basically a medium of communication is crucial to theories of second language learning and methods of second language teaching. Suppose that we assume, as transformational theory does,

---

[3]If we assume with Chomsky (1965) that a model of competence need not account for the facts of performance, then a separate performance model does indeed seem to be called for. This seems undesirable, however, because it abolishes the original definition of competence—namely, the speaker's capacity to use his language. By this definition, an adequate model of competence must account for performance, thereby obviating the need for an extra model of performance. For some of the arguments on this point, see Oller, Sales, and Harrington (1970). For a different point of view calling for a model of performance, see Fromkin (1968) and Schwarcz (1967).

that language is a self-contained system. Our emphasis in theory and practice will necessarily be structural. Clear evidence that linguistic theory has in fact encouraged an emphasis on physical structure, often at the expense of meaning, is found in the vast literature on contrastive studies done at the phonemic, morphemic, and syntactic levels. By contrast, there is an extremely sparse literature in applied linguistics on the semantic and pragmatic aspects of language. In fact, the study of the pragmatic facts of language, i.e., those having to do with the interrelationships between linguistic units, speakers, and extralinguistic information, have been almost totally neglected in applied linguistics.[4]

It was apparently because of the assumption that language is self-contained that Nelson Brooks (1964) and Rand Morton (1960, 1966) argued that manipulative skills should be acquired through pattern drills which in themselves were not related to communicative activity. Morton went so far as to insist that the acquisition of manipulative skills had to precede expressive use. That is to say that syntactic and phonological structures are best acquired by drill apart from their instrumental use. In an experiment designed to test the relative effectiveness of presenting structures apart from communicative activity and within active communication, Oller and Obrecht (1968) showed that exactly the reverse is true. The mechanical manipulation of structures is best learned in the context of communication.

A slightly weaker claim than that of Brooks and Morton has been made by Prator (1970), and Stockwell and Bowen (1968). The latter authors say "the most difficult transition in learning a language is going from mechanical skill in reproducing patterns acquired by repetition to construction of novel but appropriate sentences in natural social contexts" (Rutherford, 1968, p.vii). I maintain that there is no need at all to make this "difficult transition"; that in fact one can scarcely begin to learn a language at all without "associating

---

[4]In this paper, I am concerned mainly with the effect that a pragmatic view has on theories of the structure of language and the coding of content. However, *pragmatics also encompasses the structure of human relationships and the grammars that govern social interactional patterns.* The complexity of the latter type of grammar is surely no less than that of linguistic structure, and may have far more important implications for teaching than the kind of improvements pragmatics suggests for theories of language use and language learning. For an insightful and entertaining introduction to the application of pragmatics to human relationships, see Watzlawick, Beavin, and Jackson (1967). Also, the entire section of this volume entitled "Sociocultural and Motivational Factors" deals with the relationship aspect of communication. For a more complete discussion of the total scope of pragmatics as it applies to language teaching, see Oller (forthcoming).

appropriate sentences" with their "social contexts." Anything less is not language learning in the first place. Why create unnecessary hurdles? Why not begin learning language in its natural state, in the contexts of communication?

The usual organization of textbooks on the basis of syntactic principles rather than semantic or pragmatic ones is another reflection in second language teaching of the assumption that languages are best viewed as self-contained systems. So many textbooks fall into this category that it would be unreasonable to try to mention even a significant number of them. It seems that the criticism made by Otto Jespersen in 1904 of many foreign language textbooks of his day is as à propos as ever in the 1970's. He said, "The reader of certain foreign language texts often gets the impression that Frenchmen are strictly systematical beings who one day speak merely in futures, another day in passé définis, and who say the most disconnected things only for the sake of being able to use all the persons in the tense which for the time being happens to be the subject for conversation" (p. 17).

It has been shown (Oller and Obrecht, 1969) that sentences of a foreign language are learned more readily when they are placed in a meaningful sequence. In other words, learning is more efficient when the natural order of utterances in communicative events is preserved. The obvious explanation for this is that the student is able to capitalize on what he already knows about sentences in relation to situational settings if materials are arranged in such contexts. He has certain expectations about what sorts of information can follow from what has preceded (Oller, 1972b). This frees him in part from concentrating on decoding meanings and allows him to relate forms and meanings. McGeoch and Irion (1952) explained it this way: "When one says that material A is more readily learned than material B because A is the more meaningful, one implies that A receives more advantage from transfer effects. This in turn is tantamount to saying that the learner already knew more about A at the beginning, or that he possessed more effects of prior learning that would be brought to bear on the practice of A" (pp. 471-2).

All of the foregoing supports the assumption that the communicative function of language is an essential point of concern for any theory of second language learning which aims at adequacy. It suggests that the basic principles underlying many current theories of second language learning and practices in second language teaching may need a thorough re-evaluation. It seems that one of the most important problems for research and experimentation is the relative importance of syntactic, semantic, and pragmatic factors in second language learning. If contrastive analyses are updated to relate coding processes in different languages, we may well discover that the most important principles to be considered in program construction are pragmatic ones. A sequence of lessons which are connected in terms of the extralinguistic information they contain may be superior to lessons or series of lessons linked together only by the syntactic principles they illustrate. This is not to say that the more familiar syntactic and phonological properties of language should be neglected, but rather that perhaps they should be presented in a more realistic context from the point of view of language communication.

It seems that we would do well to reconsider the relative importance of the questions "How are units linked together in a language?", and "How do linguistic units relate to nonlinguistic settings?" We should be careful to remember that the former question presupposes the latter; that real utterances are *intrinsically* structured for communication.

3. Pragmatics as an Alternative

The argument in favor of treating language as a medium of communication was well put by Bertrand Russell in his book entitled *An Inquiry into Meaning and Truth* (1940). He was voicing a criticism of the viewpoint of certain philosophers of the logical positivist persuasion. His criticism is acutely applicable as a refutation of Chomsky's argument that language should be regarded as a self-contained system independent of its use. Russell says, "The purpose of words, though philosophers seem to forget this simple fact, is to deal with matters other than words. If I go into a restaurant and order my dinner, I do not want my words to fit into a system with other words, but to bring about the presence of food" (p. 186).

Anton Reichling (1961) has suggested that the very viewpoint which Russell was criticizing above is the historical source of transformational theory. Regardless of whether or not Reichling is correct, it should be clear that language does function to codify information about extralinguistic entities, relations, desires, etc. Thus, a theory which continues to deal exclusively with relations between linguistic units and other linguistic units cannot hope to achieve adequacy.

This would seem to be the best explanation for the current trend among a few leading transformationalists away from language as a self-contained system and toward language as a medium of communication. Rather than viewing grammar as a system with a syntactic component as its central element with no input to it as shown in Figure 1, current tendency is to view grammar as mediating between a highly-organized conceptual data set on the one hand and phonetic representation on the other, with inputs and outputs going in both directions as shown in Figure 2.

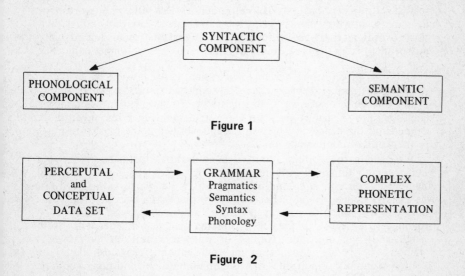

Figure 1

Figure 2

The latter model is more consonant with the fact that language is used for communicative purposes.

The importance of the relation between linguistic units and nonlinguistic settings was clearly recognized by Albert Einstein in his classic radio address entitled "The Common Language of Science" (1941). The following quotation from that talk indicates not only his realization of the pragmatic nature of language, but also his understanding of the significance of this fact for the process of language learning:

> The first step towards language was to link acoustically or otherwise commutable signs to sense-impressions. Most likely all sociable animals have arrived at this primitive kind of communication—at least to a certain degree. A higher development is reached when further signs are introduced

and understood which establish relations between those other signs designating sense-impressions. At this stage it is already possible to report somewhat complex series of impressions; we can say that language has come into existence. If language is to lead at all to understanding, there must be rules concerning relations between the signs on the one hand and on the other there must be a stable correspondence between signs and impressions. In their childhood individuals connected by the same language grasp these rules and relations mainly by intuition. When man becomes conscious of the rules concerning the relations between signs, the so-called grammar of language is established.

In an early stage the words may correspond directly to impressions. At a later stage this direct connection is lost insofar as some words convey relations to perceptions only if used in connection with other words (for instance such words as: "is", or "thing"). Then word-groups rather than single words refer to perceptions. When language becomes thus partially independent from the background of impressions a greater inner coherence is gained.

Only at this further development where frequent use is made of so-called abstract concepts, language becomes an instrument of reasoning in the true sense of the word. But it is also this development which turns language into a dangerous source of error and deception. Everything depends on the degree to which words and word-combinations correspond to the world of impression.

What is it that brings about such an intimate connection between language and thinking? Is there no thinking without the use of language, namely in concepts and concept-combinations for which words need not necessarily come to mind? Has not every one of us struggled for words although the connection between "things" was already clear? We might be inclined to attribute to the act of thinking complete independence from language if the individual formed or were able to form his concepts without the verbal guidance of his environment. Yet most likely the mental shape of an individual growing up under such conditions would be very poor. Thus we may conclude that the mental development of the individual and his way of forming concepts depend to a high degree upon language. This makes us realize to what extent the same language means the same mentality. In this sense thinking and language are linked together (Hayden and Alworth, 1965, pp. 383-5).

In this brief discussion, Einstein sets forth in an intentionally summarial fashion, some insightful fundamental propositions about the nature of language and its relation to learning and concept formation. He suggests that: (a) language consists of rule-governed sequences of signs related in stable ways to the world of sensory impressions (or, in our terminology, to "extralinguistic settings"), (b) in the initial stages, language is linked in a primitive and direct way to sensory impressions; (c) at a later stage language acquires greater freedom from any direct and obvious link to immediate sensory impressions; (d) as language becomes more complex and abstract it also becomes an instrument of reasoning and increases the possibility for inferential error; (*e*) while at the early stages language is dependent upon the linking of immediate impressions with signs, at later stages, language itself plays a part in shaping thought and conceptualization.

Einstein's remarks and the propositions concerning language which they entail are in direct opposition to Chomsky's basic assumptions that language is a self-contained system; that "innate ideas" are the basis for language learning; and that there is no discoverable relation between "deep structures" and situational settings. Frankly, I prefer the viewpoint expressed by Russell and Einstein in the above quotations over the position taken by Chomsky. It is on this basis that I have proposed a pragmatic theory of language as an alternative to Chomsky's transformational approach (Oller, 1971).

Pragmatics is defined as the study of the correspondence of linguistic forms to contexts. It logically includes syntax and semantics. Interestingly, pragmatic factors appear to be more important than phonological and syntactic ones when it comes to matters of speech perception, production, and language learning (Oller, 1972*a*). Pragmatics places emphasis not so much on entities as on their relationships within a broader perspective. It is because of the relation which linguistic forms have to extralinguistic settings that William James spoke of the "cash-value of words" (Hayden and Alworth, 1965, pp. 221-8). This value is set by the rules of usage which govern what people say in order to convey meanings. These are the rules that a child learns in acquiring language, and that the language teacher seeks to instill in his students.

If we broaden the scope of psycholinguistic inquiry from the sentence as an abstraction, to real language in use, relations and patterns which were previously concealed come into view. Old concepts take on new meanings. Innate ideas look a great deal like the principles of association and generalization built into a complex sensory mechanism and an abstract memory space. Language competence is seen as the native speaker's capacity to use his language to encode and decode messages. Deep structures appear to be pragmatic relations between situational settings (referents, actions, events, abstract concepts, etc.) and linguistic forms rather than relations between sentences and underlying sentences.

Furthermore, the concept of pragmatics has definite implications for theories of language learning and methods of language teaching. With respect to material construction, for instance, it indicates that the structures selected should be presented in meaningful contexts where normal sequences of events are observed. It also indicates that pattern drills should be designed so that instead of manipulating purely abstract elements of a verbal calculus—usually a paradigm of totally unrelated sentences illustrating a point of syntax—the student should be using language in response to a paradigm of situations. Instead of concentrating on the words coming out of his mouth, he should be thinking about the ideas in his head that he wishes to communicate.

Pragmatics defines the goal of teaching a language as inducing the student not merely to manipulate meaningless sound sequences, but to send and receive messages in the language. The necessary and sufficient means for achieving this objective is the involvement of the student in active communication in the target language. The sooner, the better. In the final analysis, language like every other blessing derives its value from its use alone.

REFERENCES

Bloomfield, L. *Language*. New York: Holt, 1933.

Brooks, N. *Language and Language Learning: Theory and Practice*, 2d. ed. New York: Harcourt, 1964.

Bruner, J., J. Goodnow, and G. A. Austin. *A Study of Thinking.* New York: Wiley, 1956.

Chomsky, N. *Syntactic Structures.* The Hague: Mouton, 1957.

———. *Aspects of the Theory of Syntax.* Cambridge, Mass.: M.I.T. Press, 1965.

———. *Cartesian Linguistics.* New York: Harper & Row, 1966(*a*).

———. "Linguistic Theory." *Northeast Conference on the Teaching of Foreign Languages*. R. G. Mead (ed.). Menasha, Wis.: George Banta, 1966(*b*). Reprinted in this volume, pp. 29-35.

———. *Language and Mind.* New York: Harcourt, 1968.

———. "Deep Structure, Surface Structure, and Semantic Interpretation," Mimeographed. Indiana University Linguistics Club, 1969.

Einstein, A. "The Common Language of Science." *Classics in Semantics*. D. E. Hayden and E. P. Alworth (eds.). New York: Philosophical Library, 1965.

Fillmore, C. J. "The Case for Case." *Universals in Linguistic Theory*. E. Bach and R. Harms (eds.). New York: Holt, 1968.

Fodor, J. A., and J. J. Katz (eds.). *The Structure of Language*. Englewood Cliffs, N. J.: Prentice-Hall, 1964.

Fromkin, V. "Speculations on Performance Models." *Journal of Linguistics*, 4 (1968), 47-68.

Harris, Z. *Methods in Structural Linguistics.* Chicago: University of Chicago Press, 1951. Reprinted as *Structural Linguistics*, 1961.

Hunt, E. B. *Concept Learning*. New York: Wiley, 1962.

James, W. "What Pragmatism Means." *Classics in Semantics.* D. E. Hayden and E. P. Alworth (eds.). New York: Philosophical Library, 1965.

Jespersen, O. *How to Teach a Foreign Language.* London: Allen and Unwin, 1904. Reprinted in 1956.

Katz, J. J. *The Philosophy of Language.* New York: Harper & Row, 1966.

Katz, J. J., and J. A. Fodor. "The Structure of a Semantic Theory." *Language*, 39 (1963), 170-210. Reprinted in Fodor and Katz (1964).

Katz, J. J., and P. Postal. *An Integrated Theory of Linguistic Descriptions.* Cambridge, Mass.: M.I.T. Press, 1964.

Lakoff, George. "Instrumental Adverbs and the Concept of Deep Structure." *Foundations of Language*, 4 (1968), 4-29.

McCawley, J. D. "The Role of Semantics in Grammar." *Universals in Linguistic Theory.* E. Bach and R. Harms (eds.). New York: Holt, 1968.

McGeoch, J. A., and A. Irion. *The Psychology of Human Learning.* New York: MacMillan, 1952.

Morton, F. *The Language Lab as a Teaching Machine.* Ann Arbor: University of Michigan, 1966.

———. "The Behavioral Analysis of Spanish Syntax." *International Review of Applied Linguistics*, 4 (1966), 170-7.

Oller, J. W. "Contrastive Analysis, Difficulty, and Predictability." *Foreign Language Annals* (1972*a*) 6, 95-106.

———. "Expectancy for Successive Elements." *Foreign Language Annals* (1972*b*), in press.

———. "Transfer and Interference." *International Journal of Psycholinguistics* (1972*c*), (cf. *Linguistics*, 89, 1972, 24-33).

———. *Coding Information in Natural Languages.* The Hague: Mouton, 1971.

———. *Pragmatics and Learning.* (forthcoming).

Oller, J. W., and D. H. Obrecht. "Pattern Drill and Communicative Activity." *International Review of Applied Linguistics*, 6 (1968), 165-74.

———. "The Psycholinguistic Principle of Informational Sequence." *International Review of Applied Linguistics,* 7 (1969), 117-23.

Oller, J. W. and B. D. Sales. "Conceptual Restrictions on English: A Psycholinguistic Study." *Lingua*, 23 (1969), 209-32.

Oller, J. W., B. D. Sales, and R. V. Harrington. "A Basic Circularity in Traditional and Current Linguistic Theory." *Lingua*, 22 (1969), 317-28.

———. "Toward Consistent Definitions of Some Psycholinguistic Terms." *Linguistics*, 57 (1970), 48-59.

Prator, C. H. "Development of a Manipulation-Communication Scale." *English Teaching Forum*, 3 (1970), 3-6.

Reichling, A. "Principles and Methods of Syntax: Cryptanalytical Formalism." *Lingua*, 10 (1961), 1-17.

Russell, B. *Introduction to Mathematical Philosophy.* London: Allen and Unwin, 1919.

Schwarcz, R. M. "Steps Toward a Model of Linguistic Performance." *Machine Translation*, 10 (1967), 39-52.

———. "Toward a Computational Formalization of Natural Language Semantics." SP a Professional Paper, 3381/000/01; Systems Development Corporation, Santa Monica, California, 1970.

Stockwell, R. P., and J. D. Bowen. "Foreword." to W. E. Rutherford, *Modern English*. New York: Harcourt, 1968.

Watzlawick, P., J. Beavin, and D. Jackson. *Pragmatics of Human Communication: A Study of Interactional Patterns, Pathologies, and Paradoxes.* New York: Norton, 1967.

PART I: DISCUSSION QUESTIONS

1. Mackey uses an example of a derivation of the pronoun "us" from A. Hill (p. 6·). He does this to illustrate that there may be little connection between the units of language and those of linguistic analysis. He goes on to say, "a learner may not be blamed for wondering whether the units and categories alleged to form the essential elements of the language exist only in the minds of those who have attempted to describe it" (p. 7). Suppose that the learner were correct. What other conclusions might be drawn from the illustration?

2. In his concluding statement, Mackey suggests that language teaching will eventually become "an autonomous discipline" which uses linguistics and psychology "instead of being used by them" (p. 13). Consider this statement in light of the current trend toward interdisciplinary studies (e.g., psycholinguistics and sociolinguistics). Refer to Chomsky where he says that "It is the language teacher himself who must validate or refute any specific proposal" (p. 32). Has the discipline already become autonomous?

3. Stern mentions a "strange interplay of the novel and the familiar, the inventive and the expected" (p. 17) in language use. Compare this view with Chomsky's statement that "new utterances that are produced and interpreted in the daily use of language are 'similar' to those that constitute the past experience of speaker and hearer only in that they are determined, in their form and interpretation, by the same system of abstract underlying rules" (p. 30). Discuss their remarks in light of the following utterances. In what ways are the following utterances novel? In what ways are they familiar?

    a.) Hello. How are you?
    b.) Eagles have long sharp talons.
    c.) Magic has blue iron wings.
    d.) It on the has why before.

4. According to Stern, the task of the language *teacher* is "to bring to the learner of English as a second language the same sense of English that enables us to use and understand English discourse" (p. 18). According to

Chomsky, the job of the *linguist* is "to discover the rules" of the generative grammar that determines the "intrinsic correlation of sound and meaning in the language in question" (p. 33). In what ways are these tasks distinct? Do the differences justify skepticism concerning "the significance, for the teaching of languages, of such insights . . . as have been attained in linguistics and psychology" (Chomsky, p. 29)? Or, is the skepticism more easily justified by questioning the validity of the supposed insights?

5. *"Why is it that first language acquisition is foolproof, whereas second language learning so frequently fails"* (Stern p. 19)?

6. Discuss Skinner's thesis referred to by Stern (p. 19) that the distinctively human behaviors involved in language are not fundamentally different from the behaviors of other animals. Consider especially the claims of Chomsky concerning the unique aspects of language mentioned by Stern (p. 20 f) and in Chomsky's own paper (p. 33 ff).

7. Evaluate the statement by Stern that "there might be a place in second language learning for the linguistic creativeness and inventiveness that the modern school of linguistics emphasizes" (p. 21).

8. To test the statement that "listening . . . is an extremely active process" (Stern, p. 24), examine a variety of errors committed by nonnative speakers in taking dictation. Refer to the list on p. 195-196.

9. What are some of the ramifications of the claims that the "existing frame of reference" of the second language learner "blocks him and cannot help him in perception" (Stern, p. 24). Similarly, "in learning a second language we have to build up a totally fresh frame of reference" (Stern, p. 24). How might these remarks be tested experimentally?

10. Discuss some of the ways in which popular pattern drill approaches fail to measure up to "meaningful situations" (Stern p. 18). Examine a course book you might be expected to teach from. Look at the most usual exercise types. Is the emphasis on faultless memorization of sentences? Stimulus-response, question-and-answer techniques? The creative use of language in realistic situations? What type of underlying theory of language do you think the author of the text supports?

11. Chomsky says, "language is not 'a habit structure' ". Moreover, there is "no known sense of 'generalization' that can begin to account for [the] . . . 'creative' aspect of normal language use" (p. 30). How might this statement be empirically tested? A word of caution: "There is . . . no obvious analogy between the experimental results obtained in studies of concept formation and the actual processes that seem to underlie language learning" (Chomsky, p. 30).

12. Evaluate a second language course book. Find out how grammatical explanations are presented to the learner. Is it by explanation? By letting the learner induce the rule from a variety of contexts? Or, is it based on

some other method? What advantages or disadvantages do you see in the approach used?

13. Consider Chomsky's statement that language is "stimulus-free" (p. 32). Does this notion accord with the fact that there is an intrinsic correlation of sound and meaning in [a] language" (p. 33)? More particularly, can it be reconciled with the fact that languages are often (if not usually) used referentially?

14. Perhaps you have observed examples of language use among nonnative speakers which involved "rule-governed creativity". Discuss some of these examples and consider what rules are being used. How are rules of the target language being violated?

15. Is the "creative aspect of language use" unique to language behavior or is it a feature of behavior in general? Consider, for instance, physical movement toward an object, or other goal-oriented behavior. What about the experiencing of objects and situations in general? Is there more repeti-tiveness and less novelty in such experiences than in language use?

16. Oller argues that linguists should "study the relationships which hold between the units of language and the extralinguistic things talked about by speakers" (p. 37). Chomsky says "it is only under exceptional and quite uninteresting circumstances that one can seriously consider how 'situational context' determines what is said" (p. 32). Consider the pros and cons of both statements.

17. In what ways might Chomsky's statement that language is "free from the control of detectable stimuli" be interpreted in order to avoid the difficulties pointed up by Oller? Or, assuming that Oller's interpretation of Chomsky's statement is correct, how might Oller's arguments be negated?

18. Consider the advantages of having an "ideal speaker-listener" as the main object of linguistic study.

PART II

LANGUAGE LEARNING PROCESSES

INTRODUCTION

The two papers in this section are concerned with the following question: What capacities does the learner possess, and how does he utilize them in acquiring a language? Macnamara notes that the first step, and possibly the most important one in answering this question, is to specify exactly what it is that is learned—i.e., to make explicit the nature of language. Papers in Part I have dealt with this first step and with some of the difficulties and controversies that are involved in it. A second and equally important step, according to Macnamara, is the specification of the mechanisms that underlie the learning process. In this regard, a key issue is the relationship between language and experience in general. Macnamara suggests that language learning is actually an inductive process whereby present contexts and their implicit meanings are used as clues to crack the code of language. Similar observations are made by Kennedy. On this basis, Macnamara argues that some of the emphasis which has been placed on *how* things are said should be redistributed to give the lion's share to *what* learners are saying or trying to say. This is a point that Oller made in Part I and that recurs in several of the papers that follow in later sections.

The relationship between linguistics and language teaching as presented by Mackey in Part I is given a somewhat different treatment by Macnamara. The latter author argues that an adequate understanding of how language functions to code information should be immanently useful to theories of how languages are learned and to methods of teaching.

An important point concerning the nature of motivation as a factor in language learning is raised by Macnamara. He suggests that the need to communicate information may be a more powerful motivator than the desire to become a part of another culture, or any other long-range goal. He seems to place the emphasis on content-level coding operations while Gardner, and Tucker, and Lambert (as we will see in Part V) emphasize relationship-level communication as it relates to attitude formation and motivation.

Some of the popular notions about an optimal age for language learning are called into question. There is little evidence to support the idea that the language learning device atrophies at an early age. The relevance of motivation to considerations of this question is discussed here, and in Part V in greater detail.

Both of the authors in this section recognize the importance of hypothesis formation and testing on the part of the learner. The learner forms expectations about what sorts of utterances will code what sorts of information, and he tests these, sometimes making errors. The importance of having the opportunity to make such errors suggests that the avoidance of situations in which students are apt to make errors may be a mistake.

The second paper, by Kennedy, observes that formal methods of language teaching have been remarkably unsuccessful when compared with the achievements of second language learners in natural settings. Kennedy takes account of the inadvisability of simplistic attempts to translate naturalistic settings into classroom methods but draws some useful and interesting parallels between first and second language learning. The two processes are probably much more similar than is commonly imagined. Kennedy anticipates to a great extent the discussion in Part V of the importance of relationship-level communication to learner motivation.

THE COGNITIVE STRATEGIES OF LANGUAGE LEARNING

John Macnamara

Some things children seem to learn naturally; others they have to be taught. Unaided, they seem to learn to walk and to perceive the world visually; on the other hand, nearly all children have to be taught arithmetic. Language is a peculiar embarrassment to the teacher, because outside school, children seem to learn language without any difficulty, whereas in school with the aid of teachers their progress in languages is halting and unsatisfactory. It is common experience that when translated to a town where their native language is not spoken children will become reasonably proficient in the new language in the space of six months. It is equally common experience that after six years of schooling in a second language, whatever the teaching method, most children emerge with a very poor command of the language. The first set of experiences shows that children are possessed of a very powerful device for learning languages; the second set of experiences shows that the school harnesses this device only in a most inadequate manner. This in turn argues that we have a poor understanding of the natural device for learning languages. My paper is about this device, about common beliefs as to its scope, and about the implications of what we know of the device for the language classroom.

The function of the human language learning device is defined with reference to a natural language such as English or French. If we could specify exactly the code which we call English, we would have taken the first and most important step in the direction of specifying the nature of the language learning device. The second step would be to specify the actual learning process whereby a person grapples with the code and masters it. The trouble with this approach is massive, however: we are very far indeed from being able to specify a code like English, and we are even farther from being able to specify the language learning process. Of any natural language we know that it has a lexicon, a sound system, and a set of structural rules. But anyone who is even vaguely familiar with linguistics knows that each is the subject of vigorous controversy. Katz and Fodor (1963) have made an interesting beginning in the description of the sort of lexicon which English users carry about in their head; Quillian (1967, 1968, and 1969) has gone further and attempted to build a computer model of a human lexicon; but I (Macnamara, 1971) have argued elsewhere not only that their work is defective in detail, but that they have taken the wrong direction. The obscurities of phonology and syntax are acclaimed in every book and paper one reads on these subjects. The work of structural and transformational linguists amounts to a very considerable deepening of our understanding of the rules of phonology and syntax. However, every linguist would, I think, agree with Lakoff's (1970) statement in a recent paper that we can scarcely claim to have done more than introduce the subjects.

The essential obscurity of language is in its loose relationship to that elusive and inapprehensible process which we call thought. A single word, like *back*, can have many meanings (e.g., rear part of a body, to wager), while a single object or idea can be expressed by several words (e.g., *drunk, intoxicated*). A single syntactic device can have quite different semantic functions (e.g., *I have a pin; I have a pain*), whereas a single semantic relationship can be signaled by means of a variety of syntactic devices (e.g., *My hair is black; I have black hair*). To make matters even worse, many ideas are conveyed without the use of any explicit linguistic device. For example, the directive, *close the door*, does not carry any explicit indication that *you* has been deleted and is understood. The problem is even more deeprooted than this example implies. The command, *put on your shoes,* does not express the *you*, but neither does it specify where the shoes are to be put (on the feet, not on the hands), nor even on whose feet (yours rather than mine). So rich and powerful is the human interpretive system that much can be left unsaid. To express everything one intends is to be a bore—it may even be impossible in principal. One result of all this is that the line which divides language and thought is a very thin one, and there is usually doubt about where it should be drawn. In this connection, see Uriel Weinreich's (1966) reintroduction of the medieval problem of relating semantic and grammatical categories. He raises serious doubts about whether one can usefully call categories such as *noun* and *verb* grammatical, while one calls categories such as *animate* and *inanimate* semantic. On the other hand, Noam Chomsky (1965) had great problems deciding whether to treat the selection restrictions on lexical items as grammatical or semantic. In other words, should we regard *The stone loved* as ungrammatical or just nonsense. All in all, then, it is difficult to say what we learn when we learn a language.

It is even more difficult to specify the learning process. Several factors which have an effect on certain types of learning have been isolated by psychological research. But I think it fair to say that the core of the process still eludes us. However, I will return to this topic later in my paper.

COGNITIVE BASIS OF LANGUAGE LEARNING

If we were to ask teachers, as I have often done, what is the essential difference between the classroom and the street as a place in which to learn a language, they would answer *motivation.* I am sure that the teachers are right; we do not seem to have adequately motivated children in classrooms to learn a language. Notice, however, that in so answering, teachers avoid the problems with which we have been dealing. They do not seek in the essential nature of language or language learning for the difference between the classroom and the street. Neither do they attribute the difference to the essential nature of the language learning device. They seem to say, rather, that whatever the nature of that device, it does not function properly unless a person is highly motivated to make it function.

I have argued elsewhere (Macnamara, 1972) that infants learn their mother tongue by first determining, independent of language, the meaning which a speaker intends to convey to them, and then working out the relationship between the meaning and the expression they heard. In other words, the infant uses meaning as a clue to language, rather than language as a clue to meaning. The argument rests upon the nature of language and its relation to thought, and also upon the findings of empirical investigations into the language learning of infants. The theory is not meant to belittle the child's ability to grapple with intricate features of the linguistic code. These must be grasped even if the clue is usually—though by no means always—to be found in meaning. The theory claims that the main thrust in language learning comes from the child's need to understand and to express himself.

Contrast, now, the child in the street with the child in the classroom. In the street he will not be allowed to join in the other children's play, not be allowed to use their toys, not even be treated by them as a human being, unless he can make out what they say to him and make clear to them what he has to say. The reward for success, and the punishment for failure, is enormous. No civilized teacher can compete. But more to the point, the teacher seldom has anything to say to his pupils so important that they will eagerly guess his meaning. And pupils seldom have anything so urgent to say to the teacher that they will improvise with whatever communicative skills they possess to get their meaning across. If my analysis of infant language learning is correct, as I believe it to be, it can surely explain the difference between the street and the classroom without placing any serious strain on the analogy between first and second language learning.

The solution then is to make the language class a period of vital communication between teacher and pupils. How simply that is said! Of course I have no practical hints. Though I was a language teacher for several years myself, that was a long time ago, and in any case I was a slave to public examinations. Moreover, there is no point in my entering into competition with talented teachers who did not surrender their minds to the last half century's talk about methods and always saw language as essentially linked to communication. Nevertheless, the theory I am proposing does suggest some broad strategies which I may mention with impunity.

An infant could not guess what his mother was saying to him unless there were a good many surrounding clues. Mother usually talks to a small child only about those things which are present to the senses, things that the child can see, feel, smell, taste, hear, things which are happening or which the child or she herself is doing. Nearly always, too, a mother's speech carries exaggerated intonational patterns. Indeed a mother's speech to an infant is intonationally often quite distinct from her speech to others. All of this, together with the mother's facial expressions, is a strong clue to her meaning or intention. It enables the child to determine her meaning and use it as the key to the code she uses to express her meaning in. The teacher, then, would be wise to provide as many aids as possible to his meaning. And he should encourage the pupils to guess. This probably implies that he should be slow to give the child the meaning in the child's native tongue.

Parents are proud of any effort which a small child makes to express himself in words. They welcome his phonological innovations; they accept his bits of words; and they understand his telegraphese. As a matter of fact, parents seldom correct a small child's pronunciation or grammar; they correct his bad manners and his mistakes on points of fact (Gleason, 1967). Somehow, when a child is vitally concerned with communication, he gradually gets over his difficulties and eradicates errors, at least to a point where society accepts his speech. That is, vitally engaged in the struggle to communicate and supported by the approval of his parents, he makes steady progress. His parents' attention is on his meaning, not on his language, and so probably is his own. And curiously he and his parents break one of psychology's basic learning rules. Psychology would advise that he should be rewarded only for linguistically correct utterances, whereas parents reward him for almost any utterance. But then the folk wisdom of the Italians, which is older than experimental psychology, has created a proverb which gives the lie to psychology and agrees with parent and child—*sbagliando s'impara* (by making mistakes we learn). Perhaps in all this there is a lesson for the schoolmaster. Perhaps he should concentrate more on what the child is saying and less on how he says it. Perhaps the teacher should lay aside the red pencil with which he scored any departure from perfection and replace it with a word and a smile of encouragement. The Irish too—not to be outdone by the Italians—have their folk wisdom: *mol an óige agus tiochfaid sí* (praise youth and it will come).

SOME DUBIOUS FOLKLORE

Just to show I'm not a complete reactionary who accepts everything from the bosom of the race, I will devote the remainder of my paper to a critical analysis of two common beliefs: (1) the child learns a language informally, whereas the adult learns it formally; (2) the adult is a much poorer language learner than the child.

From what I have said about the possibility of specifying the elements and rules of a language, it follows that the term formal learning can be applied to language in only the loosest sense. If we cannot reduce language to a formula, we cannot learn it by a formula. The extent to which we cannot formulate a language is the extent to which our learning of it cannot be formal, and this is to a very great extent. On the other hand there are useful rules or formulas which capture some of the regularities of a language. It is the case that these are often explicitly taught to adults, and they are never taught to infants. May we not speak of the adults learning as being to this extent formal, and that of the infant as informal? And if so, is this an important difference? A firm answer is of course impossible, but the issue is an interesting one which merits close attention.

We are familiar with all sorts of rules which will serve to illustrate the problem. The beginner at chess is taught the rules of the game, and when asked he is usually able to state them. On the other hand the boy who is learning to cycle is usually not taught the rules of balancing the bicycle, nor does anyone explain to him the complications of following curvilinear paths at different speeds as he alternately presses on the left and right pedals. Furthermore the cyclist cannot normally state the rules he applies. Rules, then, can be possessed in an explicit or stateable form, or they may not. Take now the man who is learning to ski. His tutor gives him many rules to follow, but he also tells him that he must not be satisfied until he has formed the rules in his legs. As he makes progress he begins to feel the rightness of the rules; they take on a new existence in him, though he still can state them in the explicit form in which he learned them.

It is my belief that in the skilled performer all rules *must* exist in a nonexplicit form; they *may* exist in an explicit form as well. It is further my belief that in the initial stages of learning explicit rules can guide the construction of structures which implicitly incorporate the rules. It is these structures, not the explicit rules, which control skilled performance. This I believe to be true even of the chess player: he does not, when playing, recall explicitly all the rules which inform his perception of the board. However, the gap between explicit rules and performance is less in chess than in skiing. From my earlier remarks on language it follows that language is closer to skiing than to chess, at least in the relationship between rules and performance.

Though we cannot be certain that infants are unconscious of all the linguistic rules which they develop, they certainly must be unconscious of many of them. Similarly, the successful learner of a second language has a great many implicit rules which he is unable to formulate. And only when he has developed structures which implicitly incorporate those rules which he learned in an explicit form will he be able to apply them with mastery.

What I want to say is this. The human language learning device serves to construct in a nonexplicit form a set of nonconscious rules which guide listening and speaking. The device can either extract the nonexplicit rules from the corpus of the language which is to be learned, or it can construct them on the basis of explicitly stated rules of the sort one finds in grammar books. The whole process is very obscure indeed, but I don't see anything against explicit rules and, with two provisos, they are probably a great help. First, the student must not expect to find rules for everything; he must trust his common sense or linguistic intuition. Second, he must learn to get on as soon as possible without explicit rules; he must be prepared to surrender himself to their automatic operation. I imagine that the only reason for distrusting explicit rules is the fact that some people have difficulty in abiding by these two counsels.

The second common belief which I wish to discuss is that one's language learning device atrophies rather early in life. The evidence for this is that babies pick up their mother tongue with what seems like great ease, and young children in suitable environments pick up a second language with little trouble, whereas adults seem to struggle ineffectively with a new language and to impose the phonology and syntax of their mother tongue on the new language. The argument has been supported with some evidence from neurophysiology (Penfield and Roberts, 1959), but the value of this evidence is dubious, to say the least.

I suspect that the evidence which most supporters of the theory draw upon confounds two phenomena, the child in the street and the child in the school. Small children don't go to school; older ones usually learn languages in school rather than in the street. We have already seen that these two phenomena must be distinguished. But besides all this many families have the experience of moving to a new linguistic environment in which the children rapidly learn the language and the adults don't. This happened frequently to English families who moved to one of the colonies, such as India. In such cases, the linguistic experience might well be attributed to unfavorable attitudes toward the new language which the parents, but not the children, adopted. However, Italian families who migrated to the United States often met with a similar linguistic fate—the children learned English, and the parents, despite favorable attitudes, did not. Is this conclusive evidence that language learning ability atrophies?

No! Let us take clear examples; let us compare a man of forty with an infant. We could not prove that the man was less skilled in language learning unless we gave the man an opportunity equal to that of the child to learn a language. We would need to remove the man from the preoccupations of his work and supply him with a woman who devoted a large part of her time and energy to helping him learn the language. Further, the woman would have to behave just like the mother of a small baby, which among other things would include treating anything the man said in his mother tongue as she would treat a child's babbling. Naturally such an experiment has never been carried out, and for that reason there are almost no grounds for the general fatalism about adults' ability to learn languages. On the contrary, what experimental evidence we have suggests that adults are actually better than children. Smith and Braine (in press) found adults superior in the acquisition of a miniature artificial language, while Asher and Price (1967) found adults superior at deciphering and remembering instructions given in what to them was a foreign language. Thus there are grounds for optimism in this area.

However there is evidence that adults and even teenagers generally have difficulty in mastering the pronunciation and intonational patterns of a new language, or even a new dialect. Labov (1966) found that persons who moved to Manhattan after the age of twelve seldom came to sound exactly like persons who grew up there. Similarly, persons who learn a language after adolescence usually sound a little bit foreign. But this does not mean that they do not communicate in that language very effectively and even quite normally. It is unwise to overemphasize their phonological difficulties. Apart from this there is no evidence that after adolescence one cannot learn a language as rapidly and as well as a small child.

CONCLUSION

One of the main tasks of linguists and psycholinguists is to make a systematic assault on the language learning device which is so remarkable in man. At present we know nothing of it in detail. We do, however, know that it is essentially geared to human thought and to its communication. It does not seem to function at all well unless the learner is vitally engaged in the act of communicating. This seems to be the reason why language teachers have laid such stress on motivation. It is my belief, however, that there has been quite a lot of confusion about the nature of such motivation. It has commonly been conceived (see for example Lambert, 1967) as a general desire to learn a language, and some attention has been paid to different grounds, "instrumental" or "integrative," for such a desire. This approach has led to interesting results. However, the logic of my paper demands a quite different emphasis; it demands that we look for the really important part of motivation in the act of communication itself, in the student's effort to understand what his interlocutor is saying and in his effort to make his own meaning clear. All this is not of course unrelated to a more general motivation to learn a language. The fact that superior attainment in language is associated with integrative motivation argues for a close relationship; after all the integrative attitude is defined as a general desire to communicate with speakers of the new language. But more pressing for most students than a general desire to be able to communicate at some future date is a specific desire to be able to communicate in some actual situation where what is being communicated is of vital concern to the persons involved. It is in the exploration of such specific motivation that I look for substantial advances in language teaching.

REFERENCES

Asher, J. J., and B. S. Price, "The Learning Strategy of the Total Physical Response: Some Age Differences." *Child Development,* 38 (1967), 1219-27.

Chomsky, N. *Aspects of the Theory of Syntax.* Cambridge, Mass.: MIT Press, 1965.

Gleason, J. B. "Do Children Imitate?" Paper read at International Conference on Oral Education of the Deaf, New York City, 1967.

Katz, J. J. and J. A. Fodor. "The Structure of a Semantic Theory." *Language,* 39 (1963), 170-210.

Lakoff, G. "Linguistics and Natural Logic." *Synthese,* 22 (1970), 151-271.

Lambert, W. E. "A Social Psychology of Bilingualism." *Journal of Social Issues,* 23 (1967), 91-109.

Macnamara, J. "Parsimony and the Lexicon." *Language,* 47 (1971), 359-74.

———. "The Cognitive Basis of Language Learning in Infants." *Psychological Review,* (1972).

Penfield, W. and L. Roberts. *Speech and Brain Mechanisms.* Princeton: Princeton University Press, 1959.

Quillian, R. "Word Concepts: A Theory and Simulation of Some Basic Semantic Capabilities." *Behavioral Science,* 12 (1967), 410-30.

———. "Semantic Memory." *Semantic Information Processing.* M. Minsky (ed.). Cambridge, Mass.: MIT Press, 1968. Pp. 216-70.

———. "The Teachable Language Comprehender: A Simulation Program and Theory of Language." *Communications of the ACH,* 12 (1969), 459-76.

Smith, K. H., and M. D. S. Braine. "Miniature Language and the Problem of Language Acquisition." T. G. Bever and W. Weksel (eds.). *Miniature Language and the Problem of Language Acquisition.* Holt, Rinehart & Winston (in press).

Weinreich, U. "Explorations in Semantic Theory." *Current Trends in Linguistics,* Vol. 3. T. A. Sebeok (ed.). The Hague: Mouton, 1966.

CONDITIONS FOR LANGUAGE LEARNING

Graeme Kennedy

Every few years there is another round of polemics over the most appropriate and successful way to teach foreign languages. This debate has been long and somewhat cyclic over many centuries and has been particularly vigorous this century. There have been advocates of direct methods, reading methods, oral methods, grammar methods, translation methods, situational methods, traditional methods, army methods, intensive methods, extensive methods, audio-lingual methods, audio-visual methods, eclectic methods, and so on (Mackey, 1965). In general, these methods of teaching have probably been comparably successful or unsuccessful in producing fluent users of foreign languages. Whereas up to half of the world's children may be fluent in two or more languages without any formal instruction, only a handful of those taught a foreign language in the classroom ever seem to reach a very high level of proficiency in that language regardless of the method of instruction used.

Each new approach and method for teaching foreign languages had tended to reflect particular educational goals, the insights of various disciplines dealing with language and language learning, the possibilities opened up by new technology, or simply the influence of individual teachers. The effect of educational goals, for example, can be seen in the influence of the Coleman Report in the U.S.A. and of the work of Michael West in making fluency in reading the primary purpose of foreign language instruction in the 1930's. Similarly, linguistic and psychological theories have also profoundly influenced foreign language teaching methodology, reflecting in turn what at the time were believed to be the linguistic parameters of the task and what was known' or believed about how humans learn. The Direct Method, for example, was an attempt to replicate what was believed to be the natural way in which children learn languages. Likewise the use of drilling and pattern practice as pedagogical devices received renewed support from the structural linguistics of the 1940's and 50's which emphasized syntactic patterns or frames as a type of habit structure forming the basis of grammars. Technical devices available as aids for teachers have proliferated in the last few decades. Radio, the phonograph, films, the tape recorder have all made it possible to expose the learner to the spoken language of native speakers of a foreign language and have encouraged the teaching of spoken language skills. This reduction of the need to rely on teachers who speak the foreign language fluently and on written material has profoundly affected the goals of foreign language instruction. Individual protagonists have always had a strong influence on the methods used for teaching foreign languages. In the seventeenth century, the great Czech teacher, Comenius, established such principles as vocabulary selection, the teaching of meaning in context, and the drill. In the last hundred years, teachers such as Plötz, Gouin, Viëtor, Sweet, Daniel Jones, H. E. Palmer, West, and Fries have given influential if often controversial support to different methods (Mackey, 1965).

The effect of such variables and the interaction among them is nowhere more apparent than in the various audiolingual methods used widely at present. Instead of foreign languages being taught mainly so that fairly small elites can have access to a foreign literature, we have seen an emphasis, especially in North America, on the teaching of speaking and listening comprehension, that is, on communication skills, to a large proportion of the school population. The theoretical foundation for audio-lingual methods came from a particular school of linguistics, American structuralism, and from behavioral psychology which contributed such concepts as habit strength, association, and reinforcement. In many cases, the linguistic and psychological insights have been reduced by language teaching theorists to series of slogans about language and language learning—"Language is structured habitual behavior"; "Habits are acquired through practice"; "Overlearning is necessary to establish habits," and so on. The use of tape recorders, language laboratories, and other electronic aids has been associated with the audio-lingual approach, and their use has been encouraged by many influential applied linguists, as well as, of course, by the representatives of electronic manufacturers.

Audio-lingual approaches vary a great deal and are widely used, but we should not be at all surprised to find our current wisdom about them being challenged. A whole series of research programs published over the last ten years has failed to substantiate on grounds of both efficacy and efficiency the more excessive claims of audio-lingual methodologists. In a widely-publicized, but method-ologically unsound study, Keating (1963) failed to find significant benefits from the use of language laboratories. Scherer and

Wertheimer (1964) showed that foreign language skills do not transfer well. That is, while students taught with an oral approach do better at listening and speaking than students taught to read and write, an oral approach does not seem to lead to improved reading and writing skills as is often claimed by supporters of audio-lingual methods. The recent controversial report on a large-scale investigation of foreign language teaching in Pennsylvania (Smith, 1970) has again failed to demonstrate that audio-lingual methods (and language laboratories) significantly improve foreign language learning.

The repeatedly ambiguous results of these and other attempts to demonstrate experimentally the superiority of one or another foreign language teaching method suggest, it would seem, not only that it is extremely difficult to compare methods experimentally, but, more important, that methodology may not be the critical variable in successful foreign language teaching. New ways of teaching foreign languages tend to be "successful" initially. The well-known Hawthorne Effect is at work to ensure this, for there is novelty and extra effort from both teachers and students.

Because of the confusion over methods of teaching it may be worth considering a switch of emphasis to see if the study of language *learning* can guide us in classroom procedures. The conditions for successful first language learning are by no means well understood, but what is known of both the context in which language acquisition occurs and of the kinds of processes which appear to be involved in the interaction between the learner and his linguistic and social environment might make us wonder whether much that passes for second language teaching may not actually interfere with the learner's capacity for language acquisition.

One of the most striking aspects of the context in which the child normally begins to acquire his first language is the richness of the linguistic environment. He is exposed to a range of unsimplified adult grammatical and lexical items, much of which he cannot comprehend. Further, as Chomsky (1965) has noted, many of the utterances the child hears consist of incomplete sentences or utterances which in some way are not well formed. Hesitations, false starts, and so on occur commonly and naturally in the enormous amount of fairly haphazard recurrence of structural and lexical features of the language. No two children are exposed to the same primary linguistic data, or the same amount of such data, and yet despite such different experience and wide differences in intelligence, almost all children are able to crack the code of the linguistic system of their culture and learn to understand and produce sentences.

The acquisition of the first language occurs within the context of a long period of physical and cognitive development and of socialization. Lenneberg (1967) has argued strongly for first language acquisition to be viewed as a "gradual unfolding of capacities," as a species-specific characteristic firmly associated with biological maturation. The hypothesis that the ability to subconsciously induce the structure of a language from haphazard primary linguistic data exists during a critical period of maturational readiness lasting up to about puberty and declining rapidly thereafter is not implausible in the light of current research on child language and of related work by researchers with other species (Marler, 1970).

On the basis of experience of the world, the developing child forms concepts and cognitive structures which can be both reflected in language and also refined through language (Carroll, 1964). The relationship between the development of language as an unfolding sequence within a critical period and the development of cognitive capacities in general can be seen in the phenomenon observed in children who, at the holophrastic and two-word sentence stages of development, know and use many individual words and can babble long sequences of sounds, yet do not string words together in longer sequences, even though adults do so in their presence. The same kind of relationship can be seen in the difficulty which some kinds of linguistic devices pose for children. For example, as Turner and Rommetveit (1967), Huttenlocher *et al.* (1968), and others have shown with various kinds of active and passive sentences, children as late as nine years of age find it more difficult to process sentences in which the logical actor-acted upon relationship does not coincide with the grammatical subject-object relationship. Similarly, comprehension of the linguistic devices used for comparing quantities has been shown to be significantly affected by the conceptual categories of equality, superiority and inferiority (Kennedy, 1970). The replication of this study with bilingual children (Young, 1971) has further demonstrated that patterns of difficulty may differ according to the first language background of the child. It seems increasingly clear that models of both first and second language acquisition, almost exclusively linked formerly to structural analyses of language, must also be linked to conceptual and semantic parameters as yet only dimly understood (Bloom, 1970).

Language serves a communicative function for the child learning it, but it is more than simply a more sophisticated means of communicating referential meaning, for language is acquired in the context of a community of speakers. To be sure, the acquisition of language enables the child to have questions answered, to make observations and requests, to state objections, to gain information, and so on. Perhaps above all, however, the language he acquires is a sign of his membership and participation in his community. His very identity and status as an individual are defined in part through the speech community.

Cracking the linguistic code of his community is thus no mere optional activity for the child. He is forced by circumstances to attempt to make sense out of the linguistic and social environment he is exposed to. Failure to do so would mean failure to join the community he finds himself in. Seen thus, as an attempt to reduce incomprehensibility, first language acquisition is achieved without apparent conscious effort on the child's part, or formal tuition, at a time, moreover, when his cognitive development is also just beginning.

As McNeill (1966) has noted, the nature of what the child actually acquires is not at all clear. The dimensions of the achievement however, are not in doubt. Speaking requires the co-ordination of several hundred neuromuscular events per second in the speech organs (Lenneberg, 1967) subsumed under the structural organization of syntactic and phonological systems so complex that no adequate description has yet been provided for any human language. Furthermore, complex sociolinguistic interactions between linguistic form and function also contribute to the learner's developing linguistic competence.

In acquiring his language, the child induces rules from the primary linguistic data he is exposed to. He acquires knowledge of something far more abstract than a set of sentence frames, namely the relationships expressed in underlying sentence structure which may not even preserve the word order of the phonetically realized surface structure of utterances (Chomsky, 1968). The child learns not only an incredibly complex system of phonology, syntax, and lexicon, but also a multitude of rules of functional appropriateness (Hymes, 1972). He learns when to speak and when not to; how to speak to his grandmother, his teacher, or the child next door; how to be tactful, direct, evasive, persuasive, inoffensive, and defensive. He has to learn to pair linguistic forms with the semantic relationships and conceptual categories underlying language use.

The creative use of language by both adults and children is one of its most striking characteristics. From the very earliest occurrences of two- and three-word sentences, the child creates novel utterances on the basis of the rules *he* has induced. Fixed phrases are only a small proportion of his utterances for he does not learn simply a stock of sentences. Instead of viewing the child's utterances as abbreviated adult sentences plus errors, psycholinguists now tend to approach the child's language as a system in its own right. A two-year-old using short sentences partly because of limited memory and processing capacity, may say *Hear tractor.* But, as McNeill (1965) has pointed out, we would assume that if he had an adult-sized memory capacity, the child would use his own grammatical rules and say *Hear tractor go window not see Mommy,* rather than the adult equivalent, *I hear a tractor going by the window, but I can't see it, Mommy.*

How the child acquires his first language is as poorly understood as what it is he actually acquires. Processes in which there is an observable interaction between the learner and other individuals in his social environment have been noted. Various cognitive processes occurring as the individual learner works on reorganizing and classifying the primary linguistic data he is exposed to are also assumed to foster language development.

Modeling has been shown to be a powerful factor in certain aspects of children's socialization (Bandura and Walters, 1963), and imitation is an obvious process in language acquisition in particular. As Brown and Bellugi (1964) have noted, however, imitation works in two directions. Other speakers imitate and expand the child's utterances, responding to the child's words, word order, and the context, and commenting on them. Thus the child's *Put box* may be expanded to become *Yes, I'm going to put it in the box.* The adult's expansions typically add omitted function words and preserve the child's word order. On the other hand, the child tends to reduce the input when he imitates. The adult's *You haven't finished your dinner yet* may become *Finish dinner.* Words with weak stress, particularly function words, tend to be omitted by the child. As Ervin (1964) has shown, children's imitations are generally not grammatically progressive. That is, the imitations are made to conform to the child's own grammatical and phonological systems. Striking examples of this phenomenon are recorded by Slobin and Welsh (in press) with a two-and-a-half-year-old subject who had rules for conjunction but not for certain types of relativization. Young children who do not yet use relative clauses may imitate sentences containing such clauses as conjoined sentences. For example, *The dog which chased the cat was barking* may become *De dog chase de cat an de dog bark.*

While imitation and expansion by adults and imitation and reduction by the child both occur when the child is acquiring his mother tongue, their precise function is unclear. For example, as

Brown and Bellugi (1964) have stated, "...it has not been demonstrated that expansions are *necessary* for learning either grammar or a construction of reality. It has not even been demonstrated that expansions contribute to such learning. All we know is that some parents do expand and their children do learn." Subsequent research reported by Brown, *et al.* (1968) confirms this finding.

The role of practice in first language acquisition is similarly equivocal. Children obviously spend a very long time acquiring their first language. Several thousand hours are spent by the child using or being exposed to language before he begins school. Many of the forms used by children, when judged alongside the grammars of adults, are deviant. Children practice these "mistakes" for weeks, months, and sometimes even years and then quite suddenly drop such forms for new ones. As Ervin (1964) has shown, the past tense in English is learned first for irregular verbs. Children say *came, went* and *did* at a time when regular verbs are still uninflected. When the regular *-ed* past tense marker is acquired it quickly dominates the previously acquired and much practiced irregular forms, often resulting in *comed*, *goed*, *doed*, and so on. There is not always a sudden clean break with the past. Klima and Bellugi (1966) have clearly shown that old forms can coexist with newly acquired ones, even when the former deviate from the ones being used by the adult models. Of course, if use of a linguistic form and practice of it by the child prevented the acquisition of competing forms, the child's language would simply cease to develop. Exposure to the language being used in communicative situations would seem to be at least as important as overt practice. This is borne out by the fact that it is not even necessary to practice speaking in order to learn to comprehend spoken language (Lenneberg, 1962).

Reinforcement is considered to be an important factor in many learning models. In language acquisition there is of course the problem of identifying precisely what it is that could be reinforced, and also the variables which could act as reinforcers (Chomsky, 1959). Parental and peer approval, and disapproval and success in communication are possible candidates. However, Brown, *et al.* (1968) have shown that children get approval for truth value rather than proximity to adult grammatical forms. For example, a child could say *That's John's* and be told, *No, it's Harry's.* On the other hand, the child could say *Dat Harry* and be told, *Yes, that's right.* At the level of phonology the operant conditioning of sound segments is plausible. Similarly, the association of word forms and their meanings could be considered to be cases of associative learning.

Other variables occurring and possibly contributing to language acquisition include a certain amount of what may be called informal tuition by adults, children's utterances being sometimes deliberately corrected and expanded, as we have noted. Brown, *et al.* (1968) report an experiment in which there was some evidence that commenting on the child's utterances by an adult may contribute to language development. Adults also sometimes use more deliberately slow and clear articulation when speaking to children directly, but this can represent only a very limited amount of the linguistic data the child is exposed to. Children ask many questions and in this way exercise some control over their linguistic environment.

One of the central issues for scholars working on the acquisition and development of language at present is the nature of the contribution by the child. Chomsky (1965) has posed the problem most directly. " . . . A consideration of the grammar that is acquired, the degenerate quality and narrowly limited extent of the available data, the striking uniformity of the resulting grammars, and their independence of intelligence, motivation and emotional state, over wide ranges of variation, leave little hope that much of the structure of the language can be learned by an organism initially uninformed as to its general character."

This innateness hypothesis has stimulated an intense debate over the last decade, a debate which initially saw a confrontation between psycholinguists using generative linguistic models and psychologists using more well-established, behavioristic learning models. Some of the major issues and the general direction of the debate can be found in Chomsky (1959), Slobin (1971), and Morton (1971). It has become increasingly clear that a dichotomy between nativistic and behavioristic theories is too simplistic, and that integrated theories which relate linguistic structure and function to cognitive processes in general must be developed, for language is just one aspect of human cognition and cannot be properly understood apart from it. Chomsky in particular has stressed (1965) that the study of language is one way of increasing our understanding of cognitive processes in general, in that a linguistic theory such as transformational grammar can be regarded as a hypothesis about "the nature of mental structures and processes."

Intimately associated with the innateness hypothesis is the question of linguistic universals, those processes, organizing principles, characteristics, and features which human languages and language users possess in common. The existence of such universals has been increasingly recognized by linguists in recent years. What is at issue is how their existence should be interpreted. Chomsky

(1968) has stated quite clearly that he sees that "the central and critical problem for linguistics is to use empirical evidence from particular languages to refine the principles of universal grammar." Such empirical work is barely under way, but the potential importance of the study of universal grammar for our understanding of the processes of language acquisition would appear to be very great indeed.

Whatever the possible nature of the contribution of innate factors, the child organizes the randomly presented primary linguistic data he is exposed to, induces rules of structure and function, and bases his own language use on such rules. He of course modifies and restructures his grammar as he gets more feedback and gradually comes to acquire a linguistic system similar to that of the adult community. He reveals himself as a problem solver rather than as a rote learner, proceeding to abandon old hypotheses about what constitutes a grammatical structure, finding the limits of applicability of new hypotheses, and generalizing old rules to new situations and contexts, for example saying *sitted* as the past form of *sit* by analogy with *fit*. As McNeill (1970) has demonstrated very clearly, processes of differentiation by which old rules are broken down into new ones appear to be of great importance at all linguistic levels and are seen particularly clearly in the acquisition of phonological features (Jakobson, 1968).

The motivation to predicate, to make statements about things, and to use language creatively, is a marked characteristic of the language acquisition process. Rather than being merely the passive recipient of a cultural tradition, the child is a creative contributor to it. The importance of this semantic and communicative imperative has frequently been underestimated.

Few teachers would be prepared to argue that learning a first or second language as a child is similar to being taught a second language in a formal educational context. The first language clearly influences the perception and production of the second. The phenomenon of "interference" in phonology and syntax especially is well known to language teachers. Hyman Kaplan is the rule rather than the exception. Because the second language learner already possesses a human language, he may have a much less urgent motivation to communicate. That is, while he may need a second language for a particular educational or vocational purpose, he can typically still use his first language to communicate with family and friends if necessary.

The age of the second language learner may also be a relevant variable. As we have noted, Lenneberg (1967) has produced some evidence that there is a critical period for first language acquisition related to neurological and cognitive maturation. However, the older second language learner may have certain factors in his favor which in part counteract the disadvantage resulting from missing an early start. He is more cognitively mature, has a longer attention span, and longer short-term memory span. Many second language learners can read, have at least a primary education, and have indeed been taught in school to reason and use reading skills in approaching new learning situations and tasks. As a result, the adult learner, especially, tends to equate language with vocabulary. It may be that he tries to identify lexical meanings of individual words rather than to make predications and thus is slower to learn syntactic rules.

But above all, the importance of the difference between the amount of time spent by the child learning his first language and that available for learning the second language should not be underestimated. It is not difficult to calculate the many thousands more hours which the first language learner has in exposure to the language he is learning in comparison with the time spent by second language learners. The second language learner is typically a part-time learner. However, it is not just amount of time *per se* which may be critical, but rather how the time is spent. And it is for this reason that it would seem worth considering further the extent to which the conditions facing the second language learner in the typical language teaching classroom usually differ from those under which the first language was learned.

Instead of having a rich linguistic environment, the second language learner is usually fed intravenously. From the incredible structural richness of a language, we, the teachers, select phonological, syntactic, lexical, and thematic items; we decide and arrange the sequence of their presentation to the student; we force him to practice the rules we think are being learned. In spite of this, however, it is likely that the learner uses a strategy similar to that used in acquiring his first language, namely a hypothesis-testing approach to induce the abstract underlying structure of the language. He has to do this, on the basis or evidence of an already highly refined and organized sample of artificial language provided by the textbook and the teacher—artificial, because such samples typically serve no genuine communicative function. Instead of using the second language, however imperfectly learned, to communicate with others in novel situations, the learner is led to memorize sentences, phrases, words, and situations. Very often, the situations are contrived so that the learner asks questions for which he already knows the answers, or gains information which he has no need of or interest in.

One article of faith for language teachers has been that the learner must be led away from making mistakes. It has generally been believed that practice of nongrammatical utterances results in incorrect habits being established. That is, deviancy from the norms of native speakers has been seen in terms of slips by the learner rather than in terms of hypotheses being tried out or in terms of redundancy reduction. Instead of a straight jacket of pattern practice, drills, memorized dialogs, and so on, designed to minimize the production of deviant forms, we should encourage the communicative use of language, giving the learner enough feedback for him to modify the hypotheses he has set up about the grammatical and functional rules of the language. This will inevitably lead to faulty hypotheses being tried out. The student may say *My dog is hungry. He needs eating,* because he assumes *needs eating* is semantically equivalent to *needs to eat* rather than *needs to be eaten.* But in all language learning, first and second, throughout a human life, a major characteristic of the learning process is discovering the limits of the applicability of rules and usages, of relating forms and functions. At the beginning of the acquisition process, the functions of both syntactic and lexical forms have to be acquired. For the mature speaker of the language it is mainly appropriate lexical usage which continues to be learned. We should therefore not try to prevent errors in the second language learner at the expense of allowing him natural communicative opportunities in which his hypothesis-testing strategies are given free rein. It is also remembering that in the final analysis we can never completely control what the learner does, for *he* selects and organizes, whatever the input. Even if we knew that translation into the first language retarded second language learning, and that audio-lingual drilling techniques facilitated learning, the learner might still translate every pattern, every drill, every dialog he was presented with.

Materials which expose the learner to the language and which exploit the motivation derived from the communicative use of language should thus, it seems, be of more concern to teachers than methods. A significant demonstration of this can be found in the research program being conducted by Lambert and his associates at McGill University in Montreal (Lambert, 1970). Children who begin school as monolingual speakers of English are being taught at school as if they were monolingual speakers of French, from the time they begin kindergarten through the primary school classes, in an attempt to achieve functional bilingualism through what has been called "a home-school language switch." With about 60% of classroom activities, including mathematics, reading, writing, and elementary science conducted in French, the children's control of spoken French has developed rapidly. The French language achievement of the experimental group has been at or above the 75th percentile when compared with children who speak French as their first language. After five years, the children are very fluent, although their production of French is still not equal to that of the native speakers. Nevertheless, they have learned far more than they would have through typical foreign language learning classes, and without any adverse effect on their English language abilities, or their academic achievement. It remains to be seen whether this promising approach can be equally successful with older learners.

Among an increasing number of attempts to explore the conditions for successful foreign language learning, age, intelligence, foreign language learning aptitude, and socioeconomic factors have been considered. There is mounting evidence, however, that the importance of complex sociological and psychological factors relating to the attitudes and motivation of the learner have been grossly underestimated in foreign language teaching programs. It seems increasingly clear that the learner's attitude toward the group whose language he is learning has a considerable effect on his success in mastering the second language. For example, if the learner feels there is little chance that he will ever be accepted by the foreign language speaking community, if he feels he will never get a chance to use the language to communicate, or if he feels negatively toward the other community, he is not likely to learn the language however much practice he does. The size, cohesion, and status of the cultural group to which a learner belongs, and the relationship between members of that group and those who speak the target language is of enormous importance (Lambert, *et al.* 1968). We are successful as second language learners to the extent that we feel that what we are doing will enable us to communicate with a group we would like to join (and which, in turn, shows signs of accepting us).

As was suggested earlier, it is not learning second languages which is difficult, but learning them in classrooms. Because humans know how to learn languages given enough data to work with, a method of *teaching* foreign languages, to be successful, must first of all not hinder language learning. The experience of the last forty years suggests that it is not enough to base methodology on modified linguistic and psychological theories, on logical rather than on empirical bases. Too often rationales, opinions, doctrines, and enthusiasms rather than results have been the source of methodological principles and practices.

While it is not yet clear what role linguistic and psychological theories have in developing pedagogy, current research in linguistic theory, sociolinguistics, and psycholinguistics is throwing light on the processes of language acquisition and language use. In particular, the revolution inspired by Chomsky's work on transformational grammar has already had a considerable effect on our understanding of language acquisition, and of the nature and structure of language.

Furthermore, there are signs that current disillusionment with the role of technology in language teaching may lead to new uses of equipment. Because of the critical importance in language learning of motivation to communicate, greater efforts to enhance the image of speakers of second languages can be made, using attractive, varied, and realistic materials on records and films, and in audio-visual laboratories, books, and magazines. Informal and formal uses of the language, different voices and accents, spoken and written language, in which communicative demands are placed on the learner, and in which it is clear to the learner that he is learning or doing things for which the new language is indispensable and which he wants to be able to do, all can contribute to successful learning.

For large numbers of children, successful foreign language learning can be a prerequisite for formal education. The goals of instruction in this case are clear. For others, the communicative opportunities and demands of a shrinking world should be evidence enough of the need for vigorous and effective programs. In both cases, methodology should provide, in the fullest sense, optimal conditions for learning and not merely a set of procedures, exercises, and techniques for the learner.

REFERENCES

Bandura, A., and R. H. Walters. *Social Learning and Personality Development.* New York: Holt, Rinehart & Winston, 1963.

Bloom, Lois. *Language Development: Form and Function in Emerging Grammars.* Cambridge, Mass.: M.I.T. Press, 1970.

Brown, R. and U. Bellugi. "Three Processes in the Child's Acquisition of Syntax." *Harvard Educational Review*, 34 (1964), 133-51.

Brown, R., C. Cazden, and U. Bellugi. "The Child's Grammar from I to III." J. P. Hill (ed.). *The Minnesota Symposia on Child Psychology*, Vol. 2. Minneapolis: University of Minnesota Press, 1968.

Carroll, J. B. "Words, Meanings, and Concepts." *Harvard Educational Review*, 34 (1964), 178-202.

Chomsky, N. "Review of B. F. Skinner's *Verbal Behavior*." *Language*, 35 (1959), 26-58.

———. *Aspects of the Theory of Syntax*. Cambridge, Mass.: M.I.T. Press, 1965.

———. *Language and Mind*. New York: Harcourt, Brace & World, 1968.

Ervin, S. M. "Imitation and Structural Change in Children's Language." E. H. Lenneberg (ed.). *New Directions in the Study of Language*. Cambridge, Mass.: M.I.T. Press, 1964.

Huttenlocher, J., K. Eisenberg, and S. Strauss. "Comprehension: Relation between Perceived Actor and Logical Subject." *Journal of Verbal Learning and Verbal Behavior*, 7 (1968), 527-30.

Hymes, D. "On Communicative Competence." *Readings in Sociolinguistics*. J. Pride and J. Holmes (eds.). London: Penguin Books, 1972.

Jakobson, R. *Child Language, Aphasia and Phonological Universals*. The Hague: Mouton, 1968.

Keating, R. F. *A Study of the Effectiveness of Language Laboratories*. New York: Columbia University Institute of Admin. Research., 1963.

Kennedy, G. D. *Children's Comprehension of English Sentences Comparing Quantities of Discrete Objects*. Unpublished doctorial dissertation. University of California, Los Angeles, 1970.

Klima, E. S., and U. Bellugi. "Syntactic Regularities in the Speech of Children." *Psycholinguistic Papers*. J. Lyons and R. J. Wales (eds.). Edinburgh: Edinburgh University Press, 1966.

Lambert, W. E., *et al.* "A Study of the Roles of Attitudes and Motivation in Second Language Learning." *Readings in the Sociology of Language*. J. Fishman (ed.). The Hague: Mouton, 1968.

Lambert, W. E., *et al.* "Cognitive and Attitudinal Consequences of Following the Curricula of the First Three Grades in a Foreign Language." Mimeographed. 1970.

Lenneberg, E. H. "Understanding Language without Ability to Speak: A Case Report." *Journal of Abnormal and Social Psychology*, 65 (1962), 419-25.

———. *Biological Foundations of Language*. New York: Wiley, 1967.

Mackey, W. F. *Language Teaching Analysis*. London: Longmans, 1965.

Marler, P. "Birdsong and Speech Development: Could There Be Parallels?" *American Scientist*, 58 (1970), 669-73.

McNeill, D. "Some Thoughts on First and Second Language Acquisition." Paper presented to Modern Foreign Language Title III Conference, Washington, D.C., 1965.

———. "The Creation of Language by Children." *Psycholinguistic Papers*. J. Lyons and R. J. Wales (eds.). Edinburgh: Edinburgh University Press, 1966.

———. *The Acquisition of Language: The Study of Developmental Psycholinguistics*. New York: Harper & Row, 1970.

Morton, J. (ed.). *Biological and Social Factors in Psycholinguistics.* London: Logos Press, 1971.

Scherer, G. A. C., and M. Wertheimer. *A Psycholinguistic Experiment in Foreign Language Teaching.* New York: McGraw-Hill, 1964.

Slobin, D. (ed.). *The Ontogenesis of Grammar: A Theoretical Symposium.* New York: Academic Press, 1971.

Slobin, D., and C. Welsh "Elicited Imitation as a Research Tool in Developmental Psycholinguistics." *Readings on Child Language Acquisition.* C. Ferguson and D. Slobin (eds.). New York: Holt, Rinehart & Winston (in press).

Smith, P. D. Jr. *A Comparison of the Cognitive and Audio-lingual Approaches to Foreign Language Instruction.* Pennsylvania: Center for Curriculum Development Inc., 1970.

Turner, E. A., and R. Rommetveit. "The Acquisition of Sentence Voice and Reversibility." *Child Development*, 38 (1967), 649-60.

Young, R. W. *Semantics as a Determiner of Linguistic Comprehension Across Language and Cultural Boundaries.* Unpublished doctoral dissertation. University of New Mexico, 1971.

PART II: DISCUSSION QUESTIONS

1. How would you answer the question raised by Macnamara: "What is the essential difference between the classroom and the street as a place in which to learn a language" (p. 59)? What are the parallels and what are the differences? What sorts of changes are necessary in order to convert the classroom setting into a more natural learning situation?

2. What kinds of language teaching exercises can be used to "make the language class a period of vital communication between teacher and pupils" (Macnamara, p. 60)? What barriers to such an objective exist? Can they be overcome?

3. Both of the authors in this section make reference to ways in which second language learning is like first language acquisition. Is there any one crucial difference, or set of crucial differences? Consider the notion of competing linguistic systems and its concomitant variable of "interference." Compare language learning with other sorts of learning where interference of a similar variety might be expected to occur.

4. Explore some of the possible causes behind the widespread failure of much formal language teaching (Macnamara, pp. 57-61, and Kennedy, pp. 66-69). How might motivational factors interact to produce some of the conflicting data? Aptitude for verbal learning?

5. Macnamara notes the indeterminate and abbreviatory nature of the relationship between utterances and extralinguistic contexts. What sorts of modifications do these observations entail for theories of learning? Consider the difficulties that a simple stimulus-response theory would encounter.

6. Discuss some of the problems involved in attempting to assign notional definitions to grammatical categories such as nouns, verbs, adjectives, and adverbs. In other words, what are some of the hurdles to be overcome by, say, a definition of a noun as "the name of a person, place, or thing". Are these hurdles insurmountable? How does this relate to language learning (see Macnamara, pp. 57-61)?

7. "Instrumental" and "integrative" motivation are defined by Gardner in Part V of this volume. The reader may wish to refer to those definitions before considering the merits of Macnamara's emphasis on the "motivation in the act of communication itself". Can coding operations *per se* be clearly differentiated from messages which involve the definition of interpersonal and intergroup relationships (see the introduction to Part V)? In what ways are they related and/or distinct?

8. Discuss some of the possible differential effects of social contexts and the different relationship definitions they entail for different social groups. How might language learners be affected by such intergroup relationships? Are the problems similar for dialect differences and the crossing of dialect barriers?

9. Consider some of the ways that expectations (of various sorts) affect your ability to understand things that are said to you. What about things that you yourself may want to say? How about the half-finished sentence that you cannot remember the rest of? In what ways might expectancies (learned in various sorts of contexts) be relevant to language learning?

10. Kennedy indicates that there is more to learning a language than merely acquiring a "more sophisticated means of communicating referential meaning, for language is acquired in the context of a community of speakers" (pp. 69-70). He goes on to refer to "the linguistic and social environment" that the child is exposed to. Can different kinds of contexts be inferred? What other kinds of contexts must be taken into account? Can a general definition of *context* be derived from these considerations?

11. Can cognitive development in general be treated as distinct from "cracking the linguistic code"? If so how, and if not, why not?

12. In what sense can the data that the child is exposed to be regarded as haphazard (Kennedy, p. 69)? Are there no constraining factors that impose order? What about the kinds of context discussed in Question 10 above?

13. Kennedy seems to assume a model of learning which is based on a process of "induction" or "generalization". According to Chomsky (see his paper in Part I), such a model cannot possibly work. Refer also to Questions 5 and 6 above in this section.

14. In what ways might the learner "test hypotheses" about grammar by making predictions or guessing? What kinds of data would he utilize in such tests? If hypothesis testing of this sort is as important as both of the authors in this section seem to believe, what consequences does it entail for methods of teaching languages?

15. Kennedy states that the child learning his first language is "exposed to a range of unsimplified adult grammatical and lexical items, much of which he cannot comprehend" (p. 68). How much adult language do you think children understand? Consider other clues to meaning besides just linguistic forms.

16. In second language teaching do you think the emphasis should be on communicative effectiveness or on production of well-formed sentences? In what ways do these notions overlap, and in what ways are they distinct?

17. Kennedy observes that children's imitations of adult-produced utterances tend to conform to their own grammatical and phonological systems. Do you know of examples that illustrate this fact? Can the same be said of adult language learners and their attempts to imitate? What sorts of indeterminacies must be accounted for?

18. What explanations can be offered for the fact that children first produce forms like *came, went,* and *did,* but later come up with incorrect forms like *comed, goed,* and *doed*? Can this be regarded as a form of hypothesis testing in the sense of Question 14 in this section? If so, what are the hypotheses, what are the data, and what are the expected changes based on the tests performed?

PART III

ASPECTS OF SECOND LANGUAGE LEARNING

INTRODUCTION

In this section several analytical approaches to problems of second language learners are discussed. Among those considered are: interference theory based on contrastive analysis; error analysis which may or may not rely on a contrastive approach; and developmental psycholinguistics. The emphasis here is on content-level coding operations. Consideration of relationship-level problems is taken up in Part V below.

The usual assumption concerning the nongrammatical utterances of second language learners is that they manifest "interference" between the target language and the native language of the learner. However, studies of first language acquisition reveal that certain errors characteristic of second language learners are also frequently present in the speech of children learning their first language. Such errors often seem to reflect testing of hypothesized rules in the grammar of the learner, thus evidencing rule-governed creativity rather than negative interference from the native language.

The first paper, by Hocking, discusses the notion of interference between the native language of the learner and the target language. He shows that by careful observation of the learner's errors, along with some expertise in the background language, the teacher should not only be able to recognize interlanguage interference when it occurs, but in many cases also be able to point to the native language feature upon which the error is based. Hocking gives numerous examples which seem best explained by assuming that the native language of the learner is in fact interfering with the second language system. However, he is cautious to point out that many of the so-called "scientific" claims for contrastive analysis in the 1940's and 1950's were exaggerations." He contends that interference from the native language can account for only part of the learner's difficulties.

Proof that only part of the errors can be attributed to interlanguage interference is provided in the following paper by Richards. In addition to elaborating on the various types of errors made by second language learners, he provides a wealth of examples of common errors among learners of English as a second language which can be traced to confusions of structures and rules within the grammar of the target language. Moreover, in a number of these instances it is possible to rule out any interference which could be attributed to the learner's native language. Richards terms these examples "intralanguage errors" and shows that they are not infrequently encouraged by the manner in which structures in the target language are presented. It is suggested that a better understanding of processes underlying second language learning may help writers of materials as well as teachers to avoid some of the traps unintentionally included in many language programs which actually encourage such errors.

Richards' second paper discusses the concepts: "transfer of training," "strategies of learning," "strategies of communication," "transitional competence," and other notions believed necessary to account for the observed outputs of second language learners. The term "transfer of training" can be identified with George's term "cross association." He compares the above-mentioned concepts with the notion "interference from the native language" and considers their relative merits as bases for explaining second language learning. He concludes that the process is sufficiently intricate that no single approach can expect to achieve adequacy. A variety of theories and viewpoints must be drawn from.

The fourth paper, by Ravem, reports on an excellent study of the acquisition of syntax by a six-year-old Norwegian child. The study extended over a period a little more than two months. Ravem argues that there is a great need for more longitudinal studies of second language acquisition. He concludes that although the situation of the second language learner is different in both obvious and subtle ways from that of the child learning his first language, the creative processes involved in both are strikingly similar.

The last paper, by George, demonstrates that processes of registering and remembering information are active and creative by nature, rather than passive as is sometimes supposed. George shows that remembering actually involves reconstruction. In a practical experiment, he presents an intriguing illustration of how material is transformed by the learner as he organizes it in terms of his own experience. The possibilities of false analogy by "cross association," which was illustrated earlier by Richards, is shown to produce natural intralanguage interference. Unfortunately, as George and Richards both mention, this is too often ignored in the preparation of teaching materials. By focusing on the learner as he actively searches for clues by means of which he may process new items, George demonstrates a practical application of certain principles of storage and retrieval of verbally coded information.

TYPES OF INTERFERENCE

B. D. W. Hocking

Interference is the adverse effect of features of a known language on the acquisition or use of another language. The teacher's concern is usually with the interference of features of a mother tongue with the acquisition or use of an L2, and this is what this paper is about; but the opposite also occurs, as many immigrants can testify, and the effect of L2s on mother tongues is undoubtedly of sufficient social importance in many communities to merit study.

The term "interference" is preferred here to "transference," also sometimes used for the same thing, since "transference" may for some people carry implications about the mechanisms through which interference takes place, and about these we know as little as, it seems, we know about the mechanisms of language learning in general. The behaviorist orthodoxy that held the field for some time has in the last ten years been powerfully attacked, but we have as yet no more than the adumbration of a theory to put in its place; we are back more or less where we started.[1] However, if we do not know how interference works, there is no doubt whatever that it does work. And there is equally no doubt that a teacher who knows why a particular mistake is made is in a better position to correct it, or even to forestall it altogether, than one who doesn't.

In the optimistic years after the war, when the ultimate breakthrough in language teaching seemed to many people to be close at hand, a proposal for dealing with interference by means of a technique of *contrastive analysis* was put forward and quickly gained the status of an orthodox pedagogic dogma, though, as we shall see, not much more. The idea was that a description of every feature of one language should be paired off systematically with descriptions of every similar or comparable feature of another one to find out precisely what similarities and differences existed between the two[2]. According to the theory, the teacher would then be able to

---

[1] Among a number of recent discussions, see Noam Chomsky, in many places, but particularly "Review of B. F. Skinner's *Verbal Behavior*," in *Language*, 35 (1959); and *Language and Mind* (New York: Harcourt, Brace & World, 1968), 3, p. 58ff.

[2] The original published exposition of the idea is Robert Lado, *Linguistics Across Cultures* (Ann Arbor: University of Michigan Press, 1957). [Actually, Fries, 1947, preceded Lado. Editor's note.]

concentrate on the points of difference that had been revealed, since it was here that difficulties of learning might be expected; the features of the target language that were similar to features of the L1 would be learned easily—in fact the impression was often given that they would virtually learn themselves. Some of the assumptions behind this were obviously right; moreover, the theory looked beguilingly complete and scientific, and it received the enthusiastic lip service that welcomed other pseudo-theories in the field of language teaching in the '40's and '50's. Contrastive analyses of small areas of various pairs of languages began appearing, and conventional studies began wearing the new label.

In spite of these attempts, the idea has never really gotten off the ground, for the good reason that it is surely quite impracticable to apply it to the whole of any two languages. It is of course perfectly feasible to make an exhaustive comparative analysis of the *phonological* systems of two languages, since such systems are invariably quite limited in scope; any teacher with a reasonable training in general phonetics (and preferably nowadays some familiarity with distinctive-feature theory as well) can do it for himself. But to carry out an analysis over the whole range of syntactic and lexico-semantic features is a different matter. The formidable set of specifications for a complete contrastive analysis laid out by Mackey[3] makes it plain that the number of permutations of elements is going to be astronomical, even if "complete" is very modestly interpreted. And even assuming that it could actually be done within any foreseeable future, which seems most improbable, the computer notwithstanding, the result would be too massive and too complicated to be useful.

Fortunately, there is no real reason to suppose that any such attempt is even theoretically desirable, much less that it is practically necessary. A more systematic and better informed application of older and simpler methods of comparison will do all that is needed, and the rest of this paper will exemplify and to some extent discuss some lines of an approach of this sort.

The prerequisites are an excellent knowledge of the target language, and at least a good knowledge of the language from which interference can be expected, usually the learner's mother tongue; the method is just systematic observation of frequently occurring faults in the target language and the search for some feature in the

---

[3]W. F. Mackey, *Language Teaching Analysis* (London: Longmans, 1965), pp. 80-97. Mackey uses the term "differential analysis."

mother tongue that may be interfering. If a regular correspondence is found between such a feature and a persistent and widespread fault, the assumption that the one causes the other is fully justified. (It is worth pointing out here that a theory of interference is and must always remain just that—a theory. Like any other theory, it postulates a causal relation between things that regularly occur together *because* they regularly occur together; that is, the usual kinds of verification are available, but no absolute, knock-down "proof.")

Interference can be expected in any of the three components of language: phonology, syntax, and lexis.

PHONOLOGY

A great deal has already been written and done in this area; many of the commonest types of phonological interference have now been well publicized, and for this reason not much will be said about them here. We have all grown fairly sophisticated about allophones and distribution, and the problem of the East African air hostess who dismissed her passengers with the hope that they had had a pleasant fright and the wish that the airline would have the pleasure of frying them again is no mystery to us. But there are still plenty of other problems that can be traced to interference, but seldom are. For example, the almost universal habit of Bantu speakers in Kenya of writing a comma after the English conjunction *that* is traceable to a prosodic feature of their mother tongues, though prosody is no doubt more properly a syntactic than a phonological matter. (See the brief discussion of contrastive stress in the section on syntax.)

However, before leaving this familiar ground, it will be well to notice that the relatively recent theory of distinctive-feature analysis[4] has provided us with a much finer tool for making phonological comparisons than we possessed before. It makes it possible to explain, for example, such previously puzzling facts as that Russian speakers learning English typically substitute [t] for [θ], whereas the Japanese learner substitutes [s], although the articulatory properties of both /t/ and /s/ are very similar in Russian and Japanese.[5] We can expect a good deal of illumination along these lines in the future.

---

[4]See R. Jakobson, G. Fant, and M. Halle, *Preliminaries to Speech Analysis* (Cambridge, Mass.: M.I.T. Press, 1963; originally published, 1955); and R. Jakobson and M. Halle *Fundamentals of Language* (The Hague: Mouton, 1956).

[5]See William C. Ritchie, "On the Explanation of Phonic Interference," in *Language Learning*, 18, Nos. 3/4 (1968).

SYNTAX

The syntactic component of historically related modern languages is usually so similar, in spite of such obvious differences as the relative degree of inflection in English and German, or the normal position of attributive adjectives in English and Spanish, that this area has received comparatively little attention. With unrelated languages, syntactic differences in the surface structure of sentences are often very great and perfectly obvious, but this, as a source of interference, is much neglected, nevertheless. Most teaching materials in use for Kenyan children (and adults) learning English, for instance, are based flatly on the totally erroneous assumption that the surface structure of sentences in the L1 is in all essentials the same as it is in English. Transformational theory would of course expect the deep structures to be the same, but the set of transformational rules operated by a speaker of, say, a Bantu language to reach his actual utterances is very different from an English speaker's. Transformational studies of particular languages promise to make life much easier for the teacher in future, by showing how it is that various languages reach the acceptable forms that their speakers actually produce, and thus what linguistic intuitions about surface structure they obey. This is of course the essence of the problem. Such studies are not yet sufficiently developed, even for English, for much direct use to be made of them, but the following examples will suggest the sort of thing that can be done without them and sometimes the lines upon which they can be expected to help in the future.

Speakers of Swahili and other Kenyan languages are very likely to produce deviant English sentences like *This law . . . its purpose is to prevent civil disorders.* Surface structures like that are perfectly normal in Swahili (which can from now on be taken as sufficiently representative of other Kenyan Bantu languages for present purposes), but deviant in English, or at any rate in written English. As far as I know, it is not yet possible to explain the transformational process by which Swahili speakers derive surface phrases like *this law its purpose* from a deep structure sentence presumably something like *this law has a purpose*, but for the teacher it is enough to know that they can. Being able to pinpoint the problem and to point out to students what they are doing when they make such a mistake and why they are doing it brings their learning or relearning task into focus; if the teacher himself does not know what is happening, the problem will remain unmanageable, since he will not even be able to tell his student exactly what the mistake *is* that he is making, and will certainly not be able to plan any teaching strategy for eliminating it.

Mistakes like that, arising from differences in the transformational rules of two languages, form an obviously important class, and this kind of interference accounts for many of the most radical syntactic troubles. But syntactic interference also arises from two other main causes: the presence of a syntactic feature in the L2 that has no analogue in the L1, and the presence of a syntactic feature in the L2 that has only a partial analogue in the L1. Examples of the first (again from Bantu speakers using English) are *They all gave me quite different advices (Bantu has no class of uncountable nouns), and *Most people now have a watch so that they could tell the time (Bantu has nothing corresponding to the English system of tense harmony between matrix and embedded sentences). A subclass of this kind of interference is the quite common case where the L2 has a certain constraint that the L1 does not have, operating upon some feature which they otherwise have in common. English, for instance, has a constraint upon the use of will and would in if and time clauses that Bantu lacks (a literal translation of *We would do it if we would be given the chance would be good Bantu), and another on what can precede a noun followed by a restrictive relative clause—with a few exceptions, a possessive cannot occur there. Bantu languages have no such constraint, and a Bantu speaker has no intuition against such a phrase as *his courage which he has shown. Such cases constitute a sort of "negative" interference, since it is not an intuition about an existing feature of the L1 that causes the trouble, but the absence of any intuition about the point at all. They are interference, just the same.

Very similar is the case of contrastive stress in English. There is simply no feature in Bantu languages, or if there is it operates in a very different way from the English device. The negative interference that results from this fact is altogether disastrous, yet to the best of my knowledge its existence has never been recognized. Certainly no grammar or teaching materials that I know mention it, or even explain what the device is or how it works. At a fairly trivial level, the result is the common faulty stressing of such sentences as *I know you are interested in politics, as I'am (for as 'I am), but the real seriousness of this particular failure of insight only becomes clear when we discover that very few Bantu speakers of English, even after completing Higher School Certificate, have any idea what the do is doing in a context like Most of our members are a bit slow in paying their subscriptions; of course, some people do pay them promptly, *but not many*.[6] That would be read by almost all the adult and frequently well educated students who come to the Kenya Institute of Administration for advanced training, with *do* completely unstressed; they take it to be just another form of the present and imitate it accordingly, quite apart from the loss of comprehension in reading and listening that it implies. The meaning of italics and underlining is of course passed over in the same way. The moral is that *no* feature of a teacher's mother tongue can be taken for granted; the most seemingly universal of them may find no echo at all in the linguistic consciousness of speakers of another language.

The remaining major cause of syntactic interference is the difference in categorization that may exist between two languages. Transitivity, to take one example from many, marks a subcategory of verbs in both English and Bantu, but what is transitive in one language is not necessarily so in the other. And the sub-subcategories are often also different. English for example, has a sub-subcategory of transitive verbs where the object is not deletable (*reach, get,* etc.); the corresponding verbs are transitive in Bantu also, but there the object *is* deletable. Knowing this enables a teacher to deal more effectively with such things as **I did not reach till 10 o'clock* and **Don't worry about your promotion; you're sure to get very soon* than he could if they simply presented themselves to him as rather perverse and inexplicable bad habits. At the very least he will deal with them more sympathetically. Another example of the kind of trouble one can expect to encounter from categorization differences is shown in the Bantu speaker's deviant **We were all more delighted*, in a context where no comparison is possible. This too is interference; *more* in English is a member of only one category, but the (approximately) corresponding words in Bantu languages, such as the Swahili *zaidi,* are both comparatives and intensifiers (as *most* is in English). Intuitions about subcategorization are extremely powerful, and for many learners the development of new ones for an L2 simply does not take place until they are made fully aware of the nature of the problem.

LEXIS

The first kind of syntactic interference we looked at arises purely from the mechanical operation of transformational rules; it has

---

[6]The most illuminating discussion of the function of *do* as a dummy element to carry contrastive stress is in Martin Joos, *The English Verb—Form and Meaning* (Madison and Milwaukee: University of Wisconsin Press, 1964). Joos' term "insistive" is really preferable to "contrastive."

nothing to do with the way people conceive the world. The last kind, arising from subcategorization differences, forms a linguistic bridge to those forms of interference that can arise in the lexical component.[7] By and large, people conceptualize the world in terms of their lexicon (though no doubt partly also in terms of their syntax, and especially of its verbal element), and some examples of interference in this area have long been language teachers' classics. But these have mostly been observed between languages that are more or less closely related and/or in constant cultural contact (English *know*, Spanish *saber/conocer*; the *faux amis* of English and French spelling and pronunciation; and so on). Their number is comparatively small, for the reason that the languages, even if unrelated, of communities in prolonged cultural contact come to conceptualize the common elements of their cultures in very similar ways; two such historically unrelated languages as Hungarian and French now have, on the whole, much the same way of dividing their concepts up among their words. But the fewness of such interferences and their frequent triviality in these circumstances should not blind anyone to their possible range and importance.

Again, a few representative examples must suffice. Where one language splits up a concept between two or more words, and the other does not, interference can be expected; *know* covering the meanings of both *saber* and *conocer, savoir* and *connaître,* and so on, is the familiar case. But between exotic languages this is so common that, as a teacher, one needs to be constantly looking for it. Relationship terms, as an obvious instance, are much more rigidly restricted in English than they are in Bantu languages (**my youngest mother*) strikes very few Bantu speakers as absurd, though they may have learned not to say it). In such cases, of course, an interference problem can only arise if it is the L2 that has the concepts lexically divided. It is interesting to notice, though, the effect that a prestigious L2 can have on a mother tongue. Swahili divides the meanings of English *ask—enquire/request* between *uliza* and *omba* respectively. Once one makes this division it is difficult to see that these concepts really have very much in common. (English, of course, *can* make the same distinction, but *need* not.) Just the same, it is not uncommon to hear *uliza* used by Swahili speakers with the meaning of *omba,* though not the other way round. The effect is as barbarous as saying **No sé a tu hermano.* (As this is heard only from

---

[7]See the discussion of the proper placing of subcategorization rules, in the syntactic or in the lexical component, in Noam Chomsky's *Aspects of the Theory of Syntax* (Cambridge, Mass.: M.I.T. Press, 1965), 2, p. 78. (Further references in Note 11 to ch. 2.)

certain speakers who are familiar with English, and is unknown from those who are not, its provenance is obvious.)

Another type of lexico-conceptual interference is exemplified in *He is very much respected because he is too just.* English conceptualizes the notion of excess (necessarily reprehensible) in one word; Bantu languages do not, though they can certainly express the notion. Presumably what happens in such a case is that the Bantu speaker, faced with this lexical oddity in English (and often, I imagine, misled by his teacher and his dictionary into thinking that *too* is the equivalent of Swahili *mno*, Kikuyu and Kamba *mũno*, etc.), puts it into the nearest lexical set he can find that is familiar to him, and assigns it a place at or somewhere near the top of the series of intensifiers. The teacher who is not expecting interference may never find out what is wrong.

As a final type, the semantic range of two words in two different languages may only partly coincide; this is of course a commonplace, but there are many normally unrecognized cases. The semantic range of Swahili *weza*, for example, is considerably wider that that of the roughly corresponding English *can*. *Weza* covers the area of *moral capacity* for doing something, and hence the condition of being quite likely or liable to do it because that is one's nature; English *can* touches this area, but only in a very restricted way, and the Bantu speaker's deviant *He's a very cruel man; he can beat his children with a hoe* is interference.

It is natural that many language teachers, working in a field where the subject matter is both immensely complex and usually ill described and where results depend upon so many factors that are very little, if at all, under their control, should have been attracted by the various nostrums and panaceas that have been offered them since 1945. Interference studies, their own and others, can undoubtedly help to solve problems for them, at least to the extent of bringing the problems sharply into focus, but they are not a panacea; there is no question of their ending all our troubles.

For one thing, the problem still remains of what to do with the information they give us when we have got it. This is not the place to discuss methods, but interference problems do not just clear up of their own accord when their causes are brought to consciousness. Experience shows that, on the contrary, they require persistent attack. And in any case, the idea that it is only the points of difference between L1s and L2s that cause serious difficulty is simply not true, though it is surprisingly often accepted as self-evident;[8] the claims about this made by the sponsors of contrastive analysis were seriously exaggerated. There are many problems of particular learners that at present seem to be merely fortuitous; there are others that clearly arise from interference within the L2 (the spelling *greatful for grateful is a trivial but typical example); and there are problems caused, as they are for a child learning his mother tongue, by the setting up of false analogies. Mother tongue interference only accounts for a part of any learner's difficulties.

Nevertheless, it is an important part. Interference problems are distinctly more persistent than others; it is not, in my experience, uncommon to find speakers of English as an L2 whose only surviving mistakes are all of this kind. The conclusion is that interference problems do indeed need special treatment, not so much, or not only, in remedial teaching situations, where there is often not sufficient time to get rid of them completely, but from the first stages of teaching.

---

[8]Mackey, op. cit., p. 80, for example, says " . . . if we subtract the characteristics of the first language from those of the second, what presumably remains [sic] is a list of the learner's differences."

A NONCONTRASTIVE APPROACH TO ERROR ANALYSIS

Jack C. Richards

The identification and analysis of interference between languages in contact has traditionally been a central aspect of the study of bilingualism. The intrusion of features of one language into another in the speech of bilinguals has been studied at the levels of phonology, morphology, and syntax. The systems of the contact languages themselves have sometimes been contrasted, and an important outcome of contrastive studies has been the notion that they allow for prediction of the difficulties involved in acquiring a second language. "Those elements that are similar to the [learner's] native language will be simple for him, and those areas that are different will be difficult."[1] In the last two decades language teaching has derived considerable impetus from the application of contrastive studies. As recently as 1967 Politzer affirmed "Perhaps the least questioned and least questionable application of linguistics is the contribution of contrastive analysis. Especially in the teaching of languages for which no considerable and systematic teaching experience is available, contrastive analysis can highlight and predict the difficulties of the pupils."[2]

Studies of second language acquisition however have tended to imply that contrastive analysis may be most predictive at the level of phonology, and least predictive at the syntactic level. A recent study of Spanish-English bilingualism for example, states "Many people assume, following logic that is easy to understand, that the errors made by bilinguals are caused by their mixing Spanish and English. One of the most important conclusions this writer draws from the research in this project is that interference from Spanish is not a major factor in the way bilinguals construct sentences and use the language."[3]

*I am grateful to William F. Mackey, Bernard Spolsky, and John Macnamara for comments on earlier versions of this paper.

[1] Robert Lado, *Linguistics Across Cultures* (Ann Arbor: University of Michigan Press, 1957), p. 2.

[2] Robert L. Politzer, "Toward Psycholinguistic Models of Language Instruction," *TESOL Quarterly*, 2.3, 151.

[3] Gail McBride Smith, "Some Comments on the English of Eight Bilinguals," *A Brief Study of Spanish-English Bilingualism* Donald M. Lance. Research Project Orr-Liberal Arts-15504. (College Station, Texas: Texas A and M University, 1969).

This paper focuses on several types of errors observed in the acquisition of English as a second language, which do not derive from transfers from another language. Excluded from discussion are what may be called *interference* errors; that is, errors caused by the interference of the learner's mother tongue. A different class of errors are represented by sentences such as *did he comed, what you are doing, he coming from Israel, make him to do it, I can to speak French.* Errors of this nature are frequent regardless of the learner's language background. They may be called *intralingual* and *developmental* errors. Rather than reflecting the learner's inability to separate two languages, intralingual and developmental errors reflect the learner's competence at a particular stage and illustrate some of the general characteristics of language acquisition. Their origins are found within the structure of English itself and through reference to the strategy by which a second language is acquired and taught.

1. Distinguishing Interference, Intralingual and Developmental Errors

Before we can analyze intralingual and developmental errors, we need to be able to distinguish them from interference errors in a sample of second language speech. Initially, contrastive analysis or a knowledge of the learner's mother tongue, allows for identification of instances where the characteristics of one language are being carried over into another. We then locate errors which are common to learners who have quite different mother tongues. They may also occur with children acquiring English as a mother tongue and with deaf children learning written English.[4] A sample of such errors is shown in Tables I-VI (see *Appendix*). These are representative of the sort of errors we might expect from anyone learning English as a second language. They are typical of systematic errors in English usage which are found in numerous case studies of the English errors of speakers of particular mother tongues. They are the sort of mistakes which persist from week to week and which recur from one year to the next with any group of learners. They cannot be described as mere failures to memorize a segment of language, or as occasional lapses in performance due to memory limitations, fatigue, and the like.[5] In some learners they represent final grammatical competence; in others they may be indications of transitional competence.

---

[4]Cp: Vivian Cook, "The Analogy between First and Second Language Learning," *IRAL*, 7, p. 207-16; H. H. Stern, "Foreign Language Learning and the New View of First-Language Acquisition," *Child Study*, 30/4, 25-36; Paula Menyuk, *Sentences Children Use*, (Cambridge, Mass.: MIT Press, 1969).

[5]S. P. Corder, "The Significance of Learner's Errors," *IRAL*, 5, p. 161-9.

2. Sources of the Present Study

Tables I-VI are taken from studies of English errors produced by speakers of Japanese, Chinese, Burmese, French, Czech, Polish, Tagalog, Maori, Maltese, and the major Indian and West African languages.[6] From these sources, I have selected those errors which occurred in a cross section of the samples. By studying intralingual and developmental errors within the framework of a more adequate theory of second language learning than a purely contrastive approach suggests, and through examining typical cases of the teaching of the forms from which they are derived, it may be possible to see the way toward teaching procedures that take account of the learner's strategy for acquiring a second language.

3. Types and Causes of Intralingual and Developmental Errors

An examination of the errors in Table I-VI suggests that intralingual errors are those which reflect the general characteristics of rule learning, such as faulty generalization, incomplete application of rules, and failure to learn conditions under which rules apply. Developmental errors illustrate the learner attempting to build up hypotheses about the English language from his limited experience of it in the classroom or textbook. For convenience of presentation, Tables I-VI will be discussed in terms of: (1) overgeneralization; (2) ignorance of rule restrictions; (3) incomplete application of rules; (4) false concepts hypothesized.

3.1 Overgeneralization

Jakobovits defines generalization or transfer, as "the use of previously available strategies in new situations . . . . In second language learning . . . some of these strategies will prove helpful in organizing the facts about the second language but others, perhaps

---

[6]Major sources for Tables I-VI are F. G. French, *Common Errors in English* (London: Oxford University Press, 1949); L. Dušková, "On Sources of Errors in Foreign Language Learning," *IRAL*, 7 (1969), 11-36; J. Arabski, "A Linguistic Analysis of English Composition Errors Made by Polish Students," *Studia Anglica Posnaniensia*, 1, Nos. 1 & 2, 71-89; C. Estacio, "English Syntax Problems of Filipinos," *Proceedings of 9th International Congress of Linguists* (The Hague: Mouton, 1964), p. 217-23 (esp. comments by Meyerstein and Ansre); Jack C. Richards, "Language Problems of Maori Children," *Comment* (Wellington, N.Z.), No. 36 (1968), p. 28-32; A.W.S. Bhaskar, "An Analysis of Common Errors in P.U.C. English," *Bulletin of the Central Institute of English* (Hyderabad, India), No. 2 (1962), p. 47-57; S. Grelier, *Recherche des principales interférences dans les systèmes verbaux de l'anglais du Wolof et du francais* (Sénégal: Centre de Linguistique Appliquée de Dakar, No. 31; E. F. Aguas, "English Composition Errors of Tagalog Speakers and Implications for Analytical Theory." Unpublished doctoral dissertation, University of California, Los Angeles, 1964.

due to superficial similarities will be misleading and inapplicable."[7] Overgeneralization covers instances where the learner creates a deviant structure on the basis of his experience of other structures in the target language. For example (see Table I.1,3,4,8) *he can sings, we are hope, it is occurs, he come from.* Overgeneralization generally involves the creation of one deviant structure in place of two regular structures. It may be the result of the learner reducing his linguistic burden. With the omission of the third person *-s*, overgeneralization removes the necessity for concord, thus relieving the learner of considerable effort. Dušková discussing the omission of third person *-s* notes "Since [in English] all grammatical persons take the same zero verbal ending except the third person singular in the present tense . . . omissions of the *-s* in the third person singular may be accounted for by the heavy pressure of all other endingless forms. The endingless form is generalized for all persons, just as the form *was* is generalized for all persons and both numbers in the past tense . . . . Errors in the opposite direction like *there does not exist any exact rules* may be explained either as being due to hypercorrection . . . or as being due to generalization of the 3rd person singular ending for the 3rd person plural."[8]

Overgeneralization is associated with redundancy reduction. It may occur, for instance, with items which are contrasted in the grammar of the language, but which do not carry significant and obvious contrast for the learner. The *-ed* marker in narrative or in other past contexts, often appears to carry no meaning, since pastness is usually indicated lexically in stories, and the essential notion of sequence in narrative, can be expressed equally well in the present. *Yesterday I go to the university and I meet my new professor.* Thus the learner cuts down the tasks involved in sentence production. Ervin-Tripp suggests that "possibly the morphological and syntactic simplifications of second language learners correspond to some simplifications common among children [i.e., mother tongue speakers] learning the same language."[9]

---

[7]Leon A. Jakobovits, *A Psycholinguistic Analysis of Second-Language Learning and Bilingualism* (Institute of Communications Research: Illinois, 1969), p. 32. See also, Jakobovits, "Second Language Learning and Transfer Theory," *Language Learning*, 19, 55-86.

[8]Dušková, ibid. (See footnote 6.)

[9]Susan M. Ervin-Tripp, "Comments to 'How and When Do Persons Become Bilingual'," L. G. Kelly (ed.), *Description and Measurement of Bilingualism*, (Toronto: University of Toronto Press, 1969), p. 33.

Certain types of teaching techniques increase the frequency of overgeneralized structures. Many pattern drills and transform exercises are made up of utterances that can interfere with each other to produce a hybrid structure:

Teacher	Instruction	Student
He walks quickly.	Change to continuous form	*He is walks quickly.*

This has been described as overlearning of a structure.[10] At other times, *he walks* may be contrasted with *he is walking, he sings* with *he can sing*, and a week later, without any teaching of the forms, the learner produces *he can sings, he is walks*.

3.2 Ignorance of Rule Restrictions

Closely related to the generalization of deviant structures is failure to observe the restrictions of existing structures, that is, the application of rules to contexts where they do not apply. *The man who I saw him* (Table III, 2) violates the limitation on subjects in structures with *who. I made him to do it* (Table VI) ignores restrictions on the distribution of *make*. These are again a type of generalization or transfer, since the learner is making use of a previously acquired rule in a new situation. Some rule restriction errors may be accounted for in terms of analogy; other instances may result from the rote learning of rules.

Analogy seems to be a major factor in the misuse of prepositions (Table IV). The learner, encountering a particular preposition with one type of verb, attempts by analogy to use the same preposition with similar verbs. *He showed me the book* leads to *he explained me the book; he said to me* gives *he asked to me; we talked about it*, therefore *we discussed about it; ask him to do it* produces *make him to do it; go with him* gives *follow with him*. Some pattern exercises appear to encourage incorrect rules being applied through analogy. Here is a pattern exercise which practices *enable, allow, make, cause, permit*.[11]

It is followed by an exercise in which the student is instructed to complete a number of statements using verbs and prepositions from the table.

---

[10]David K. Wolfe, "Some Theoretical Aspects of Language Learning and Language Teaching," *Language Learning*, 17, 3.4 (1967), 180.

[11]A. J. Herbert, *The Structure of Technical English* (London: Longmans, 1965), p. 10.

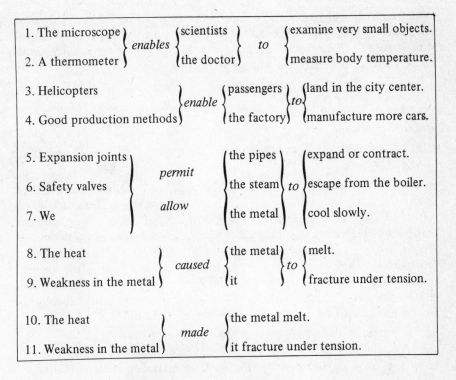

1. The microscope ⎱ enables ⎧ scientists ⎱ to ⎧ examine very small objects.
2. A thermometer ⎰ ⎩ the doctor ⎰ ⎩ measure body temperature.

3. Helicopters ⎱ enable ⎧ passengers ⎱ to ⎧ land in the city center.
4. Good production methods ⎰ ⎩ the factory ⎰ ⎩ manufacture more cars.

5. Expansion joints ⎱ permit ⎧ the pipes ⎱ ⎧ expand or contract.
6. Safety valves ⎱ ⎨ the steam ⎬ to ⎨ escape from the boiler.
7. We ⎰ allow ⎩ the metal ⎰ ⎩ cool slowly.

8. The heat ⎱ caused ⎧ the metal ⎱ to ⎧ melt.
9. Weakness in the metal ⎰ ⎩ it ⎰ ⎩ fracture under tension.

10. The heat ⎱ made ⎧ the metal melt.
11. Weakness in the metal ⎰ ⎩ it fracture under tension.

The rise in temperature _____ the mercury _____ rise up the tube.
The risk of an explosion _____ the workers _____ leave the factory.
The speed of the train _____ it _____ leave the rails on the curve . . . .

From a class of 23 with mixed language backgrounds, no fewer than 13 produced sentences like *the rise in temperature made the mercury to rise up the tube.* Practicing *make* in the same context as *allow it to, permit it to, enable it to*, precipitates confusion. Other instances of analogous constructions may be less easy to avoid. Table III, 2, includes *this is not fit to drink it, the man who I saw him.* By analogy with the learner's previous experience of *Subject + Verb + Object* constructions, the learner feels that there is something incomplete about *that's the man who I saw*, and so adds the object after the verb, as he has been taught to do elsewhere.

Failure to observe restrictions in article usage may also derive from analogy, the learner rationalizing a deviant usage from his previous experience of English. This may happen even when the mother tongue is close to the English usage. F. G. French gives the following example of how a common article mistake is produced by rational analogy.[12]   In English we say *The sparrow is a small bird. Sparrows are small birds.* Since the statements are exactly parallel a logical substitute for the second sentence would be: *The sparrows are small birds.* In Burmese, the equivalents would be

sa gale thi	nge thaw	nget	pyit thi
The sparrow	small	bird	is

and in the plural

sa gale mya thi	nge thaw	nget mya	pyit kya thi
The sparrows	small	birds	are

Instead of following the form of the mother tongue, however, the learner, having first produced *The sparrows are* from *The sparrow is,* sees a parallel between *sparrows* and *birds* and produces the common error, *The sparrows are the small birds.* A similar example is noted by Aguas, from Tagalog-speaking students.[13] In her study, she found a number of examples where sentences such as *Robot is like a human being* were produced, instead of *A Robot is like a human being.* Aguas rules out the possibility of transfer from Tagalog, since this would have required a determiner before the noun.

Ang	robot (ay)	parang	tao.
(N-m)	robot____	like	human being.

Here the analogy is from a somewhat comparable structure such as *Robots function like human beings.*

3.3 Incomplete Application of Rules

Under this category we may note the occurrence of structures whose deviancy represents the degree of development of the rules required to produce acceptable utterances. For example, across background languages systematic difficulty in the use of questions can be observed. A statement form may be used as a question, one of the transformations in a series may be omitted, or a question word may simply be added to the statement form. Despite extensive teaching of both the question and the statement forms, a grammatical question form may never become part of competence in the second language. Redundancy may be an explanatory factor. The second language learner, interested perhaps primarily in communication, can achieve quite efficient communication without the need for

---

[12]French, ibid, p. 9. (See footnote 6.)

[13]Aguas, ibid, p. 49. (See footnote 6.)

mastering more than the elementary rules of question usage. Motivation to achieve communication may exceed motivation to produce grammatically correct sentences. A further clue may be provided by classroom use of questions.

The use of questions is a common teaching device. Typically they are used, not to find out something, but as a means of eliciting sentences. Alternatively the statement form may be used as a means of eliciting questions through a transform exercise. Classroom observation suggests that the use of questions may be unrelated to the skills it is meant to establish. Here are some examples:

Teacher's Question	Student's Response
Do you read much?	*Yes I read much.*
Do you cook very much?	*Yes I cook very much.*
Ask her what the last film she saw was called.	*What was called the last film you saw?*
What was she saying?	*She saying she would ask him.*
What does she tell him?	*She tell him to hurry.*
What's he doing?	*He opening the door.*
Ask her how long it takes.	*How long it takes?*
Will they soon be ready?	*Yes they soon be ready.*
How much does it cost?	*It cost one dollar.*
What does he have to do?	*He have to do write the address.*
What does he ask his mother?	*He ask his mother for the address.*

As the above samples illustrate, when a question is used to elicit sentences the answer often has to be corrected by the teacher to counteract the influence of his question. Some course books proceed almost entirely through the use of questions; others avoid excessive use of questions by utilizing signals to indicate the type of sentence required. These may reduce the total number of deviant sentences produced.

3.4 False Concepts Hypothesized

In addition to the wide range of intralingual errors which have to do with faulty rule learning at various levels, there is a class of developmental errors which derive from faulty comprehension of distinctions in the target language. These are sometimes due to poor gradation of teaching items. The form *was*, for example, may be interpreted as a marker of the past tense, giving *one day it was happened* (Table I, 2) and *is* may be understood to be the corresponding marker of the present tense; *He is speaks French*

(Table I, 1). In Table II, 5, we find the continuous form instead of the simple past in narrative; elsewhere we encounter confusion between *too, so,* and *very*, between *come* and *go*, and so on. In particular instances I have traced errors of this sort to classroom presentation, and to presentation which is based on contrastive analysis of English and another language or on contrasts within English itself.

Here is an example of how the present continuous came to be understood as a narrative tense. The simple present tense in English is the normal tense used for actions seen as a whole, for events which develop according to a plan, or for sequences of events taking place at the present moment.[14] Thus the sports-commentator's *Now Anderson takes the ball, passes it to Smith . . .* and the cooking demonstrator's *I take two eggs, now I add the sugar. . . .* How do we find this use represented in textbooks for teaching English as a second language?

Typically one finds that the continuous form has been used instead for these functions. A recent audio-visual course contains many sequences like the following:[15]

> The lift is going down to the ground floor. Ted
> is getting out of the lift. He is leaving the
> office building. Ted is standing at the entrance
> of the office building. He is looking up at the sky . . .

This is not a normal use of English. The usual tense for a sequence of events taking place "at the moment" is the present tense, the continuous being used only when a single event is extracted from a sequence, the sequence itself being indicated by the present forms. This presentation of the continuous form led a number of my students to assume that the continuous form in English is a tense for telling stories and for describing successions of events in either the present or the past.

The reasons for the occurrence of untypical verb uses in many course books appears to be related to a contrastive approach to language teaching. In this example, the course designer has attempted to establish the use of the continuous form in a context in which the present form is appropriate. It is often felt that a

---

[14]W. H. Hirtle, *The Simple and Progressive Forms* (Quebec: Laval University Press, 1967), p. 40-41; R. A. Close. "Concerning the Present Tense," *English Language Teaching*, 13 (1959), p. 59.

[15]L. G. Alexander, *The Carters of Greenwood*, Elementary Workbook, Cineloop II (London: Longmans, 1966).

considerable amount of time should be devoted to the continuous form, since it does not exist in most learners' mother tongues. Excessive attention to points of difference at the expense of realistic English is a characteristic of much contrastive-based teaching. My experience of such teaching confirms Ritchie's prediction: "A course that concentrates too much on 'the main trouble spots' without due attention to the structure of the foreign language as a whole will leave the learner with a patchwork of unfruitful, partial generalizations . . . . " [16]

It is evident why this is often the case. The linguist who writes a contrastive description of two languages is interested primarily in the areas where the two languages differ. When such a description is used as the basis for teaching materials, we may well misrepresent the actual facts of English usage, since the parts of the language which are most often needed are not necessarily those which are most different from the learner's mother tongue. The translation of techniques of language description into techniques of language teaching has been a major feature of many schools of applied linguistics. The fad for minimal pair drills, for example, was largely based on the fallacy that, since phonological distinctions depend on the criterion of meaning, distinctions of meaning must depend on phonological distinctions, and that failure to maintain all the distinctions in a second language will mean failure to communicate.

Many courses progress on a related assumption, namely, that contrasts within the language are an essential aid to learning. "Presenting items in contrast can lighten the teacher's and the student's work and consequently speed up the learning process." [17] Here are some examples of actual learning from materials thought out in terms of contrast.

George notes that a frequent way of introducing the simple and continuous forms is to establish the contrast:

is = present state, is + -ing = present action. [18]

The contrast is in fact, quite false to English. When the past is introduced it is often introduced as a past state. *He was sick.* This

---

[16] William C. Ritchie, "Some Implications of Generative Grammar," *Language Learning*, 17, p. 129.

[17] Ruth Hok, "Contrast: An Effective Teaching Device," *English Language Teaching*, 17, 3, p. 118.

[18] H. V. George, "Teaching Simple Past and Past Perfect," *Bulletin of the Central Institute of English* (Hyderabad, India), 2 (1962), 18-31.

lays the groundwork for the learner to complete the picture of present and past in English by analogy:

is = present state   *is* + *-ing* = present action.
was = past state   ∴   *was* + *-ing* = past action.

Thus, *was* or *was* + *-ing* may be used as past markers. Used together with the *verb* + *-ed* it produces such sentences as *he was climbed the tree*. Interpreted as the form for "past actions" it gives *I was going down town yesterday* instead of *I went down town yesterday*.

Table III shows examples of the confusion of *too, so,* and *very*. Other substitutions are common, such as the use of *teach* for *learn*, of *do* for *make*, of *come* for *go*, of *bring* for *take*. Learners often feel that the members of such pairs are synonyms, despite every attempt to demonstrate that they have contrastive meanings. Such confusion is sometimes attributable to premature contrastive presentation.

Here are the occurrences of *too* and *very* in a first reader which tells the story of a group of children who light a fire in the snow in front of an old house: [19]

> *The house is empty because it's old. . . . I'm very*
> *cold. England is too cold. . . . The fire is very*
> *big. . . . It's very big. It's a very big fire. The*
> *firemen are going to put water on the fire because*
> *it's too big.*

The course designers intended to establish a contrast between *too* and *very*, but in so doing they completely confuse the meaning of the two forms. From the presentation—and from the viewpoint of a young learner—they have the same meanings. Thus we have the parallelism between:

> *It's too big, and it's dangerous.*
> *The fire is dangerous. It's very big.*

How could a child, following such a presentation, avoid saying *This is a too big house? Too* would be more safely taught out of association with *very*, and in contexts where it did not appear to be a substitute for *very*, as, for example, in a structure with *too* + *adjective* + *infinitive—this box is too heavy to lift*.

Other courses succeed in establishing confusion between *too, so,* and *very* by offering exercises like these:

1. Reword the following sentences, using *too*.
   This coffee is so hot that I can't drink it.

---

[19]*Scope,* Reader 7 (London: School Council Publications Co., 1969).

I've got so fat that I can't wear this dress now . . . .

Example. *This soup is very hot. I can't drink it.*
This soup is too hot (for me) to drink.

2. Remake these sentences using *too.*
This hat is very big; he's only a little boy.
This grammar is very difficult; a child can't
understand it. [20]

This type of exercise leads to the errors in Table III, 4. The common confusion of *since* and *for* (Table IV, 4) is sometimes reinforced by similar exercises, such as those which require choosing the correct preposition in sentences like:

I have been here (for/since) a week.
We have been in Canada (for/since) 1968.

Constant attempts to contrast related areas of English can thus have quite different results from those we intend. As yet, there is no substantial confirmation that a contrastive approach to teaching is likely to be *a priori* more effective than any other approach. Nor is there any evidence that contrasting items within a language plays an important role in language acquisition. Classroom experience and common sense often suggest that a safer strategy for instruction is to minimize opportunities for confusion by selecting nonsynonymous contexts for related words, by treating them at different times, and by avoiding exercises based on contrast and transformation.

CONCLUSIONS

An analysis of the major types of intralingual and developmental errors—overgeneralization, ignorance of rule restrictions, incomplete application of rules, and the building of false systems or concepts—may lead us to examine our teaching materials for evidence of the language learning assumptions that underlie them. Many current teaching practices are based on the notion that the learner will photographically reproduce anything that is given to him, and that if he doesn't, it is hardly the business of the teacher or textbook writer. It has been remarked that "Very surprisingly there are few published descriptions of how or what children learn. There are plenty of descriptions of what the teacher did and what materials were presented to the children but little about what mistakes the children made and how these can be explained, or of what

---

[20]These examples are taken from Paul Nation, *Too, So, Very*, Working Paper, English Language Institute, Victoria University of Wellington, 1967.

generalizations and learning strategies the children seem to be developing . . . . It may be that the child's strategy of learning is totally or partially independent of the methods by which he is being taught." [21]

Interference from the mother tongue is clearly a major source of difficulty in second language learning, and contrastive analysis has proved valuable in locating areas of interlanguage interference. Many errors however derive from the strategies employed by the learner in language acquisition, and from the mutual interference of items within the target language. These cannot be accounted for by contrastive analysis. Teaching techniques and procedures should take account of the structural and developmental conflicts that can come about in language learning.

APPENDIX
Tables I-VI

TYPICAL INTRALINGUAL AND DEVELOPMENTAL ERRORS

Table I. *Errors in the Production of Verb Groups*

1. *be + verb stem* for *verb stem*

   We are live in this hut.
   The sentence is occurs . . .
   We are hope . . .
   He is speaks French.
   The telegraph is remain . . .
   We are walk to school every day.

2. *be + verb stem + ed* for *verb stem + ed*

   Farmers are went to their houses.
   He was died last year.
   One day it was happened.
   The teacher was told us.
   They are opened the door.

3. wrong form after *do*

   He did not found . . . .
   He did not agreed . . .
   The man does not cares for his life.
   He did not asks me.
   He does not has . . .

---

[21]J. Dakin, "The Teaching of Reading," *Applied Linguistics and the Teaching of English*, (eds.), C. Fraser and W. H. O'Donnell. (London: Longmans, 1969), p. 107-11.

4. wrong form after modal verb

Can be regard as . . .
We can took him out.
I can saw it.
It can drawing heavy loads.
They can used it.
It can use in state processions.
She cannot goes.
She cannot to go.
They would became.
We must made.
We can to see.
We must worked hard.

5. *be* omitted before *verb + stem + -ed* (participle)

He born in England.
It used in church during processions.
They satisfied with their lot.
He disgusted.
He reminded of the story.

6. *-ed* omitted after *be + participle verb stem*
The sky is cover with clouds.
He was punish.
Some tree are unroot.

7. *be* omitted before *verb + ing*

They running very fast.
The cows also crying.
The industry growing fast.
At 10:30 he going to kill the sheep.

8. *verb stem* for *stem + -s*

He alway talk a lot.
He come from India.
She speak German as well.

Table II. *Errors in the Distribution of Verb Groups*

1. *be + verb + -ing* for *be + verb + -ed*

I am interested in that.
The country was discovering by Columbus.

2. *be + verb + -ing* for *verb stem*

She is coming from Canada.
I am having my hair cut on Thursdays.

3. *be + not + verb + -ing* for *do + not + verb*

I am not liking it.
Correct rules are not existing.
In French we are not having a present continuous tense and we
are not knowing when to use it.

4. *be + verb + -ing* for *verb + -ed* in narrative

. . . in the afternoon we were going back. On
. Saturday we were going down town, and we were
seeing a film and after we were meeting my brother.

5. *verb stem* for *verb + -ed* in narrative

There were two animals who do not like each other.
One day they go into a wood and there is no water.
The monkey says to the elephant . . . .

6. *have + verb + -ed* for *verb + -ed*

They had arrived just now.
He had come today.
I have written this letter yesterday.
Some weeks ago I have seen an English film.
He has arrived at noon.
I have learned English at school.

7. *have + be + verb + -ed* for *be + verb + -ed*

He has been married long ago.
He has been killed in 1956.

8. *verb (+ -ed)* for *have + verb + -ed*

We correspond with them up to now.
This is the only country which I visited so far.

9. *be + verb + -ed* for *verb stem*

This money is belonged to me.
The machine is comed from France.

Table III. *Miscellaneous Errors*

1. wrong verb form in adverb of time

I shall meet him before the train will go.
We must wait here until the train will return.

2. object omitted or included unnecessarily

We saw him play football and we admired.
This is not fit to drink it.
This is the king's horse which he rides it every day.
That is the man who I saw him.

3. errors in tense sequence

He said that there is a boy in the garden.
When the evening came we go to the pictures.
When I came back I am tired.

4. Confusion of *too, so, very*
I am very lazy to stay at home.
I am too tired that I cannot work.
I am very tired that I cannot go.
When I first saw him he was too young.
Honey is too much sweet.
The man became so exhausted and fell on the floor.

Table IV. *Errors in the Use of Prepositions*

1. *with* instead of	∅	met with her, married with her
	from	suffering with a cold
	against	fight with tyranny
	of	consist with
	at	laughed with my word
2. *in* instead of	∅	entered in the room, in the next day
	on	in T.V.
	with	fallen in love in Ophelia
	for	in this purpose
	at	in this time
	to	go to Poland
	by	the time in your watch
3. *at* instead of	∅	reached at a place, at last year
	by	held him at the left arm
	in	at the evening; interested at it
	to	went at Stratford
	for	at the first time
4. *for* instead of	∅	serve for God
	in	one bath for seven days
	of	suspected for, the position for Chinese coolies
	from	a distance for one country to another
	since	been here for the 6th of June
5. *on* instead of	∅	played on the piano for an hour
	in	on many ways, on that place, going on cars
	at	on the end
	with	angry on him
	of	countries on the world
	to	pays attention on it
6. *of* instead of	∅	aged of 44, drink less of wine
	in	rich of vitamins
	by	book of Hardy
	on	depends of civilization
	for	a reason of it
7. *to* instead of	∅	join to them, went to home, reached to the place
	for	an occupation to them
	of	his love to her

Table V. *Errors in the Use of Articles*

1. omission of *the*

    (a) before unique nouns

    Sun is very hot
    Himalyayas are . . .

    (b) before nouns of nationality

    Spaniards and Arabs . . .

    (c) before nouns made particular
    in context

    At the conclusion of article
    She goes to bazaar every day
    She is mother of that boy

(d) before a noun modified by a participle	Solution given in this article
(e) before superlatives	Richest person
(f) before a noun modified by an *of*-phrase	Institute of Nuclear Physics

2. *the* used instead of Ø

(a) before proper names	The Shakespeare, the Sunday
(b) before abstract nouns	The friendship, the nature, the science
(c) before nouns behaving like abstract nouns	After the school, after the breakfast
(d) before plural nouns	The complex structures are still developing.
(e) before *some*	The some knowledge

3. *a* used instead of *the*

(a) before superlatives	a worst, a best boy in the class
(b) before unique nouns	a sun becomes red

4. *a* used instead of Ø

(a) before a plural noun qualified be an adjective	a holy places, a human beings, a bad news
(b) before uncountables	a gold, a work
(c) before an adjective	... taken as a definite

5. omission of *a*

before class nouns defined by adjectives	he was good boy, he was brave man

Table VI. *Errors in the Use of Questions*

1. omission of inversion

What was called the film?
How many brothers she has?
What she is doing?
When she will be 15?
Why this man is cold?
Why streets are as bright as day?

2. *be* omitted before *verb + -ing*

When Jane coming?
What she doing?
What he saying?

3. omission of *do*

Where it happened?
How it looks like?
Why you went?
How you say it in English?
How much it costs?
How long it takes?
What he said?

4. wrong form of auxiliary, or wrong form after auxiliary

Do he go there?
Did he went?

Did he finished?
Do he comes from your village?
Which road did you came by?

5. inversion omitted in embedded sentences

Please write down what is his name.
I told him I do not know how old was it.
I don't know how many are there in the box.

ERROR ANALYSIS AND SECOND LANGUAGE STRATEGIES

Jack C. Richards

The field of error analysis may be defined as dealing with the differences between the way people learning a language speak, and the way adult native speakers of the language use the language. Such differences may create interest for a variety of reasons. We may begin with the interests of those who study language "for its own sake." Since language is not simply a more complex instance of something found elsewhere in the animal world, Chomsky suggests that the study of human language is the most fruitful way of discovering what constitutes human intelligence. Some of the most insightful notions about what language is have come from observing how language is acquired by children. By looking at children's speech, comparing it with adult speech, and trying to account for the differences, psycholinguists have been able to speculate about the nature of the mental processes that seem to be involved in language.

While the mother-child relationship and other language-crucial activities of the child's experience do not include any consciously incorporated instructional strategies, in the field of second language teaching elaborate instructional procedures are often defended as being essential components in successful second language learning. Since the goal of the language course is to lead the learner toward adult uses of the new language, differences between the way the learner and the native speaker speak the language have been studied in the hope that methods of overcoming these difficulties might be devised. Errors in second language learning, it is sometimes said, could be avoided if we were to make a comparison of the learner's mother tongue and the target language. The sum of the differences would constitute his learning difficulties, and it is here that teaching strategies would be optimal. Alternatively, interpretation of errors in second language learning along the lines of errors in first language learning suggests that second language errors are not, by nature, different from those made by children learning English as a mother tongue, hence they should not be of undue concern to language teachers. The purpose of the present paper is to look at recent and less recent ideas on errors in second language learning, in the hope that such an examination might illuminate the experience of second language teachers.

1. "Errors" in First Language Learning

What sort of ideas about language and language learning have been deduced from differences between children's and adult speech? Firstly, considerable support for current notions of language have been found in studies of child language development. It used to be thought that speaking was simply the exercise of our individual verbal habits, and that these were acquired through repetition, reinforcement, and conditioning, in much the same way as animals can be trained to perform certain tasks through the use of appropriate conditioning techniques. It is suggested that this is an inadequate account of language and of language learning. In children, it appears that the process of formulating language is an active and creative process, yet a process that follows similar patterns in children across quite differing learning circumstances. All children learning English as a mother tongue seem to follow a similar sequence in their acquisition of grammar, for instance. If we listen to the speech of English-speaking children at about three or four years old for example, we hear them using question forms like this (Bellugi, 1968):

> What he can ride in?
> Where I should put it?
> Why he is doing it?

These questions share a common structural feature that makes them different from adult questions. In these questions, that part of the sentence that normally comes after the subject in the statement form—the *can* in *He can do it*—has been left in this position in the question form, instead of being put before the subject as in the adult sentence *What can he do*? Now at about the same time as children are producing sentences like this, they *are* able to make questions that do not require a *wh*-word such as *where* or *why*. They have no difficulty in saying *Can he ride in a truck*? but when they use a *wh*-word they fail to change the word order and produce *What he can ride in*?

It is clear from instances like this in children's language that the children are not simply imitating the speech of their parents, for sentences like this do not appear in adult speech. If we were to compare the sentences that the child is capable of producing at this stage with those of an adult, we would have an illustration of the child's *competence* at age three or four compared with adult competence.

Child's competence

He possesses the rules permitting questions with the form: *Can he go? Where he can go?*
He cannot produce: *Where can he go?*

Adult's competence

He possesses the rules permitting questions with the form: *Can he go? Where can he go?*

By looking at the differences between the child's sentences and those of the adult we see evidence of the way the child appears to be formulating hypotheses about the English language, some of which he will eventually abandon in favor of the rules of adult language. Since the differences between children's and adult speech are *systematic*, found wherever children learn English, psycholinguists have been able to postulate universals that seem to be crucial for language development (Slobin, 1970).

Now the crucial elements in first language acquisition would seem to center on the psychology of learning, that is, those strategies employed by the child as he teaches himself his mother tongue, the development of his other faculties such as intelligence, cognition, perception, and so on, and the structure and rules of the particular language he is acquiring, in this case, English. These would appear to shape and formulate the sentences he produces in a systematic way. It has been suggested that the differences between the way a second language is often spoken and the way the language is spoken by native speakers are systematic, just as children's language follows a definite norm and developmental sequence of its own, as we saw with the example of the use of questions. Corder believes that errors in second language speech reveal a systematic attempt to deal with the data, and that they should play the same role in our study of second language learning as differences between child and adult speech play in the study of first language acquisition. "It is in such an investigation that the study of learners' errors (in second language learning) would assume the role it already plays in the study of child language acquisition, since the key concept . . . is that the learner is using a definite system of language at every point in his development, although it is not the adult system in the one case, nor that of the second language in the other. The learner's errors are evidence of this system and are themselves systematic" (Corder, 1967).

2. The Significance of Errors in Second Language Learning

If learners' errors in second language acquisition are systematic, in what ways are they organized, and what do they suggest about the nature of second language acquisition? Selinker calls the speech output in a second language an *Interlanguage*, since it invariably differs from the target language, and he uses the term *fossilization* to refer to permanent characteristics of the speech of bilinguals irrespective of the age at which the second language is acquired or the amount of instruction or practice in it. He characterizes fossilization in the following way: "it is my contention that the most interesting phenomena in interlanguage performance are those items, rules and subsystems which are fossilizable. . . . If it can be experimentally demonstrated that fossilizable items, rules and subsystems which occur in interlanguage performance are a result of the native language then we are dealing with the process of *language transfer*, if these fossilizable items, rules and subsystems are a result of identifiable items in training procedures, then we are dealing with *transfer-of-training*, if they are a result of an identifiable approach by the learner to the material to be learned, then we are dealing with *strategies of learning*, if they are the result of an identifiable approach by the learner to communication with native speakers of the target language, then we are dealing with *strategies of communication*, and finally if they are the result of a clear overgeneralization of target language rules then we are dealing with the *reorganization of linguistic materials*. I would like to hypothesize that these five processes are central processes in second language learning and that each process forces fossilizable material upon surface Interlanguage utterances, controlling to a very large extent the shape of these utterances" (Selinker, 1969*a*, 1969*b*).

I should like to focus on Selinker's description of interlanguage characteristics as a basis for an account of typical errors in second language communication in English. As data I will begin with an analysis of samples of English speech elicited from two speakers, one whose mother tongue is European French, the other whose mother tongue is Czech. To obtain the six speech samples presented in Figure 1, the speakers were given a number of short texts in English; they were instructed to read the texts and then asked to relate the content of each text in their own words without referring to the texts. In what ways does their performance of this task illustrate systematic approaches to second language communication?

3. Interference

Perhaps some of the most apparent examples of fossilizable items in second language communication are those described as instances of language transfer or interference. This may be defined as the use of elements from one language while speaking another and may be found at the level of pronunciation, morphology, syntax, vocabulary, and meaning. Examples 1, 2, 3, 4, and 7 in Sample 1 for example, reflect the use of elements of French morphology and syntax. In Example 1, the plural -*s* is omitted, perhaps because plurals are not pronounced in French. A French structure is used in Example 2—*has allowed to capitalist man*—following the French structure—*a permis au capitaliste de*—. In Example 3, French article usage is reflected in the use of—*the money*—following the French—*pour investir l'argent*—. In Example 7, the influence of French likewise seems evident, *have the possibility to do great profits* follows the French—*ont la possibilité de faire de grands profits.*

These examples of interference might appear to confirm some of the claims that have sometimes been made for the possibility of predicting instances of interference by contrasting the grammatical or other systems of two languages. "We can predict and describe the patterns that will cause difficulty in learning and those that will not cause difficulty, by comparing systematically the language and culture to be learned with the language and culture of the student" (Lado, 1957). Many such contrasts between languages have been attempted, though they have been criticized because they make demands on linguistic theory that our present knowledge about language is simply not ready to meet. We do not know enough about the higher-level organization of particular languages to make the neat sort of contrasts that such statements imply either feasible or meaningful. Most of the contrasts that have been made have been based on practical knowledge of two languages rather than on any systematic application of a theory of contrastive analysis (see Wardhaugh, 1970). Yet the instances of interference we have looked at seem so evident that it might appear that second language data can be entirely described in such terms. Indeed it often has been. What happens in fact is that in analyzing second language data it is tempting to see all errors as effects of the interference of the mother tongue, ignoring all other relevant phenomena. Both Samples 1 and 2 provide examples of errors that require alternative interpretations.

Figure 1. Samples of Second Language Speech

Sample 1 (French)

The fact that land and minerals are very cheap in inaccessible *region*[1] and the development of new techniques *has allowed to capitalist man*[2] to invest *the money*[3] in this region and exploit *the minerals.*[4] It's . . . this *is occurs*[5] in Australia where man has exploited huge *mounting*[6] of minerals in this region. And they *have the possibility to do great profits*[7] in this part of the country.

1. Interference (plural not pronounced in French)
2. Interference (a permis au capitaliste de . . .)
3. Interference (l'argent)
4. Interference (les minéraux)
5. Overgeneralization
6. Overgeneralization
7. Interference (ont la possibilité de faire de grands profits)

Sample 2 (Czech)

In the first part of the article the *author give*[1] us reasons for investment in inaccessible regions. The reason for . . . to invest in *this regions*[2] is the *possibility to buy*[3] land, minerals and deposits at very low cost. Another factor which *permits to invest*[4] in this region is the development of new technology which *permits to connected*[5] *this inaccessible regions*[6] in *short time*[7] with the regional . . . the regions which are civilized.

1. Overgeneralization
2. Overgeneralization
3. Overgeneralization
4. Overgeneralization
5. Overgeneralization
6. Overgeneralization
7. Interference

Sample 3 (French)

The human eye may be compared to a camera. The camera functions with a lens . . . *would*[1] *enregistrate*[2] by a lens and a screen behind it which *enregistrate*[3,4] the image. Once the image is developed *it stay*[5] here. *In contrary*[6] in movies the image *disappear*[7] from the screen. The eye-human eye functions like . . . like the camera. It is *composed with*[8] a lens and behind the lens is *little*[9] screen coated with cells and *enregistrates*[10] the light.

1. Performance error
2. Interference (French borrowing)
3. Interference (French borrowing)
4. Overgeneralization (Omission of -s)
5. Overgeneralization
6. Interference (au contraire)
7. Overgeneralization
8. Overgeneralization
9. Performance error
10. Interference (French borrowing)

Sample 4 (Czech)

The author of the article compares the function of a camera and the function of the human eye. In an ordinary camera we have *lens*[1] which *concentrate*[2] beams of light on the film which is in the back of *camera.*[3] This light *can impress the film and in this way to fix*[4] the image of the film. The function of the human eye is very similar. We have the same lens in our eye and the film which is found in *camera*[5] is replaced in our eye by *retina,*[6] an organic matter which is *composed by*[7] light sensitive cells.

1. Interference
2. Overgeneralization
3. Interference
4. Performance error
5. Interference
6. Interference
7. Overgeneralization

Sample 5 (French)

Steam engine[1] is *composed with*[2] a cylinder in which a piston can move easily and which *fix*[3] *well the cylinder.*[4] This piston is *actionated*[5] by the steam and it is connected to a wheel

1. Performance error
2. Overgeneralization
3. Overgeneralization
4. Interference (fixe bien le cylindre)
5. Interference (actionné)

(continued on next page)

which it *makes turned*.[6] The steam ... this
engine *has been discovered*[7] in the 18th
century, but James Watt is the person who
ameliorate[8] it and who *give*[9] it *his actual
form*.[10]

6. Interference (le fait tourner)
7. Interference (a été découvert)
8. Interference (French borrowing)
9. Performance error
10. Interference (sa forme actuelle)

Sample 6 (Czech)

The article is about the invention of *steam
machine*.[1] *Steam machine*[2] was invented in
17th century[3] by an Englishman, James Watt.
The principle of the steam machine is ... the
basis of the steam machine is *piston*[4] which is
pushed by the pressure of *steam*.[5] This piston is
connected with[6] a wheel by a rod and in this
way the motion of the wheel is possible.

1. Interference
2. Interference
3. Interference
4. Interference
5. Interference
6. Overgeneralization

4. Overgeneralization

In Samples 1 and 2 we find examples of a similar type of error,
illustrated by *this is occurs* (Example 5 in Sample 1) and *the author
give us* (Example 1 in Sample 2). Here we have a similar type
of error from both the French and Czech subjects. These illustrate
what Selinker calls overgeneralization of target language rules, or the
reorganization of linguistic materials. Jakobovits (1970: 111-12)
defines generalization as "the use of previously available strategies in
new situations. ... In second language learning some of these
strategies will prove helpful in organizing the facts about the second
language, but others, perhaps due to superficial similarities will be
misleading and inapplicable." In Sample 1 the French speaker seems
to have generalized the form *is occurs* from his experience of forms
like *it is made of* and *it occurs.* In the Czech example in Sample 2 the
omission of the third person *-s* in *the author give us* may result from
the pressure of other forms in English without *s.* Dušková (1969)
remarks, "Since (in English) all grammatical persons take the same
zero verbal ending except for the third person singular in the present
tense . . . omissions of the *-s* in the third person singular in the
present tense may be accounted for by the heavy pressure of all the
other endingless forms. The endingless form is generalized for all
persons."

These examples of overgeneralization are the effects of particular
learning strategies on items within the target language, and since such
learning strategies appear to be universally employed when a learner
is exposed to second language data, it is not surprising that many of
the errors found in second language communication are identical
despite the background language of the speaker. The elements that

differ are those effects of language transfer or interference while those that we find in common are the results of other learning strategies. One aspect of generalization has often been referred to in studies of first language acquisition. It has frequently been remarked that children learning English as their mother tongue will produce forms like *comed*, and *goed*, by analogy with past tense formation in regular verbs. Among children acquiring French as their mother tongue we likewise find things such as *on poudra* instead of *on pourra* (we will be able . . .) by probable analogy with *on voudra* (see Kinzel, 1964). Likewise both French-speaking children and people learning French as a second-language produce sentences like *je serai très malcontent* instead of *je serai très mécontent* presumably on the analogy:

   heureuse/malheureuse   content/malcontent

Similar processes seem to account for common preposition mistakes in English. The pressure of one English construction on another as the learner tests out his hypotheses about the structure of English may account for forms like *permits to invest* and *permits to connected* in Sample 2 and the other examples of overgeneralization by analogy noted in the other samples. (Sample 1, Example 6; Sample 2, Example 3, 4, and 5; Sample 3, Example 8; Sample 4, Example 7; Sample 5, Example 2; Sample 6, Example 6).

In Sample 3 we have an interesting demonstration that the French speaker is not simply transferring the grammar of his mother tongue into English. In Example 8 he uses *composed with* instead of *composed of*. The Czech speaker in Sample 4, Example 7, likewise uses *composed by* and in Sample 5, Example 2, the French speaker again produces *composed with* instead of *composed of*. Had the French speaker followed the grammar of his mother tongue here he would have produced the correct English form. In French the equivalent would be *composé de* which is the English equivalent of *composed of*. The French·equivalent of the form the French speaker used (*composé avec*) would in fact be inappropriate in French in this context. Both the French and the Czech speaker are evidently trying to work out the particular rules of English structure, being guided here not by the grammar of the mother tongue but by what they already know of English, and by their own intuitions. As Wolfe (1967) comments: "Once the student grasps the idea that the new language differs from his native language in many matters of structure, he will not know when it is safe to operate in terms of his native language (it seldom is) and he may try to create his own structures on the basis of previous contact with the new language. . . . Some students, not knowing a correct form, will make up a form which does not parallel either the native or the target language. Or a student will persistently fail to make a grammatical distinction in the target language which he actually does make in his mother tongue." We see examples of this from the French speaker, who fails to use the past tense in Sample 5, Example 9, although this would be required were he recounting the text in French. The psychological parameters in second language learning thus cannot be identified exclusively with the linguistic ones.

The effect of rules within the target language has been described in more formal terms by Falk in this way: "Few if any of the rules of the syntactic component are completely independent of the other rules. The formulation of one rule will invariably affect other rules in the grammar. . . . Because this is so, the construction of a subgrammar, i.e., of some subset of the rules for a particular language, is a complicated task. Some of the rules in such a subgrammar will inevitably be ad hoc since the limited nature of the undertaking excludes detailed consideration of all the linguistic facts which may affect the rules" (Falk, 1968).

So far I have talked about interference and overgeneralization as if they were independent factors. The facts are not quite so consistent. In Samples 4 and 6 the Czech speaker consistently omits articles, and this I have attributed to interference, since articles are not present in his mother tongue. Dušková (1969:18) notes, however, "Although the difficulty in mastering the use of articles in English is ultimately due to the absence of this grammatical category in Czech, once the learner starts internalizing their system, interference from all the other terms of the (English) article system begins to operate as an additional factor." This no doubt leads to diffidence and hesitancy in the use of articles by the Czech speaker.

5. Performance Errors

If language learning both in a first and second language setting involves trying out hypotheses about the language from one's experience of it (and in the case of second language learning, from one's experience of other languages), and abstracting the rules that permit us to produce sentences in the language, then we shall need to go further than looking at simple examples of interference, overgeneralization, and analogy. These processes are in themselves insufficient to account for the complexity of language learning. The samples we have looked at do not enable us to say whether these mistakes are occasional, or represent permanent states in the speaker's competence. In Sample 3 for instance, the speaker says (Example 9) *behind the lens is little screen*, omitting the article. But what does this error really represent? There are several possibilities. First, we may exclude interference from the mother tongue, since this would have required the use of the article in French. A second possibility is that the speaker realized the mistake as he said it but forgot to correct it—that he would have corrected it if he had had more time to think about it. In fact when looking at the transcribed text the speaker did correct this mistake himself.

Now this is something that the child who says *What he can ride in?* is unable to do. The child's competence is represented by that particular sentence, whereas this particular article error by the French speaker is simply the sort of error anyone is likely to make speaking under normal circumstances. It is therefore an error at the level of *performance* rather than competence. Performance errors are quite normal aspects of language use. When we are tired or hurried, we all make errors of this type. There is a similar error in Sample 4, Example 4. The Czech speaker was able to recognize the mistake in *This light can impress the film and in this way to fix the image of the film*. This error was probably a function of the length of the sentence the speaker was trying to produce, hence it is related to memory limitations rather than to competence. Clearly if we want to have a more certain idea of someone's competence in a second language, we need to take a much closer and more detailed look at his speech output to find out if his sentences consistently display particular interlanguage characteristics, that is, to find out if the speaker has internalized a system of some sort that does not correspond to that of the native speaker.

6. Markers of Transitional Competence

Just as we need to be able to distinguish between performance and competence errors in the analysis of second language data, so it may be necessary to distinguish between those errors that indicate the learning sequence by which particular grammatical rules are built up, and those that represent the final state of the speaker's competence. In our example of first language learning for example, sentences like *What he can ride in?* seem to be produced by all English speaking children before they are able to use the form of the adult grammar—*What can he ride in?* Are some of the errors observed in second language learning also representative of developmental sequences by means of which the learner masters the rules of the

English grammatical system? This question cannot be answered from the data I have presented here, and I know of no studies that could confirm or reject such a hypothesis. What is needed are detailed longitudinal studies of an adult learner's progress with a second language, documenting the appearance and development of particular structures. The types of short-term errors attributed here to overgeneralization and analogy could then be placed within the overall sequence of language development. It may be that the innate ability to generate and hypothesize rules, so evident in first language acquisition, becomes subordinate in adult second language learning to secondary learning strategies, such as generalization, borrowing, and memorization, for purely biological reasons. It should also be noted that I am using terms like interference, analogy, and generalization, without relating them to a psycholinguistic model of language. They are used here simply as convenient ways of classifying observable phenomena at the level of speech, though this does not explain how they are represented at the level of language. Psycholinguistic models (such as that of Jakobovits, 1970: chapter 4) have been proposed that do try to account for such factors as interference and generalization.

If we were to try to locate our Czech speaker's article errors at the level of competence, we would require a close developmental study of his article usage as he acquires English, to find out if after some exposure to English, his use of articles was entirely haphazard, or whether he had worked out some consistent way of dealing with them. Is his learning task the same as that of the child faced with the appearance of articles in his mother tongue?

Jones (1970), in his study of child language development, places the development of the article system as coming logically and necessarily after the development of the substantive or noun. It is a further conceptualization of the substantive, permitting a point of view that conceptualizes it either as a universal or a particular. Leopold (1939-) found that articles were not used at all by his child subject in the first two years but later took on systematic usage. With an adult acquiring the system as a second language, however, cognitive development has already occurred, hence he may have to resort to other strategies to develop rules to deal with the article system in English.

7. Other Forms of Interference

Before looking at other aspects of second language learning strategies, I should like to refer to an aspect of interference that is not manifest in the particular samples we have looked at so far, but which is nevertheless quite widespread. This has to do with contrasts between styles across languages. We may regard style as the choice we have within a language of a particular mode of expression, such as formal or informal, and colloquial or officious. In some speech communities differences of this sort are so marked and have become so institutionalized that they may be regarded as quite distinct varieties of the same language. In Baghdad, according to Ferguson (1959), the Christian Arabs speak a "Christian Arabic" dialect when talking among themselves but speak a general Baghdad dialect "Muslim Arabic" when talking in a mixed group. This phenomenon, where two distinct varieties of a language exist side by side in a community, with each having a definite and distinct role to play, is what Ferguson called *diglossia*. What typically happens is that particular functions are assigned to each variety of the language, the most fundamental distinction being between what may be called High and Low uses of the language. The High form is generally regarded as superior to the Low form and is compulsory for certain types of situations. Ferguson gives sample situations, with indications of the appropriate form of the language to be used:

sermon in church or mosque	H	
instructions to servants, waiters, clerks, workmen		L
personal letter	H	
speech in Parliament	H	
university lecture	H	
conversation with family, friends, colleagues		L
news broadcast	H	
radio soap opera		L
newspaper editorial, news story, caption on picture	H	
caption on political cartoon		L
poetry	H	
folk literature		L

Now the differences between the High and Low forms of languages that exhibit this phenomenon, and it is very widespread—Arabic, Modern Greek, Swiss German, and many Asian languages for example—are much greater than those between what we may call a formal or informal style in English. In diglossic communities the High style may have striking differences in grammar and in word order, and in the area of the vocabulary the High style may have a much more learned and classical lexicon than the Low.

People who belong to language communities that manifest this phenomenon may come to expect such switching between distinct language varieties to be a universal feature of languages. In other words, when they come to write something in English that would demand a high style in their mother tongue, they may feel a pressure to give their English a correspondingly high style. Thus one finds people who write English clearly and faultlessly, exhibiting what I call "diglossamania" in certain situations. In English for example, we do not feel that there is a low status about words of high frequency, in the vocabulary we use in normal everyday situations. A Tamil-speaking student however may prefer the feel of *I instructed him to obtain it for me* over *I told him to get it for me.* There may be a distinct preference for archaic words or for words of low frequency, whereas the native speaker of English prefers a simple style. You may have noticed this in written English from Greek or Arabic students, for example, depending on the topic they choose to write about.

The effects of the High/Low distinction in the student's mother tongue may also be evident at the grammatical level in his written English. Kaplan, in a 1967 article dealing with composition difficulties of Arab students, remarks that Arab students appear to prefer certain devices of conjoining sentences over others, thus the sentences:

The boy was here.
He drank the milk.

may be more frequently conjoined with *and* by Arab students, producing *The boy was here and he drank the milk* in preference to *The boy who was here drank the milk.* (See also Macmillan, 1970:146). This may be attributed to the influence of the grammar of a high style in Arabic. This use of balancing devices to create a more aesthetic style produces among certain Indian students sentences like:

While I am still a student, and yet I still have plenty of time.
Whenever I see him, then I feel happy.
Even though I am poor, yet I am happy.

Here are two examples from a letter-writing manual for students of English written by an Asian with a diglossic mother tongue. As a model for a personal letter he uses a distinctly high style:

With the warm and fragrant breath of Spring, here approaches the bliss of Eastertide. May it shower joy and happiness upon you all. The tide brings to my mind the old memories of several Easters feted with you and the decorated eggs placed on my dresser.

For an order however, the writer presents a normal low style as a model:

I want to order from you a copy of the latest edition of __ book. In this connection please let me know what will be the total cost.

The prevalence of artificially high style uses of English among Indians has been called "Babu English" and it is well parodied in a novel by F. Anstey (1902):

After forming my resolution of writing a large novel, I confided it to my crony, Mr. Ram Ashootosh Lall, who warmly recommended to persevere in such a magnus opus. So I became divinely inflated periodically every evening from 8 to 12 p.m., disregarding all entreaties from feminine relatives to stop and indulge in a blow-out on ordinary eatables . . . and at length my colossal effusion was completed, and I had written myself out: after which I had the indescribable joy and felicity to read my composition to my mothers in law and wives and their respective progenies and offsprings, whereupon, although they were not acquainted with a word of English, they were overcome by such severe admiration for my fecundity and native eloquence that they swooned with rapture. . . .

In examining instances of interference or language transfer we thus need to consider more than just the linguistic variables and their distribution across languages; we need also to consider social reactions to different aspects of language use, since these too may be carried from one language to another, influencing the sort of sentences that may be formulated in the second language.

8. Strategies of Communication and Assimilation

The shape of the utterances produced in the second language may be influenced by additional factors, not related to interference or to aspects of generalization and analogy. Under communication strategies we may include errors that derive from the fact that heavy communication demands may be made on the second language, forcing the learner to mold whatever he has assimilated of the second language into a means of saying what he wants to say, or of getting done what he wants to get done. The learner may simplify the syntax of the language in an effort to make the language into an instrument of his own intentions. Errors deriving from such efforts may be attributed to strategies of communication. Errors attributable to the learner's attempts to reduce the learning burden of what he has to assimilate may be closely related, and they may be referred to as strategies of assimilation.

Perhaps the clearest examples of alterations in language structure as a result of strategies of assimilation and communication are to be found in pidgin languages—languages used by people whose mother tongues are different, in order to facilitate communication between them. In the process of becoming a pidgin a language often loses some of its vocabulary, or is simplified in its phonology or grammar. Simplification is one way in which speakers of different languages can make a new language easier to learn and use (see Samarin, 1962).

We frequently find instances of a similar process in a normal second language setting. The communicative demands made on the second language may far outpace the speaker's actual competence in the second language, thus the speaker may have to create the means of expressing relations for which the language course has not prepared him. The school English course, for example, may begin with the present tense, the present continuous, and following concepts of linguistic grading or sequencing, delay the introduction of other tenses until the present and present continuous have been mastered. Supposing however, that the English program is that of an English-medium school in a multilingual context, where English provides the only lingua franca among Chinese-, Malay-, and Tamil-speaking children. The children in their use of English as a lingua franca outside of the classroom cannot wait until the past and "future" tenses have been taught before they will begin talking about past and planned events. They will have to establish their own way of dealing with past and planned events, and in so doing there will be considerable simplification of syntax, and extension of the uses of known forms into other areas. This may produce what has been called "dormitory English" and "playground English," which can function as an entirely efficient form of communication: *You are not knowing what Boonlat is do. He is open stand-pipe . . . water is not coming, so he go ask . . .* (example from a working paper by H. V. George).

This may seem an extreme example, but in any situation where the second language actually has to be used outside the classroom in real situations, inevitably the learner finds himself having to cope with circumstances that the school syllabus has not covered or for which he may not have the linguistic resources available. Looking at such language samples, we are often not able to say whether a particular error is attributable to a strategy of communication, or to a strategy of assimilation, that is, an identifiable approach by the learner to the material being learned.

My own acquisition of French in Quebec has provided me with many examples of the effects of communication and assimilation strategies, since on arrival in Quebec extensive demands were immediately made on whatever I had been able to pick up of the language. As an example of assimilation strategy, I found the form *je vais* (I'm going to) easier to learn than the future tense in French, and I quickly developed the means of expressing futurity or intention with the use of this construction. This however led me to use the *going to* form in situations where the future tense was appropriate, and now I frequently have to correct a tendency to use the *going to* form in sentences like *Je vais vous téléphoner ce soir* (I'm going to telephone you tonight) when what is really intended is *Je vous téléphonerai ce soir* (I'll telephone you tonight).

As an example of a communication strategy my acquisition of the conditional passé tense in French is illuminating. A language need that soon presented itself was the need to express intentions in the past that I was unable to fulfill. Since I did not acquire the grammatical means to do this until fairly late, I had to find alternative ways of expressing the same content. This I did by lexical means, through the use of a longer construction. Thus instead of saying, "I would have liked to have seen the film last night"—*J'aurais voulu voir le film hier soir*—I would say, "I had the intention of seeing the film last night, but . . . "—*J'avais l'intention de voir le film hier soir, mais . . .*

Similar strategies may account for the frequent misuse of the present tense as a narrative form, since the present tense is usually introduced first in language courses and the additional learning burden involved in acquiring the past tense can be avoided if the past is simply expressed lexically. A word like *yesterday* will thus suffice to locate the time setting and the speaker will continue in the present. *Yesterday we go for a drive and we stop near the beach and we . . .* Thus the speaker is able to expand the functional capacities of his knowledge of the second language, while keeping to known or sure ground.

The selection and gradation of items in a language course should therefore take account not merely of linguistic factors, such as the frequency or complexity of items to be introduced, but also the demands that will be made on the language and how the learner will adapt what he is given to his particular needs.

9. Errors and the Teacher

Teachers, as Pit Corder remarks, are more concerned with how to deal with errors than with what causes them, and in this there have been several schools of thought. "One is that if we were to achieve a perfect teaching method the errors would never be committed in the first place, and that therefore the occurrence of errors is merely a sign of the present inadequacy of our teaching techniques" (Corder, 1967). This attitude is illustrated in the introduction to a recent elementary English course. "One of the teacher's aims should be to prevent mistakes from occurring. In the early stages while the pupils are wholly dependent on the teacher for what they learn, it should be possible to achieve this aim" (Lee, 1970).

It is difficult to reconcile this approach with what we know or can observe about language learning. Children do not themselves acquire language by correctly imitating sentences they hear. "A child learns his language by interacting with it, by actively coping with and manipulating his environment. He does this on the basis of unsystematic, usually unplanned language input on the part of his parents" (Moores, 1970). Does this lead to an essential casualness on the part of the teacher towards the nature of the sentences his students produce? After all, current views of language learning emphasize that language cannot be taught, but must be learned by the child. Attempts to teach language by direct imposition of an adult grammatical model seem psycholinguistically inconsistent.

However, in assessing the teacher's role in second language teaching we are faced with the fact that although the child learning his mother tongue begins by producing sentences which do not duplicate adult sentences, gradually building towards an adult grammar, in second language learning what is usually the end point in the learning process is an Interlanguage, that is, a form differing from the target language characterized by interference both internal and external to the language. What we would have to postulate then is the encouragement of those types of sentences that indicate language development, and the minimization of opportunities for fossilization, for the establishment of permanent deficiencies in the learner's competence. In the present state of our knowledge about second language acquisition this is not a realizable goal, since we have so little information about which types of errors in second language learning are positive and which are negative. A form like *What he is doing?* may represent transitional competence in first language acquisition, but fossilization in the second language learner's speech. In the present state of our knowledge, we need to be careful not to be overoptimistic about the relevance to second language teaching of studies of first language acquisition.

At the same time, all language teaching techniques can be seen to produce transfer-of-training effects, where the general effects of memory on the material taught are apparent in reconstruction and retroactive inhibition as well as generalization and analogy. It is possible to try to arrange teaching materials to minimize the unwanted effects of such factors, but we have no way of knowing whether this is ultimately of any advantage to the learner. Questions, for example, invariably influence in unintended ways the form of the sentence the student uses in his answer. *What was the woman saying?* used to elicit sentences about a film will tend to elicit *The woman saying she will. . . . Ask her how long it takes* will produce *How long it takes?* and so on. Or if we introduce a text for practicing comparative constructions including *is as big as, is bigger than*, some of the students will produce *is as bigger as, is as big than.* Such effects might be minimized by separating the forms that interfere with each other and teaching them at different times, but we cannot say very much about what the results of particular instructional approaches will be on the final competence of the learner. It may make no difference at all, since there is no evidence that the linguistic and instructional variables—the points we select to teach and the order and manner in which we teach them—are the same as the psychological variables, the actual nature of the process by which the language items become part of the speaker's competence.

Despite the inadequacies of our present knowledge about the relevance of particular approaches to language instruction, there are excellent social motivations for teachers' drawing their learners' attention to examples of fossilization, to those errors that seem to have become a permanent rather than a transitional feature of their speech. In looking at the social justification for the correction of certain errors we can keep in mind, however, that linguistically we may simply be trying to modify our learner's performance rules. Even if his competence is represented in sentences like *Yesterday I go down town*, conscious attention to the way he speaks may assist him to modify his performance so that he produces *Yesterday I went down town*. If grammmatically deviant speech still serves to communicate the speaker's intentions, why should we pay further attention to it?

Simply because speech is linked to attitudes and social structure. Deviancy from grammatical or phonological norms of a speech community elicits evaluational reactions that may classify a person unfavorably. In sociolinguistic terms " . . . our speech, by offering a rich variety of social and ethnic correlates, each of which has attitudinal correlates in our own and our listener's behavior is one means by which we remind ourselves and others of social and ethnic boundaries, and is thus a part of the process of social maintenance (or change)" (Williams, 1970). Psychologists have investigated the way listeners will provide a range of reliable cultural, social class, and personality associations upon hearing speech samples. These are usually measured by playing recordings of speakers, and having them rated on a series of characteristics, such as intelligence, character, good looks, and so on. I propose that the adult second language learner's deviation from grammatical norms elicits evaluational reactions that can be measured in similar ways. My evidence is largely anecdotal. Here is an extract from a recent UNESCO report. "Individuals who learn new languages later in life, especially after the age of 15 or so, characteristically have more difficulty with new structures than with new vocabulary, and the difficulty seems to increase with age. It is not uncommon to characterize such people as 'having a foreign accent' or 'speaking brokenly,' even though their vocabulary and general fluency may be quite satisfactory in the acquired language. Although they have little difficulty in being understood for practical purposes, they are apt to be considered as perpetual foreigners or outsiders" (Noss, 1967).

My observations of native speakers' reactions to grammatical deviancy suggest that not all instances of deviancy, not all errors, are evaluated in the same way. We don't react to *I'm going in Paris next week* in the same way as we react to *I is going to Paris next week* or to *He come from India*. Omission of a third person *-s* or a plural seems to grate rather violently, whereas a misplaced preposition may not affect us so much. Deviancy in article usage may elicit a "baby-talk" evaluation. You may have noticed this in your own relations with nonnative speakers of English. One almost automatically corrects certain types of mistakes while we let others pass without too much thought.

Native speakers' reactions to systematic variation in grammatical or other features could be measured using the psychologists' techniques for measuring reactions to different dialects. This would demand systematically varying the nature of deviancy in oral or written texts and having native speakers assess the personality traits of the speakers.

Here is an example of a passage in which article usage is deviant:

I remember war period very clearly. I remember big bomb which exploded near house I was living in in 1940. First wall began to crack and window broke and I hurried out of house just before chimney fell down. I saw that big tree in front of house was broken.

Here is the same text with article usage restored but past tense omitted:

> *I remember the war period very clearly. I remember a big bomb which explode near the house I live in in 1940. First the wall begin to crack and the window break and I hurry out of the house just before the chimney fall down. I see that a big tree in front of the house is broken.*

Information on the reaction of native speakers to particular aspects of grammatical deviancy would thus enable us to say which examples of fossilization the second language teacher should pay most attention to.

CONCLUSIONS

To draw together some of the points I have touched upon here, I have first of all tried to suggest why people who speak second languages may not speak or write them with native-speaker-like fluency. I have suggested that deficiencies in their knowledge may be the results of interference, the use of aspects of another language at a variety of levels; of strategies of learning such as overgeneralization and analogy by means of which the learner tests out his hypotheses about the structure of the language; of strategies of assimilation, in which the learner makes his learning task easier; and of strategies of communication, whereby the learner adapts what he knows into an efficient communication model, producing an optimal utility grammar from what he knows of the language.

At the same time we need to distinguish between performance and competence errors. The former are occasional and haphazard and are related to such factors as fatigue, memory limitations, and so on. The latter are systematic and may represent either a transitional stage in the development of a grammatical rule or the final stage of the speaker's knowledge. While our knowledge about second language learning is still largely speculative, excluding the possibility of prescribing recipes for teachers, I hope that this account of errors and learning strategies has at least suggested some of the reasons for what we hear from our students of second languages.

REFERENCES

Aguas, E. F. "English Composition Errors of Tagalog Speakers and Implications for Analytical Theory." Unpublished doctoral dissertation. University of California, Los Angeles, 1964.

Anstey, F. *A Bayard from Bengal*. London: Methuen, 1902.

Bellugi, U. "Linguistic Mechanisms Underlying Child Speech."(ed.), E. M. Zale. *Proceedings of the Conference on Language and Language Behavior*, pp. 36-50. New York: Appleton-Century-Crofts, 1968.

Corder, S. P. "The Significance of Learners' Errors." *IRAL*, 5 (1967), 161-169.

Dušková, L. "On Sources of Errors in Foreign Langauge Learning." *IRAL*, 7 (1969), 11-36

Falk, J. "Nominalizations in Spanish." *Studies in Linguistics and Language Learning V*. Seattle: University of Washington Press, 1968.

Ferguson, C. "Diglossia." *Word* 15 (1959), 325-40.

French, F. G. *Common Errors in English*. London: Oxford University Press, 1949.

George, H. V. "Teaching Simple Past and Past Perfect." *Bulletin of the Central Institute of English* (Hyderabad, India), 2 (1962), 18-31.

Jakobovits, L. A. *Foreign Language Learning*. Rowley, Mass.: Newbury House.

Jones, R. *System in Child Language*. Aberystwyth: University of Wales Press, 1970.

Kaplan, R. "Contrastive Rhetoric and the Teaching of Composition." *TESOL Quarterly*, 1.4 (1967), 10-16.

Kinzel, P. *Lexical and Grammatical Interference in the Speech of a Bilingual Child*. Seattle: University of Washington, 1964.

Lado, R. *Linguistics Across Cultures*. Ann Arbor: University of Michigan Press, 1957.

Lee, W. R. *The Dolphin English Course; Teacher's Companion.* London: Oxford University Press, 1970.

Leopold, W. F. *Speech Development of a Bilingual Child*. 4 vols. Evanston: Northwestern University Press, 1939-1949.

Macmillan, M. "Aspects of Bilingualism in University Education in Sudan." (ed.), T. Gorman. *Language and Education in East Africa*. Nairobi: Oxford University Press, 1970.

Moores, D. F. "Psycholinguistics and Deafness." *American Annals of the Deaf*, 39 (January, 1970).

Noss, R. *Higher Education and Development in South East Asia*. Paris: UNESCO, 1967.

Richards, J. C. "A Non-Contrastive Approach to Error Analysis." *English Language Teaching*, 25 (1971), 204-219. (This volume, pp. 96-113.)

Samarin, W. J. "Lingua Francas, with Special Reference to Africa." (ed.), F. Rice, *Study of the Role of Second Languages in Asia, Africa, and Latin America,* pp. 54-64. Washington: Center for Applied Linguistics, 1962.

Selinker, L. "The Psychologically-relevant Data of Second Language Learning." Paper read at the Second International Congress of Applied Linguistics, Cambridge, England, 1969a. In P. Pimsleur and T. Quinn (eds.) *The Psychology of Second Language Learning*. Cambridge University Press, 1972, 35-44.

        "Language Transfer." *General Linguistics,* 9.2 (1969b), 67-92.

Slobin, D. "Suggested Universals in the Ontogenesis of Grammar." Working Paper 32, Language Behavior Research Laboratory, University of California, Berkeley, 1970.

Wardhaugh, R. "The Contrastive Analysis Hypothesis." *TESOL Quarterly*, 4.2 (1970), 123-30.

Williams, F. "Language Attitude and Social Change." (ed. id.), *Language and Poverty*, Chicago: Markham, 1970.

Wolfe, D. K. "Some Theoretical Aspects of Language Learning and Language Teaching." *Language Learning*, 17, 3-4 (1967), 181.

LANGUAGE ACQUISITION
IN A SECOND LANGUAGE ENVIRONMENT

Roar Ravem

The present paper is a report on a study of a Norwegian six-year-old child's acquisition of English syntax in a second language environment. The study was undertaken with my son as the informant when I was a student of applied linguistics at the University of Edinburgh in 1966. It arose out of a general interest in language acquisition *per se* and more particularly out of an interest in relating studies of language acquisition to the teaching of foreign languages in kindergartens and at early elementary school stages. The more we know about language learning the more likely we are to be successful in our teaching of a second language. However, the gap between a child acquiring his first language and a child learning a second language, at a time when he already possesses "language," is likely to be so big that any direct application of our knowledge is difficult, the more so because our knowledge in the first place is still extremely shaky. I hope that the present study will make a small contribution to filling the gap.

More recent studies of the acquisition of syntax have been concerned with the linguistic competence of the children at different stages of their linguistic development, and an effort has been made to write generative grammars for these stages. The investigators have been interested in the obtained data only to the extent that they throw light on the child's system of internalized rules for generating language. According to the language acquisition model suggested by Noam Chomsky,[1] a distinction is made between "performance"—the actual utterances—and the underlying "competence" on which performance is based. Chomsky's basic tenet is the notion that linguistic theory should provide an adequate characterization of the native speaker's knowledge of his language, i.e., the native speaker's intuition of what is grammatical in his language should be capable of being described in a logically consistent way. Even if it were possible, in Chomsky's terms, to give a descriptively adequate account of an adult native speaker's linguistic competence, an adequate description of a child's competence is very much more difficult, both because the child's intuition of what is grammatical is not available and also because the child's competence is continually developing.

---

[1] N. Chomsky, *Aspects of the Theory of Syntax* (Cambridge, Mass.: M.I.T. Press, 1965), 1.

In the present study no serious attempt has been made to go beyond capturing the syntactic regularities of my informant's speech at the times of observation. An attempt has been made to present some of these regularities in the form of rewrite rules, but as they are based on what appear to be the most productive patterns as shown by performance data, they do not claim to be generalized rules characterizing my informant's competence. They are at best a reflection of it.

The sentences singled out for closer scrutiny were interrogative and negative sentences of the kind that in adult language require a *do*-transformation. These are of particular interest because the comparable sentences in Norwegian are made by inversion of subject noun phrase and verb.

BACKGROUND AND METHOD

My informant, Rune, was six and a half when the study began. He had a rudimentary knowledge of English, acquired during a previous stay in England and from being read to occasionally in English. He had been exposed to the language, but had never had any systematic teaching of it. He started school in the middle of January, 1966 in Scotland and was allocated to a class of children of his own age group. Basing one's judgement on a purely subjective impression, one can say that Rune appears to be slightly ahead of his age group with respect to intelligence and perhaps language development too.

The material was collected from two main sources: free conversation and a translation test. Rune, who is a talkative child, did not seem to be affected by the fact that the conversations were recorded, and thus it was not difficult to elicit utterances from him. With the help of my eleven-year-old daughter, who is bilingual in Norwegian and English, we managed to steer the conversation in different directions to elicit from Rune different kinds of sentences, referring to both past, present, and future.

The translation test, involving about fifty negative and interrogative sentences requiring an auxiliary in adult speech, was given at regular intervals. The object of the translation experiment was to compare the utterances with the data obtained in free conversation in order to get an indication of the validity of prompted utterances of this kind. The stimulus took the form of a request (in Norwegian) like "go and ask Mother if ... " or "tell Ranny that. ... " The indirect sentence provided Rune with less of a clue to the syntactic structure of *his* sentence than a direct sentence would have done; the clue was further reduced by putting the sentence to him in Norwegian (notably in such cases where *do* is used). By prolonging the time gap between the stimulus and Rune's response it was hoped that the effect of the stimulus as a clue would be further reduced. The validity of the translation experiment was supported by the obtained utterances in free conversation. There were some clear cases of interference from Norwegian, but they were of the same kind as found in the conversation material.

The conversation data were collected at four different "Times," starting on 31st December 1965 and finishing on 6th March 1966. The translation test was given within a week of the conversation recordings. It was seen to be an advantage to record intensively at 3-4 week intervals rather than more frequently and less intensively.

SOME FINDINGS

Only negative and interrogative sentences have been singled out in the study for analysis. However, some examples of declarative sentences were included for comparative purposes. Our special concern was with Rune's acquisition of *do* as a tense marker. If Katz and Postal are correct, which they probably are, the only meaning of *do* is to be a carrier of tense[2]. Being semantically empty it does not appear as a morpheme in deep structure, and the task of the learner of English is to discover the particular function of *do* as a tense carrier. This might help to explain the reason why *do*-transformations constitute a particular difficulty for foreign learners of English. In this respect *do* does not have the same status as the modal auxiliaries, which behave, along with *have* and *be*, roughly in the same way as the equivalent auxiliaries in Norwegian. On this basis we would expect that Rune would acquire these auxiliaries more quickly than *do*. The following examples show that this is in fact the case: *I not like that* (C.1)[3], *eating you dinner to-yesterday?* (T. 2), *what you did in Rothbury?* (C. 3), *climb you?* (C.2) compared with *can I give that to Sooty?* (C.1), *oh, I mustn't take that aeroplane open and . . .* (C. 1), *I have try that, "men"*[4] *I can't do it* (C. 1).

---

[2] J. J. Katz and P. Postal, *An Integrated Theory of Linguistic Description* (Cambridge, Mass.: M.I.T. Press, 1964), p. 8.

[3] *C* refers to Conversation data, *T* to Translation. The number refers to Time of recording.

[4] Norwegian for *but*. Rune made use of Norwegian vocabulary items frequently and without hesitation, as if they were available English words. One interesting observation is that even at Time 1, before he knew any written English (or Norwegian), the Norwegian words were often given an English pronunciation. Somehow he was able to translate from one phonological system into another. Examples are: *tak* /ta: k/(roof), pronounced by Rune as /teik/; *ratt*/rɑt/ (steering wheel pronounced as /raet/.

1. Declarative sentences.

The following typical declarative sentences have been included for comparative purposes:

a)   All crying.
     We climbing Friday.
     I drawing and do something.
     I fall down again (i.e., prob. *fell*).

b)   He can see the moon.
     I will hear what you will say.

c)   I have say it.
     I have lost it.
     I have eating and play.

On the basis of data of the kind represented by (a) above we would suggest, very tentatively, the following rule:

$$S \quad NP + \left\{ \begin{array}{c} (be) + V \\ V \end{array} \right\} + (X) + (adv.\ t)$$

Both modals and *have* have been excluded. Rune uses *have* for "completed" aspect, but the participle morpheme *-en*, is not normally realized. The only available verb forms at this stage are, on the whole, verb stem (V) or V_{ing}. That V and V_{ing} are not free variants, except possibly in (a) above, is indicated by the almost exclusive use of V in sentences with modal auxiliaries. The following obtained sentences uttered in succession illustrate this:

I singing out yesterday.
I can sing Blaydon Races for you.

We can only venture a guess why Rune makes such an extensive use of the *ing*-Form of the main verb, more often than not without the auxiliary *be*. Is it because he has been exposed to English at an early stage so frequently in situations where the present progressive is used that· he has generalized his own usage on this basis? An interference from Norwegian is out of the question as Norwegian has no expanded tense form.

The concept of tense is available to Rune, but he appears not to have discovered how to realize it in English. Time relations are sometimes expressed by help of an adverb of time as in the obtained sentences *I singing now/yesterday/ all the day* (i.e., every day). The nonoccurence of *-ing* with such verbs as *like* and *think* and the fact that *be* occurs optionally only in the context of V_{ing}, not V, might indicate a beginning differentiation between the simple and progressive forms.

2. Negative Sentences

In adult grammar *do* is used when the verb phrase does not contain another auxiliary verb. As with the modal auxiliaries the negative element, *not*, follows or is attached to *do* and not to V. The sentences below exemplify the similarities between the use of modal auxiliaries and *do* in negative sentences in English as contrasted with Norwegian.

I cannot come.	Jeg kan ikke komme.
I could not come.	Jeg kunne ikke komme.
He does not work.	Han arbeider ikke (he works not).
We did not take it.	Vi tok det ikke (we took it not).

Since *do* is not yet available at Time 1, one prediction would be that Rune, in keeping with Norwegian structure, lets *not* follow the main verb and produces sentences of the form NP + VP + *not*. What we find, however, are such sentences as *I not like that, one is not crying. I not looking for edge.* The negative sentences at this stage correspond to the pattern for declarative sentences. We need only insert *not* after the subject NP in our formula.

3. Interrogative Sentences

The following types of interrogative sentences, all of them requiring *do* in adult grammar, were studied: (a) sentences beginning with a question word (*what, when,* etc.); (b) sentences requiring *yes* or *no* as an answer; (c) negative versions of (b); (d) negative questions beginning with *why*.

Again we find a high degree of syntactic similarity between English and Norwegian in the use of modal auxiliaries and *have* ("ha"), but there is no equivalent to *do* as shown by the following examples:

(a)	What did he say?	*Hva sa han?* (What said he?)
(b)	Did you do it?	*Gjorde du det?* (Did you it?)
(c)	Don't you like ice cream?	*Liker du ikke iskrem?* (Like you not ice cream?)
(d)	Why don't you like ice cream?	*Hvorfor liker du ikke iskrem?* (Why like you not ice cream?)

A reasonable prediction would be that Rune at Time 1 would make use of Norwegian syntactic structure to form English sentences of the types in brackets above, i.e., by inversion of subject NP and V.

If *do* is semantically empty, these sentences differ from adult grammar only in their transformational history. They would sound foreign, but would be perfectly understandable.

As we shall see later this happens to both affirmative and negative versions of Q-*yes/no*-sentences, but interestingly enough not to Q-*wh*-sentences. These seem to be generated on the basis of the rule for declarative sentences with a prefixed Q-*wh* morpheme. If we take the sentence (a) *What you reading to-yesterday?* (T. 1) to represent a simple tense sentence and (b) *What she (is) doing now?* (C.1) to represent progressive tense, they both retain the word order NP + V of declarative sentences.[5] Both sentence types then appear to have developed from the same basic pattern—that of declarative sentences. We could illustrate this hypothesis by help of the following structural description.

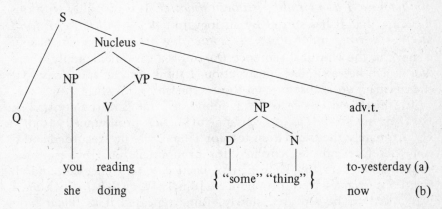

On the basis of this pattern we could make various predictions about the line of development for (a) and (b).

That Rune, like L1 learners, makes use of the pattern of the declarative sentence in Q-*wh*-sentences is, as we have already pointed out, rather surprising in view of the inversion of subject NP and V in Norwegian. It would be reasonable to expect both (a) and (b) to come out as *What reading you to-yesterday?* and *What doing you now?* This happens with *yes/no*-questions, where typical examples are *Climb you?* and *Like you food?* Again we could speculate as to whether Rune in these types of sentence makes use of inversion as a question signal from lack of a question word. Negative

---

[5]The only justification for letting (a) represent a simple tense sentence is the fact that this and similar sentences in the translation test later develop into simple past tense sentences of adult grammar.

yes/no-questions and negative *why*-questions are structured differently, but on a par with the respective affirmative sentences. These sentences were included in the Translation test only at Time 3. The Q-*why*-*Neg*-sentences proved much more resistent to the *do*-transformation than the other types of sentence included in the study. Typical sentences before the introduction of the *do*-transformations are:

I singing out yesterday.   Why we not live in Scotland?
I not sitting on my chair.   Drive you car to-yesterday?
What you reading to-yesterday?   Like you me not, Reidun?

4. The Development of *do* as a Tense Marker

Do occurs from the beginning frequently in the context of a few isolated verbs, where it is probably a lexical variant of *not*, e.g., *I don't know, I don't think, It doesn't matter.* It is probably with this meaning that it has spread by analogy to *I don't will more, I don't talking to you,* and *I don't say something more.* It appears also at Time 2 in the elliptical sentence *Do you?*, a case incidentally where Norwegian has a similar construction. I think we can safely say that the auxiliary *do* is absent from Rune's speech at this stage.

The next occurrence of *do* is found at Time 2 in the context of *you*, most likely as a variant of *you*, pronounced [dju:]. Unfortunately the translation test for Time 2 was not recorded and it can therefore not be checked for pronounciation. However, the conversation data for Time 2 have been carefully checked, and all eight occurrences were pronounced [dju:]. When *What d'you like?* was asked to be repeated slowly, Rune repeated it as *'What 'you 'like.* It is not unthinkable that *do* is acquired by children by first being a variant of *you*.

Time 3 is a transition stage. *Do* is clearly emerging as a tense carrier. The fact that Rune is now in the middle of a process of acquiring *do* is likely to be responsible for the greater lack of stability found at this stage than at the other times of observation. It is as if Rune is searching for a morpheme to attach tense to. The following examples illustrate the vacillation:

I not sitting on the chair.   What you did in Rothbury?
I don't sit on the chair.   What you do – in the hayshed?
What d'you do to-yesterday?   Like you ice cream?
What d'you did to-yesterday?   Did you drive car to-yesterday?
When d'you went there?

By Time 4 *do* has clearly emerged as a separate element, with both a present and past tense form. *Did* is more often than not used in sentences requiring the past tense, but there are also examples which show that the distinction is not fully established. Where *do* occurs it is almost invariably followed by the infinitive form of the main verb.

Contrary to the findings of Susan M. Ervin[6], there does not appear to be any significant time lag between the introduction of *do* into negative and interrogative sentences in Rune's case. This might be accounted for, however, by Rune's greater linguistic maturity and faster rate of learning.

At this stage *yes/no*-questions, both negative and affirmative, also fall into line with Q-*wh*-sentences as shown by the following examples: *Did you not see on TV to-yesterday?* as compared with the Time 3 *See you not on TV to-yesterday?* and *Did you not say it to Daddy?, Don't you like me, Reidun?* as compared with the Time 3 *Say it you not to Daddy?, Like you me not, Reidun?* Except for the Q-*why*-Neg-sentences, which throughout the time of study have consistently been of the type *why* + NP + *not* + VP (or alternatively *why* + *not* + NP + VP), the other structures under study should at Time 4 be capable of being described by a single set of related rules, as is the case of adult grammar.[7] These are by no means as stable as in adult grammar. Rune still frequently produces sentences which syntactically correspond to earlier structures.

CONCLUSION

The study reported here was not undertaken to test any particular hypotheses relating to certain theories of language learning. The only purpose was to conduct a study within the framework of recent L1 syntax studies to find out something about developmental sequence as compared with first language learners.

Recent first language syntax studies have shown that children exposed to a language at an early age internalize rules by help of which they are able to generate sentences. Attempts have been made with some degree of success to give a characterization of the sets of rules that are operative at various stages of development. The studies have shown that a large measure of creativity enters into the process of language acquisition.

---

[6]S. M. Ervin, "Imitation and Structural Change in Children's Language," E. H. Lenneberg (ed.). *New Directions in the Study of Language* (Cambridge, Mass.: M.I.T. Press, 1964), p. 184.

[7]To find out what had happened to Q-*why*-neg-sentences after the termination of the study, Rune was asked (January '67) to translate some of these from Norwegian. In addition to some earlier structures, such as *Why not Ranny come home?*, most of them were in the main in keeping with adult grammar, e.g., *Why do we not live in Oslo? Why doesn't we go to Oslo?* But also the obtained *Why didn't Mammy don't make dinner?* was attested by Rune as correct.

The situation of the learner of a second language is clearly different from that of the L1 child. The most obvious difference is that the task of the foreign learner is not to learn "language," which he already possesses and the knowledge of which must affect his acquisition of a second language. The process of learning the second language might therefore conceivably be qualitatively different. Nor is he very often exposed to "primary linguistic data" in the sense that an L1 learner is, but rather to carefully graded language items presented in small doses for a few hours a week.

The present study has, I believe, shown what we would expect to find, namely that a normal six-year-old child at all levels of language is greatly facilitated by the linguistic competence he already possesses through his first language. The six-year-old's greater maturity makes for a faster rate of learning. The first language, especially when it is as closely related to English as Norwegian is, is a source the learner can draw on. The detrimental effect of first language interference can only be assessed properly after the learner has achieved a good command of the second language.

What is perhaps more striking is the extent to which second language acquisition in an environment where no formal instruction is given seems to be a creative process not unlike that of first language acquisition. The similarities between Rune and L1 learners in the developmental sequence of negative and interrogative sentences are in many ways more revealing than the differences.

It does not follow from this that the appropriate methodology for teaching a foreign language at an early stage is to expose the children to a "language bath" and let them develop for themselves internalized generative rules which ultimately develop into those of adult grammar. We do not know if second language acquisition can be speeded up by children being exposed to selected and linguistically graded language patterns. And even if we have accepted that language learning is not merely a question of habit formation and reinforcement of correct responses, we cannot exclude the possible transfer value of well-established basic sentence patterns, especially if they are acquired in contextualized situations.

Perhaps a larger measure of language exposure and a freer scope for creative and self-corrective language learning than permitted by a graded course would be appropriate in early foreign language teaching in a school setting. Only a series of carefully controlled experiments could provide an answer to this question.

TWO PRACTICAL EXPERIMENTS WITH TEACHERS-IN-TRAINING AND SOME CONCLUSIONS

H. V. George

Probably many trainers of teachers have found that an effective way of reaching teacher-students is to establish reference points in their immediate experience. This is particularly useful when the "students" are grown-up, for they tend to idealize their recollections of their own learning, and often lack imaginative insight into the typical learner-states of not-knowing and half-knowing. In these pages I describe two practical ways of providing such reference points, an experiment in remembering, and a five-lesson course in a foreign language.

I. AN EXPERIMENT IN REMEMBERING

Foreign-language learning is much concerned with registration and memory, and few teachers appreciate the things that can happen to lesson material they "present," when it is received and stored for recall in a human brain. For this reason I have always anticipated these topics in my Methods Courses by collection of data from immediate experience. I will describe the procedure and the findings accumulated over eight courses.

The experiment

At the beginning of a lecture period I give out slips of paper—on which the students write their "serial numbers." I announce that, wishing to collect data for subsequent discussion of remembering, I am going to read a short piece of prose and ask questions to which one-word, or brief, answers should be given.

Here is the passage, which has proved to elicit evidence for all the psychological processes one may profitably discuss, followed by the questions, which are asked briskly and not repeated:

> The well-preserved corpse and personal effects of a warrior who died probably 600 years ago have been discovered in North West China. The discovery was made in the large Tsaidam Basin in Chinghai Province during the course of oil-prospecting. The man is believed to have lived during the Yuan Dynasty, about 600 to 700 years ago. The corpse was excavated from a small earth mound, was wrapped in a woollen blanket and clad in a fur coat with light armor fixtures. He was also wearing a fur hat with a red feather. Beside him lay a horse's tail, a saddle, a bow made of horn, and eleven arrows

whose delicately shaped arrowheads were still sharp. The climate of the region—hot and dry in summer, and intensely cold in winter—probably accounted for the good state of preservation. On the neck, there was a wound, and a silk bandage. The warrior may have been Mongolian.

1. In what province was the corpse found?
2. In what part of China is this province?
3. What is the climate of the province in summer?
4. What is the climate of the province in winter?
5. What were the discoverers looking for?
6. What had been the profession of the man whose corpse was discovered?
7. When had he lived?
8. Give the name of the ruling family at that time.
9. What is presumed to have been his race?
10. How had the body been buried?
11. With what material was the body clothed?
12. With what material was the body wrapped?
13. What was the ornament of his hat?
14. What color was it?
15. What was around the neck?
16. What was the bow made of?
17. How many arrows were there?

After the last question I collect the slips quickly, asking for no discussion to take place until I have "analyzed" the results, then turn to another topic. Five minutes before the end of the period I give out fresh slips of paper, and, to the surprise and amusement of the students, repeat the questions.

Sometimes it has been feasible to give a third opportunity for recall, a few days later, but as students *may* have been interested in each others' recollections, no consequence can be attached to the findings. Occasionally it has been possible to bring in a student who has attended a previous course, several months or a year or two before, to answer the questions, of course without hearing the passage again.

Two marks were given to Question 1, one part of the name, *Chinghai*, often appearing correctly and the other wrong, to Question 3, with the two-part answer *hot and dry*, and to Question 8, where an allowance was made for approximations to *Yuan*. The maximum score was, therefore, 20.

The data

The average score (366 students) at the first attempt was 8.47, and at the second attempt 8.94. Each of the eight groups of students showed an improvement, the minimum increment being 0.2, and maximum 0.9. This improvement surprised the participants, who felt they should have forgotten something.

The answers themselves exemplify all the interferences which take place through uncontrolled, or random associations.

Questions 11 and 12 provide opportunity for straightforward cross association through juxtaposition of similar items and result in much confusion.

There is further cross association between Questions 1 and 8, the names, or distorted versions of them, getting interchanged.

Aural perceptions are, for many people, both impressionistic and lasting; moreover a "satisfactory" aural impression easily transcends any logical or semantic incongruity. Question 4 asked for recall of the phrase *intensely cold*. This has given *extense cold, immensely cold, intensively cold*, and *intentionally cold*, each repeated at the second attempt. (Needless to say, the graduates writing and repeating such phrases were perfectly able to distinguish the meanings of *intensely, intensively* and *intentionally*.) Question 10, *in an earth mound*, produced *in the ground*, which makes sense, and *in an earth mountain* which sounds sufficiently like the original to satisfy the writer. *Wrapped in an earthern pot* is an assortment of aural reminiscences superbly defying reason.

There is persistent interference from previous knowledge, often accompanied by a rationalizing of the items recalled. For example, *Chinghai* became *Shanghai*. Chinghai has been placed in N. W. China; but the geographical knowledge of the student preventing Shanghai from appearing in that quarter, the answer to Question 2 became *S. E. China*.

Rationalizing frequently appeared in answers to Question 5. Instead of "oil-prospecting" the discoverers were looking for *archaeological remains*. One of the answerers in this vein rationalized throughout: the corpse was the body of *a ruler* (Question 6) and was *preserved in balm* (Question 10).

The burial was frequently described as in *a coffin, an urn, a tomb.*

A bow made of *horn* obviously carred slight credibility, though in point of fact one would have thought it better entitled than some of the alternatives proposed: *wood, bone, ivory, bamboo, iron, copper.*

Interference frequently occurred for "aesthetic" reasons. To balance the two-item answer to Question 3 (*hot and dry*), the answer to Question 4 became *cold and moist, moist* being derived from *dry* to provide a rational as well as an item-for-item balance. Other "balancing" answers, but giving less intellectual satisfaction, were *cold and . . . chilly, icy, freezing.* One participant had *neither too hot in summer, nor too cold in winter.*

There was a persistent tendency to "refine" the vocabulary. The *feather* often became a *plume*; the *silk* bandage tended to be *silken*, the mundane *bandage* becoming a *band*, a *ribbon* or (perhaps associatively via *silk handkerchief*) a *kerchief*. A *scarf duly bandaged* sounds a "school-mistressy" contribution, rather than a refinement; and objectivity exacts mention of the opposite phenomenon, restricted however to two exceptional degradations: a *muffler*, and a *piece of cloth. Red* was translated to *scarlet* and the *hat* to a *helmet.*

The reliability of answers to questions where there exists the possibility of complete accuracy was low; dates and figures being changed very frequently and drastically. To Question 7 the majority of participants gave correct answers, but *600 to 700 years ago* appeared unblushingly as *6-7,000 years ago, 7th century B.C., 600 A.D.* and so on. The *eleven* arrows were often reduced to the rhyming *seven*, but every number from *two* to *sixteen* achieved representation.

The names were more often than not omitted and rarely appeared unmutilated. Sometimes they were replaced by anything vaguely Chinese. *Chinghai* appeared as *Shanghai, Hanoi, Yang Tse, Manchuria, Ming*, and *Ho*; and by a real flight of aural fantasy, as *Germany*[1], *Yuan* competed with *Chinghai* for *Manchu, Ming* and *Yang Tse*, and brought *Chu Yang, Hun* and *Confucius* into the field.

There is no correlation between the frequency with which particular items were recollected, and the significance which students would attribute to these items if they were asked to make a summary of the printed passage. The "insignificant" detail of the *red feather* was generally registered and faithfully reproduced, while many "important" facts were represented largely by blank spaces on the answer slips.

The conclusions

Here are the conclusions I usually elicit during discussion of the results.

1. The generally unexpected high score links with the "challenge" aspect of the single reading ("I am going to read the passage once.") and the single opportunity to register the questions. This is a very pertinent point. Many teachers conscientiously remove the challenge to student effort from their classroom work. (Why should a student

---

[1] The *Ch-* of *Chinghai* is easily transformed into the *Ge-* of *Germany*. The second syllable, *man* may echo the *an* of *Yuan*, or may derive from the rather common background of *Manchu*.

ever listen *now*, when he can rely upon indefinite repetition from the teacher?)

2. The improvement of recall can be attributed (*a*) to the provision of time for consolidation of what the brain has registered (*b*) to the provision of opportunity for the repetition of the effort to recall. The second point seems worth stressing. It is not repetition which conduces to learning, but repetition of *effort*. Though, as already stated, no conclusion can be drawn from performance at a third hearing of the questions, a few days afterwards, it is of casual interest that the average score shows a further slight improvement. After intervals of months, or longer, exstudents have scored 7 (1 student), 6 (1), 5 (2), 2 (1), and 0 (1).

3. I spend a good deal of time over cross association, since most teachers, and, to be frank, most course designers, are unsuspecting of its occurence.

Wrapped in and *clad in* easily interchange their accompanying items, *wool* and *fur*. There are, in fact, two mental operations involved if a student is placed in a learning situation like this, namely *registration* of each item, and the *separation* of one item from the other; and since there are no significant context items by association with which each might be held in "its" context, the separation probably requires far more effort than the registration.

Evidently the very association of ideas that underlies the methodical description produces the juxtaposition of items allowing cross associations in the "learning." A teacher or course designer has to be cautious in presenting a series of items. An item which for him is a "methodical," that is, associational development of a previous item may well prove an associational hazard for the learners. Here is an actual example of such a juxtaposition in a course: *This book is blue; it is a blue book.* If the first item is completely established for all the learners before the second is presented, the establishment may be successful; though wasteful of learning effort. In other circumstances we can predict that *This book is a blue* and *it is blue book* will emerge as stable variants.

4. Occurrences such as *intentionally cold* and *wrapped in an earthern pot* produce a good deal of amusement, but they are instructive too. First of all there is the fact that a graduate teacher making an effort to achieve aural recollection may "accept" nonsense, and then there is the fact that having once accepted it, he repeats it, without further reference to outside criteria.

Teachers are often astonished to discover that reasonably intelligent children produce *My brother is a book* with no consciousness of anything untoward, and that, after patient explanation, after persistent drill, of *is* and *has, My brother is a book* is as firmly there as ever.

After one year of English, the annual Examination papers, 1962, of a Hyderabad class of eleven-year-olds showed the following distribution with respect to establishment of the *is/has* distinction.

Pupils:	44
Successful:	7
Unsuccessful, unmarkable:	3
Unsuccessful, confused:	34

"Confused" means containing one or more of the following:

He is a garden.	*Her name has Anita.*	*I am a house.*
Raj is a sister.	*He has rich.*	*I was a good meal.*
He is a big house.	*My mother is rice.*	*Raj has a good boy.*

In many courses, *is* and *has* come too close, and perhaps if the children have been permitted only an aural impression, the sound *iz* has already been associated with "possession," before *has* is introduced.

Sometimes the grammatical associations of the course designer lead him to introduce, in fairly close succession, the three common spoken plural forms of nouns, *-s -z -iz*, the three spoken 3rd-person-singular endings of verbs in the Simple Present, *-s -z -iz*, and the three spoken forms of apostrophe *s, -s, -z -iz*. By the end of a few months, the teacher of the course may hopefully expect the separation, of *Das is* from *Das's, brush is* from *brushes* (verb and noun), *Das's brush is* from *Das's brushes*, not to forget *Das brushes.* With class teaching and the usual amount of pupil absence from lessons, it is safe to say that the expectation will be disappointed.

5. More often than not, the course designer and teacher visualize the material, with standard word forms and separation, and background grammar—taken for granted. The learner, with no such knowledge, attempts to attach each new item to what is already apprehended; in traditional terms, to link the unfamiliar with the familiar. What to the person who *knows* is so unlikely that he does not think of it—is not for this reason improbable to the learner. A native English child for instance, has no worry about the form *I might 'of' known it*: this is how he hears the sentence, and how he writes it, until "correction" replaces the middle item in his conception of the expression by *have*. However remote from the course designer's associations, there is no improbability about *Das is book is on the desk, This is Tom is box* for a school child, and the *-iz*

of *Das's* is easily identified with the *-iz* of *Das is*, the *-iz* of *boxes* with the *-iz* of *box is*, and so on.

This point, I find, has to be emphasized repeatedly. I usually bring forward a battery of examples, ranging from the classic "child she-bear" interpretation of the hymn (the "child she bare") to the occurrence of the very day—for instance, on the day this is written, a teacher-student's question whether one *can* say "go to shore" (which turns out to be interpreted from my own spoken words "went ashore"). With these and students' own reminiscences, one endeavors to establish the fact that new aural impressions are linked by learners to previous aural impressions; that when *satisfaction* is experienced in aural terms (grammaticality or rationality being irrelevancies in this respect) it will prove extraordinarily difficult to change the aural impressions; and that a course which is not planned in aural terms may prove capricious and elusive if the presentation is "aural."

6. The rationalizing examples lead to the realization that remembering is *reconstruction.* In some contemporary foreign language teaching theory, stress is laid on the establishment of automatic responses through drills. It is said that the native speaker "accepts" what he hears, and repeats it "naturally," and that foreign learners may be trained to accept and reproduce "natural" English simply through sufficient hearing and repetition of what is presented.

There may be some truth in this statement, but it is easy to get evidence for rationalization in our learners' use of English and I feel that it is a risk not to take it into account.

7. No student-teacher fails to recognize the working of analogy to produce *He suggested me to go . . . He explained me that. . . .* The frequent doubling of past-time markers, *Did he discovered it He began to talked* are by rational analogy. From *the little/great knowledge* we get *the some knowledge* (perhaps with an aural recollection of *the sum total . . .*) *He did it yesterday* allows *He did it previous day.*[2]

8. The aesthetic influences of a different cultural background show themselves particularly in the writing of the more advanced

---

[2]While rationalizing usually appears as construction of analogous forms, we have occasional refusals to accept normal English English usage by open and formally expressed objection, on "factual" grounds. This kind of objection has produced a definite divergence of usage between English English and Indian English with respect to tense forms in subordinate clauses, when the verb in the leading clause has the Simple Past form. Native speakers prefer the concord of "sound" to "representation of fact" (*I knew he was married* versus *I knew he is married*); Indian speakers prefer the "representation of fact." *I would be grateful if you will . . .* is, one supposes, now standard Indian English, the preterite of Modesty being accepted, but the future time expression retained too.

learners. In many foreign languages high and low styles are further apart than in English, and the foreign student often feels that a word occurring late in the course is "better" than one learned earlier; in this way there is much discrepancy between word frequencies in mother tongue and in foreigners' English. One notices too an avoidance of repetition, where the mother tongue speaker of English would probably find repetition effective. In syntax we note the feeling for balance behind what is now standard Indian English: *Though he didn't do it, 'yet' he . . .* and *Though he didn't do it, 'but' he. . . .*

I have outlined the kind of use I find one can make of a very straightforward experiment in registration and recall. There are implicit conclusions, which I do not draw then and there in the course but allow to develop, if they do. Later in the session, I attempt to bring the teacher-students into personal contact with the psychological features of foreign language learning, through a short course in a foreign language. Reference can then be made to the more general observations of the "memory experiment."

II. A COURSE IN MALAY

Malay is sufficiently unlike any Indian languages to create problems equal to those of Indian learners of English. I give five consecutive lessons and a test and keep a record of the performance of each group of teachers-in-training, so that I can refer to procedures and results on previous courses, citing figures to show that the extent of the learning does indeed depend on whether the teaching exploits, ignores or works in opposition to the associational psychology studied in the "memory experiment." The course is not primarily a "demonstration" of methods in the usual way, but a means of providing data for comparison and assessment.

Here are a few notes on the learning. All figures represent correct answers. No account is taken of the variation in numbers of "candidates" from group to group (from 40 to 50) as only clear contrasts are discussed. "Picture" and "pictorial" refer simply to blackboard sketches, and English translations are used for the Malay words referred to. On the "test" paper there is a cyclostyled sketch of a Malay house with background, and a list of Malay words *most* but not all of which were presented in the "Course." The "students" had to write on the picture the Malay names of any objects the word for which was on the list.

1. *Water* and *rain* identified on two Courses on which they occurred in a picture
   context: 16 and 6; 4 and 6. The same words on two Courses on which they

occurred in a picture context, and also during an exposition, with a diagram, of the "water cycle": 24 and 36; 29 and 37. The figures illustrate the effect of repetition of opportunity for learning effort.

2. *Door* and *window* confused by "careless" cross association: 11 and 13 with 9 transpositions. The Malay words sound quite unalike[3], but the presentation "situations" were identical (*going to the . . . opening the . . .*). Here are the corresponding figures for two courses on which the words were presented on separate occasions and with care to keep them distinct: 26 and 30; 21 and 36. On this course the words *Open the door* also occurred in a Malay song: 35 and 36.

3. Here are the stilt supports of the Malay house, *tiang*, presented on a picture in cross association with the steps to the raised doorway, *tangga*. *Tiang*: correct 7, incorrect 7; *tangga*: correct 11, incorrect 13. The unpresented word *lada* was chosen by 13 examinees to represent the steps.

4. *Smoke* and *tree* "carelessly" taught from a picture: 9 and 7. The Malay words differ by one letter (*rokok, pokok*). Here is *smoke* with the same presentation but *tree* occurring in a picture story about a snake attempting to catch a female bird on a nest in a tree and being driven off by the male: 6 and 39. Here is *smoke* on a picture (house), by mime (cigarette) and again on a picture (ship's funnel) with *tree* presented as above: 38 and 35.

5. *Fruit* with pictorial representation only (3 courses): 19, 3, 1. Here is the same word with pictorial representation, but with curiosity aroused by its "strange" occurrence (*one "fruit" ship, two "fruit" school*) as a numerative, followed by a brief explanation: 39, 43.

6. *Sun (matahari)* with every reinforcement (a few know the words beforehand, as a famous spy's "name"). A large *eye* on the blackboard has rays added to transform it to the *eye of the day, a daisy (day's eye)* is drawn on the blackboard and is reduced to an '*eye*': 38, 38, 42, 50, 50. Only four students have "failed" on this; and all through the persistence of previous knowledge, in an interesting way: *Api* is *fire, atap* the *roof*. These are transposed and *atap*, understood as *fire*, is identified with *aftab*, the Persian word for *sun*.

The sentence part of the test has fourteen questions in Malay, to which answers are allowed in Malay, or English. Some are general, and answers to these are mainly a matter of recollection: *Where is your town, in the South, the East, the North, the West or in the middle of your country? Are you a teacher or a student here?*

A "noun" in Malay has no singular/plural distinction, and "noun"–"noun" juxtaposition implies a relationship. Though the grammar may be grasped, a *series* of such juxtapositions may defeat

---

[3]The word for *window* (jendela) is a Portuguese loan word and recognized by a few students from Kerala.

the "pupils." Here are figures from two courses (*a*) with "intuitive" (*b*) with explicit grammar:

	(*a*)	(*b*)
name lord (your name)	44	45
name city lord (the name of your city)	29	45
name race human land Malay (the names of the races of the people of Malaya)	2	12

(The word *tuan* (lord) caused much curiosity, appearing as *you your he him Sir yes* and *I beg your pardon.* I used it to call attention to the parallel diversity of the English -*iz.*)

One group of sentences has a variety of comparatives and superlatives: *Who is the tallest of these people? Is Ali taller than Idris?* (Sketch provided) *What is the largest city of India? Is there a city in Malaya where Indians form the majority of the inhabitants?* The area is instructive, as Malay expresses these relationships very differently from English. Going over the answers, one sees that all individual words and constructions in a sentence may be known—as evidenced by other answers—yet the sentence may remain uninterpreted. Students who have succeeded on such questions usually say that it is by rapid scanning and general reconstruction (or "guess"). From, for instance: *Is - question marker - one - "fruit" - city - in - land - Malay - where - human - India - which - many* the successful answerer has picked out rapidly: *Malay city, Indian many?*

From the description of these two attempts to provide experience for teacher-students, some of my own views on language teaching have probably become apparent.

Clearly I think language teaching should take learner interest as a first premise. Without effort there is no learning, without interest there is unlikely to be sustained effort. I think, too, that efficient teaching has to accord with the psychology of perception and remembering.

Both from the viewpoint of interest and from that of opportunity for separation of associations, I find I require variety of context. However, we teach English not so that our students shall learn "English," but so that they shall learn through English: throughout the course, the means and end seem to me to offer a possibility of harmony.

Variety of context implies a varied vocabulary, and, at each level, a fairly large *recognition* vocabulary. By *large,* I do not mean *uncontrolled*, but I do mean *large*. A figure under 3000 words is being cited as an aim for a six-year school course, and this seems to me, for a recognition vocabulary, that is, as equipment for further learning through English, inadequate.[4]

I do not think the grammar of the language is likely to be the basis of an efficient course, with vocabulary and context restricted to the requirement of the grammar teaching. In such subordination of vocabulary and course content there seems a methodological fallacy. Genuinely useful "structural items" occur unequivocally and frequently; each context we exploit lends itself to, indeed cannot avoid their exemplification and repetition. A construction which genuinely recurs in a wide range of contexts "supports" a large, varied vocabulary, and this should be both our reason for teaching it, and our means of teaching it. The grammatical associations of course designers and the impressions of native speakers seem unable to provide trustworthy indications of the *relative importance* of the items proposed for inclusion in courses, and if we do not allow variety of context—size and range of vocabulary—to exercise some control over the grammatical items, we neglect a very necessary assurance that our students are working usefully. Until there is adequate statistical information, the next best control is that of representative context, from which, of course, on a wider scale, the statistical information must itself derive.

There remains the aural-oral aspect to consider.

It is not uncommon to hear of prescriptions of some weeks, or months, of oral work before reading and writing are begun, though untrained, nonnative speakers of the language would have to do the teaching, to large classes and with course materials based mainly on syntactic content. I do not myself endorse these prescriptions. Obvious drawbacks are the reliance on a single type of impression and response, and relative inability of the learners to work independently of the teacher. I would add as a disadvantage an insufficient amount of receptive experience by comparison with the productive.

I do not think any teacher would opt to rely wholly on one kind of impression, unless there were some special reason. The alleged special reason is, of course, the interference of the written English with the spoken impressions. This interference is not imaginary, but

---

[4]A few students have taken up a suggestion that they should try to make a list of *all* the Malay words they could recall from five lessons. The number has been from 130 to just over 200. One must keep in mind the relative experience of the learners, and also the fact that only interested students take the trouble to make a list (they have not always been the *best* learners however). Nevertheless the rate of learning indicated by these figures contrasts strangely with official targets of a recognition vocabulary of 2,600 to 3,000 words, for a 1,000 hour school course; and a probable achievement of 1,500 words.

as our class experiments—and classroom experiences—show, excluding the written form does not exclude interference; the whole range of cross associations among the aural impressions being uncontrolled.

In many courses with recommendations for entirely aural presentations, one looks in vain for any systematic teaching of reading and writing, at any stage. Since many unskilled teachers use these courses as reading materials one realizes that such efficiency as the teacher might achieve is thereby negated.

To be efficient a course taught through aural impressions would have to be thought out in those terms. However if cross associations were avoided by careful design it would seem wayward not to make the phonic-graphical associations which would allow great reinforcement of impressions, the possibility of some independence for the learners and a more reasonable proportion between receptive and active aspects.

PART III: DISCUSSION QUESTIONS

1. Hocking opens his paper by defining "interference" as "the adverse effects of . . . a known language on the acquisition . . . of another language" (p. 87). Are there other kinds of interference? Do all of them involve the confusion of features of one system with those of another? Are there other explanations for problems besides some sort of interference?

2. What are some possible explanations for the fact that some items which are very different between the native and target language may present less difficulty to the learner than items which are similar?

3. Hocking concludes that although interference theory brings many problems of second language learner's "sharply into focus . . . the problem still remains of what to do with the information . . . when we have got it" (p. 94). In what ways is the teacher better off for knowing the source of certain errors?

4. What is the difference between "final grammatical competence" and "transitional competence" as distinguished by Richards (p. 97) and Ravem (p. 142).

5. Discuss the implications of the observation that "simplifications of second language learners correspond to some simplifications common among children learning the same language" (Ervin-Tripp, as cited by Richards, p. 99).

6. In his discussion, *Ignorance of Rule Restrictions*, Richards notes that certain violations in this category "are again a type of generalization or transfer, since the learner is making use of a previously acquired rule in a new situation" (p. 100). Later he says that "analogy seems to be a major factor in the misuse of prepositions." Consider the examples used to support these statements in the light of Chomsky's remark that "there is no known sense of 'generalization' that can begin to account for this . . . 'creative' aspect of normal language use. The new utterances that are produced and interpreted . . . are 'similar' to those that constitute the past experience of speaker and hearer only in that they are determined . . . by the same . . . abstract underlying rules" (p. 30).

   Are Richards' examples of student outputs "creative" in the sense of Chomsky? In what ways are they "similar" to previously experienced utterances? In what ways are they novel? What "abstract underlying rules" may be posited? Can such rules be learned by "generalization," "analogy," or transfer . . . ? (Note that Richards is not saying that a certain example resulted in the production of a certain other example; rather, certain types of structures, by analogy, resulted in the production of a deviant form.)

7. Is it possible to interpret the examples of *Incomplete Application of Rules* (pp. 102-103) as "generalizations"?

8. What are some of the factors which might influence the writers of textbooks to produce abnormal usages like those mentioned by Richards? Under what circumstances might the narrative discussed on p. 104 be appropriate? In other words, when would the present continuous be used as a narrative form?

9. Examine some second language teaching materials to see if you can find exercises which encourage faulty generalizations. Errors such as these, derived from textbook presentation of items, are referred to as "transfer-of-training" errors in Richards' second paper. Do you think such errors can or should be avoided?

10. In what ways are errors derived from "strategies of communication" different from the other categories mentioned?

11. How much effort do you think the teacher should expend in helping learners to avoid errors? Could you draw up a hierarchy of difficulty for a given language based on common errors you have observed?

12. Richards notes how different conceptions of appropriate styles may be carried from one language to another. Can you suggest examples in a specific language of social features that differ from the conventions of English, e.g., greeting behaviors, invitations, status distinctions, etc.?

13. Collect some samples of errors made by second language learners and attempt to explain them. Can they all be fitted into the categories suggested by Richards in his second paper?

14. Ravem refers to the "gap between a child acquiring his first language and a child learning a second language." Just how great is this gap? What are the differences and similarities?

15. Compare the difficulties in describing the linguistic competence of a child with those involved in describing that of an adult. Is the adult's linguistic intuition more or less available? More complex or less? More subject to change or less? Refer to Ravem p. 137-138.

16. It is hypothesized by Ravem that "*do* as a tense marker ... being semantically empty," should be acquired later than auxiliaries like *have* and *be*. This was true at least for Rune. Why should we expect this to be the case? What assumptions about learning does Ravem's hypothesis imply?

17. Why might Rune have made such extensive use of *ing*-forms in verbs? Is it possible that the present progressive is more easily learned by generalization and association than forms which are less directly related to the immediate experience of the child? What other explanations can be given? See Ravem p. 139.

18. Consider the acquisition of time markers in general. Why should time adverbs ("yesterday", "today", etc.) be used before tense markers in verb forms are acquired?

19. What do you think is the source of Rune's invention "to-yesterday"?

20. Discuss the contrasts between English and Norwegian negative constructions as exemplified on p. 140. What predictions would be made from these contrasts based on interference theory? Are they confirmed or not in Rune's sentences?

21. What are some of the implications of Ravem's study for translation as a testing device? Teaching technique? Did Rune seem to be influenced negatively by Norwegian structures as a result of translation?

22. Towards the end of Ravem's study, "Rune still frequently produces sentences which syntactically correspond to earlier structures" (p. 143). What implications does this observation have for theories about the acquisition of syntactic rules?

23. Ravem concludes that "the similarities between Rune and L1 learners in the developmental sequence of negative and interrogative sentences are in many ways more revealing than the differences." However, he cautions that "it does not follow ... that the appropriate methodology for teaching a foreign language at an early stage is to expose the children to 'a language bath' " (p. 144). Why not? What essential features of the real world setting for language acquisition are missing in the classroom?

24. Repeat the first experiment described by George. Analyze and compare your results with his.

25. In view of George's findings and conclusions (which are similar in many ways to those of other authors in this volume) what attitude should the teacher

take toward errors? Should it be an uncompromising one? Consider the fact that certain errors are apparently a normal if not a necessary part of the learning process.

26. How can confusions between phonologically similar forms such as "has" and "is" be avoided? What assumptions about learning mechanisms must be made in order to account for the confusions in the first place? How can these theoretical assumptions aid in practice to minimize the problem?

27. Notice the footnote on p. 151 discussing the "occasional refusals to accept normal English [as opposed to, say, Indian English] usage" on the part of nonnative speakers. Try repeating a deviant syntactic construction such as "I would be grateful if you will do it" several times. Do you sense a point at which the grammatical irregularity stops seeming unnatural? What implications does this phenomenon have for learning? Is the notion "habit" relevant?

PART IV

ASPECTS OF TESTING

INTRODUCTION

Articles in this section deal with a broad range of topics in testing. The first three papers deal primarily with coding operations and the testing of skills in this domain. The paper by Spolsky considers some theoretical issues which have important implications for techniques of language testing. In particular the distinction between competence and performance proposed by Chomsky is seen to have serious consequences for methods of measuring proficiency as well as for teaching practices. Spolsky contends that this distinction brings into question the technique of testing which concentrates on one point of grammar at a time. This thesis sets the stage for the article by Upshur which follows.

Upshur reports on a promising approach to the testing of productive communication skills. He also focuses on the practical and theoretical differences between discrete-point tests and tests of integrative skills. This discussion is continued in the third article by Oller. He agrees with Upshur and Spolsky that tests which aim at specific points of grammar are less effective as measures of communicative competence than tests that require the integration of skills. The latter type of test more closely parallels the communicative use of language.

The fourth paper, by Upshur, considers the functional uses of language-skill tests in total educational settings. On the basis of an analogy with information processing systems, several ways in which tests constitute decision-making procedures in educational programs are illustrated. Upshur's paper also serves to make clear the important and intimate interrelations between teaching, learning, and testing.

Brière, in the last paper of this section takes up some of the linguistic and sociocultural aspects of tests in general. His discussion carries us well beyond the testing of content-level coding operations in a second language situation. The functional validity of tests which employ language and procedures that may be appropriate for middle-class white Americans may be entirely inappropriate for children from other sociocultural backgrounds. Biased tests convey important relationship information to the child. They say that his world, in some sense, is inappropriate. It is in this manner that culturally biased tests are "criminal" in their effects. The problem is crucial with such tests because they lead to false conclusions about the "mental ability" and related skills of the child and they ultimately contribute to a definition of the child as inferior. These falsehoods must inevitably lead to decisions that will significantly limit the opportunities available to the culturally different child in a hostile educational setting.

WHAT DOES IT MEAN TO KNOW A LANGUAGE; OR HOW DO YOU GET SOMEONE TO PERFORM HIS COMPETENCE?

Bernard Spolsky

If we wish to speak of the process of second language acquisition, we must first consider the end result and consider the notion "knowing a language." How do we know that someone has learned a language? What does it mean when we say that someone knows a language?

Consider first the definition offered by Charles Fries:

> A person has 'learned' a language when he has thus first, *within a limited vocabulary* mastered the sound system (that is, when he can understand the stream of speech and achieve an understandable production of it) and has, second, made the structural devices (that is, the basic arrangements of utterances) matters of automatic habit.[1]

Fries arrives at this position after first showing the inadequacy of the notion that knowing a language means knowing its vocabulary. He points out that even a native speaker's knowledge of the words in his language is limited by his experience; we never finish learning all the words and their many meanings, as even a few minutes' study of a dictionary will prove. On the other hand, he claims, we early finish with the business of mastering the sound system—a child of four can recognize all the sounds of his language and produce recognizable variants of them—and of mastering "the fundamental matters of word order and the patterns of form"—by the time he goes to school, a child has learned the basic grammar of his language. It is natural, then, that we tend to believe that second language learning is a matter of doing in another language what we are conscious of doing in our own, namely, learning words, rather than what we did unconsciously as young children when we mastered our phonology and grammar.

Fries argues then that vocabulary need not be stressed in initial phases of language learning:

> Accuracy of sound, of rhythm, of intonation, of structural forms, and of arrangement, within a limited range of expression, must come first and become automatic habit before the student is ready to devote his chief attention to expanding his vocabulary.[2]

---

[1] Fries (1945), p. 3.
[2] *Loc. cit.*

It is interesting to see what happens when Fries' definition of knowing a language is translated into practical terms by preparing a test to see whether a student knows a language. Let us assume first that knowing a language consisted only in knowing (that is, in being able to recognize definitions or synonyms of) the words of the language. Obviously, we wouldn't test the student with every word in the dictionary before we decided whether he came up to the criterion. We would make use of some appropriate statistical technique to select a representative sample of words, find out what percentage our student knows, and compare his performance with that of a native speaker of the language. Obviously, the process is not simple, but it is feasible, for we are dealing with a more or less finite number of items (the words of a language) from which we can choose a more or less representative sample; we need have little hesitation in generalizing our results.[3]

Can this same degree of finiteness be found if we move from the area of vocabulary that Fries rejects as irrelevant to the areas he names, the "sound system" and the "structural devices"? The answer is yes, if we consider that each of these systems is a matter of listing items and listing patterns for arrangement. For the former, one would list the segmental phonemes, the suprasegmentals, and the possible combinations. The list of phonemes would be quite small, no more than sixty or so items, so that it would be quite easy to test each item, although when one started to worry about all the possible combinations, the list would get much larger, and sampling would be necessary.[4] Similarly, if one follows Fries, the "structural devices" are equally straightforward, a matter of a list of items and possible arrangements. He points out that English uses three structural devices: word order, inflection, and function words. It is possible, he says, to select from these a minimum set that will provide for the production of "one pattern for each of the situations in which the language is actually being used"[5] and a larger set for recognition, chosen on the basis of frequency of occurence in the speech of native speakers of the language. It is possible to list the items in these sets[6] and to use the list as a universe from which we can draw a

---

[3]The words "more or less" are used advisedly, for there is a real sense in which the lexicon of a language is an open set; new words (and meanings) are being added and old ones dropped all the time. But at any given time, the words of a language are listable, in a way that the sentences of a language cannot conceivably be.

[4]One particular type of sampling that has been proposed is to test only those items or combinations that do not occur in the subject's native language. See Lado (1961). For counterarguments, see Upshur (1962).

[5]Fries (1945), p. 33.

[6]See for example the *Appendix* to Fries (1945).

representative sample to decide whether a student has learned the language or not.[7]

Fries thus rejects the layman's notion that knowing a certain number of words in a language is the criterion for knowing that language, but maintains a related notion, that knowing a language involves knowing a set of items. He speaks of lists of individual elements (sound segments, sentence patterns, lexical items) to be mastered, and says that to learn a language, one must make each of these items a matter of automatic habit.

While it may be true that the layman's idea of *learning* a language is learning words, his criterion for *knowing* a language is usually expressed quite differently. When he judges his own or anyone else's control of a language, he is much more likely to make a functional statement: "I know enough French to read a newspaper," "He can't speak enough English to ask the time of day." Statements such as these refer to language use and not to grammar or phonology. The question then arises, how does one go about deciding when someone knows "enough" to carry out a specified function. One approach is of course to give him a language-using task to perform. If we want to know whether someone knows enough English to understand a lecture on thermodynamics, we can have him listen to such a lecture and then check his comprehension.[8] Another approach is to attempt to characterize in linguistic terms the knowledge of the language required to function in this way, that is to say, to describe the linguistic knowledge which correlates with the functional ability.[9] If Fries is working in a correct framework, the procedure is relatively clear. We say that underlying any functional use is a number of discrete elements; the functional use is thus an integrated system. Functioning in a language then involves, among other things, mastery of the sound system. Mastery of the sound system includes knowing a given number of phonemes. A test that finds out whether a subject knows these phonemes gives evidence of part of his knowledge of the language. By adding the results of similar tests of grammatical

---

[7] A detailed examination of the nature of language tests that follow from these principles is given in Lado (1961). While he does discuss various types of tests of the "integrated skills," he spends more than twice as much space on specifications for tests of the "elements of language": the sound segments, stress, intonation, and grammatical structures (which he defines as "the patterns of arrangement of words in sentences and the patterns of arrangement of parts of words in words").

[8] The point of this example is that you have to know some physics as well as some English to understand such a lecture; in fact, the more physics one knows, the less English one needs.

[9] In the terms proposed by Carroll (1961), to list the discrete points that make up the overall ability.

structures and of vocabulary, we can finish up with a clear picture of his knowledge. The results of batteries of tests like these can then be compared with his actual functioning in the language.

There are many reasons why this approach has not proved successful;[10] one of the fundamental reasons is that it fails to take into account two vital truths about language, the fact that language is redundant, and the fact that it is creative.

Redundancy is a concept developed as part of the statistical theory of communication.[11] In this theory, a message carries information to the extent that it effects a reduction in uncertainty by eliminating certain probabilities. The greater the reduction, the greater the information. Thus, the result of throwing a die (with six possibilities) carries greater information than the result of the toss of a coin (with only two possibilities). Or consider a more linguistic example. I ask someone to write down his first name. When I see him write the letter *P*, the uncertainty has been reduced by a large amount, for he has excluded all names that begin with any other letter. When he adds *a*, uncertainty is further reduced as names like *Peter* and *Phillip* are ruled out. Adding the letter *u* makes it pretty easy to guess the final answer; *l* makes me almost positive, and his lifting the pen merely serves to confirm my guess. From this example, we can see again the way in which different parts of the message carry varying amounts of information. The letter *p* gave the most information, for it cut down the possibilities from the whole set of possible men's names to the set of names beginning with *P* a reduction, let us say, to 1/26 of the original.[12] The letter *a* reduced the possibilities to an even smaller set, but by a smaller proportion. This is because of the fact that in English only thirteen letters can follow the letter *p*. There just aren't any words in English that start with the letter *p* and have as their next letter *b,c,d,g,j,k,m,p,q,v,w,x,* or *z*, so that the information value of *a* in this case is 1/13 rather than 1/26. As more letters are added, the amount of information conveyed by each letter becomes less, until certainty is reached. Now, the interesting thing here is the relation between the amount of information and our ability to guess. Our guessing, which gets easier as we go on (as the remaining elements contain less information) has depended on the knowledge that we have of the probabilities of occurrence of the various elements in the order they appear. It is our

---

[10]See Spolsky (1968).
[11]See Shannon and Weaver (1949).
[12]The exact value is of course different, for the number of first names starting with each letter varies.

knowledge of the rules of English that permits us to rule out 50% of the possibilities for the second letter of the word. If English were not restricted in this way, the second letter would convey as much information as the first. The probability relations between the two letters, effected by the rules of English spelling and phonotactics, reduced the amount of information carried by the second letter. In a language without such restrictions, more information could be conveyed using fewer units. In natural languages, more units are used than are theoretically necessary; that is to say, natural languages are redundant.

Redundancy may seem wasteful of effort, but it is in fact of great use, for it reduces the possibility of error and permits communication where there is some interference in the communicating channel. The technical term for this interference is noise. Consider an example. We might wish to set up a system of bells to communicate with a secretary in the next office. Say we set up a code as follows:

one ring: "Come in for dictation."
two rings: "Send the visitor in."
three rings: "Come and show the visitor out."
four rings: "Don't disturb me."

In such a code, each message has one and only one interpretation, and the difference between each is minimal. Any accident—the telephone ringing at the same time, touching the bell accidentally, pressing the bell once too often, losing count while pressing—will lead to misunderstanding and an annoyed secretary. The system then is efficient, but liable to error and open to interference. One way of reducing the chance of error or interference is to add redundancy; for instance, to say that the signal will be repeated after ten seconds, or to add a system of lights or flags confirming the message. In a redundant system, I can be more sure of the message getting through.

When one considers all the interferences that occur when natural language is used for communication, it is clear that only a redundant system would work. The redundancy of natural language can be illustrated in many ways. It is possible to understand messages with many words omitted; not just in telegrams

HAVING WONDERFUL TIME SEND MORE MONEY

which are unambiguously reconstructable, but when words have been left out in a purely statistical way:

when, for _____, every third _____is left _____, it is _____possible to
_____ . When it is every sixth _____, it is really so simple _____you can
read it as _____as if all are there. But _____ second _____is_____
difficult.

In much the same way, it is possible to guess at words with letters
left out. One becomes most conscious of what is involved when one
is doing a crossword puzzle. Note the three types of information that
one is given to help guess: the number of letters in the word, the
meaning of the word, and, as one goes on, certain of the letters. But
note also the help one gets from knowing the rules of English
spelling; as soon as a *q* appears, one is almost completely certain as to
the next letter. Another clear example is when there is noise
interfering with the understanding of a spoken message. Talking on a
telephone, or using radio-telephony, or conversing at a cocktail party
are clear cases of understanding messages even though only a portion
of the original signal gets through. The important point to note is
that in all these examples, there has been no linguistic principle
involved in the omissions, simply a random interference. That is to
say, messages in normal language can be understood even though a
good proportion of them is omitted or masked; or in other words,
every message contains many elements (defined statistically rather
than linguistically) that can be omitted without breaking down
communication.

But if we give these distorted or incomplete messages to someone
who doesn't know the language well, we find that there is a
considerable difference. He just cannot function under these
conditions: he needs the full normal redundancy, and at times even
that is not enough. Consider for example how when we speak to
someone whose native language is different, we speak more slowly,
more clearly, with added gesture and frequent repetition. Or take
some experimental evidence. In some studies we made of the
possibility of using the redundancy principle in testing[13] we
compared the performance of native speakers of English and
nonnatives (including some with very high competence) in writing
down English sentences that were read to them on a tape to which
varying amounts of noise had been added. We were not surprised to
find that the more noise we added, the more mistakes were made;
nor were we surprised to find that some nonnatives did as well or
better than natives when there was no added noise; but what was

---

[13]Spolsky, *et al.* (1968).

important was the clear distinction that one found between natives and nonnatives as soon as any noise was added. This is to be explained by the nonnative's inability to function with reduced redundancy, evidence that he cannot supply from his knowledge of the language the experience on which to base his guesses as to what is missing. In other words, the key thing missing is the richness of knowledge of probabilities—on all levels, phonological, grammatical, lexical, and semantic—in the language. It is possible to factor out each of these elements and explore the exact nature of the language learner's mastery of each item, but in the broad matter of functioning in a language, all combine to form an integrated whole, the exact contribution of each part being indefinable. In a nonredundant language system, the absence of any single element would reduce communication by a specific amount; language, however, permits communication to continue even when a large portion of the signal, and a random portion at that, is masked or missing.

Two implications follow. The first is that knowing a language involves the ability to understand a distorted message, to accept a message with reduced redundancy. A model of understanding speech must then include the ability to make valid guesses about a certain percentage of omitted elements. From this follows the usefulness of such language testing techniques as the noise test referred to and the cloze procedure. The second implication is to raise some serious theoretical (but not necessarily practical) questions about the value of deciding a person knows a language because he knows certain items in the language. The principle of redundancy suggests that it will not be possible to demonstrate that any given language item is essential to successful communication, nor to establish the functional load of any given item in communication. Consider the ease with which speakers of different dialects, dialects even with different number of phonemes, manage to converse, or the ways in which speakers constantly handle the forgetting of a specific word. All of this suggests then that while testing specific linguistic items is likely to be valuable in the control of instruction, the assessment of proficiency in a language must rather be based on functioning in a much more linguistically complex situation than is provided by the one-element test.

Knowing a language involves knowing the items that make up the language, but it also involves being able to supply these items when they are missing, or being able to do without them. Even were we able to list all the items, we could not show that to know a language you need know any one of them.

The creative aspect of language was for some time lost sight of in the behavioristic models that dominated linguistics in the first half of the twentieth century. Chomsky (1964) points out the two conflicting views of the essential nature of language that had been held in the nineteenth century. On the one hand was the Humboldtian view: the essence of language is its *Form*, a constant and unvarying factor underlying each new linguistic act.

It is by having developed an internal representation of this form that each individual is capable of understanding the language and using it in a way that is intelligible to his fellow speakers.[14]

Contrasted with this is the view expressed by Whitney: "Language in the concrete sense. . . [is]. . the sum of words and phrases by which any man expresses his thought . . . . "[15] Saussure, under Whitney's influence also regarded *langue* as an inventory of elements: it was perhaps for this reason that he relegated the sentence to *parole*.

De Saussure's personal bent was probably to understate the creative act and to emphasize the mechanical process, just because the former, at first sight, seems to be the very essence of speech.[16]

It was the understatement of the creative aspect, then, that marked linguistics until Chomsky restated the Humboldtian position, tracing it in fact back to Descartes. In *Cartesian Linguistics*, he sets forth Descartes' insights about language, and his conclusion that

man has unique abilities that cannot be accounted for on purely mechanistic grounds, although, to a very large extent, a mechanistic explanation can be provided for human bodily function and behavior. The essential difference between man and animal is exhibited most clearly by human language, in particular, by man's ability to form new statements which express new thoughts and which are appropriate to new situations.[17]

Descartes considered the possibility of a machine which would give a specific number of responses to a specific number of cues, but pointed out that one could not conceive of a machine that could reply appropriately to everything said to it, as every human being can. However imperfect a man is, he can arrange words together to express his thoughts: however perfect an animal, it cannot. The distinction is basic and not just connected with peripheral organs, for a parrot can utter words, but cannot speak; a deaf mute cannot

---

[14] Chomsky (1964), p. 56.
[15] Quoted by Chomsky (1964), p. 59.
[16] Godel (1966), p. 492.
[17] Chomsky (1966), p. 3.

produce words, but can use language. Consider the parrot for a moment. We can easily train him to produce a number of sets of sounds that seem like utterances. With more care and appropriate use of reinforcement, we can train him to produce each of these "utterances" on appropriate cues. There should be no difficulty in training the bird to utter sounds that seem like "Please feed me" in order to receive food, or like "It's a pellet of food" when the food appears from the hopper. By the definitions of behavioral psychology these utterances could be classified as a *mand* and a *tact* respectively, essential elements of what Skinner calls verbal behavior.[18] But I do not think that many of us would be prepared to call such behavior language. What is missing is the creative element: the parrot's repertoire of utterances remains limited and closed: we do not find it one day saying "Please give me a pellet" unless it has been exposed to that particular sentence.

And the central fact in support of the creative aspect is that humans produce (and of course understand) many sentences that they have never heard before. For the parrot to learn English by memorizing all the sentences of English would be a clearly impossible task, for there are about 10^{30} possible English sentences of twenty words or fewer (by comparison, there are about 3×10^9 seconds in a hundred years). This creativity is the basic distinction between what I have called languagelike behavior and knowing a language.[19] While precise specification may not be possible, for there is a continuum, the interpretation of each is relatively clear. Thus, languagelike behavior refers to the parrot trained to speak, and equally well to the student who is able to recite a number of sentences in a second language but not to modify them and use them in a free conversational situation. This example of the students learning a second language makes the continuum clear, for there is a stage at which the student may be able to use his stock of sentences to answer a finite set of questions. But this is not the same as knowing a language, which involves the ability to produce an indefinite number of sentences in response to an indefinite number of stimuli. One is said to know a second language when one's competence is like that of a native speaker. Performance need not however be identical, for it is accepted that someone knows a language even when he speaks hesitantly, with many errors, or with a foreign accent, or when he understands it with some difficulty under conditions of noise. What

[18]Skinner (1957).
[19]Spolsky (1968).

confuses the distinction between languagelike behavior and knowing a second language is a third category, speaking a second language with the grammar of the first. It is thus normal for a person who knows one language and has developed languagelike behavior in a second to be able to adjust this behavior in accordance with the grammar of his first language. It is this that differentiates the human language learner from the parrot. Again, it is a matter of degree, but we would not normally want to say that such a person has learned a language until he has developed linguistic competence in it, and until he is able to understand and create novel sentences in it according to its grammar and not just to the grammar of his first language.[20]

The creative aspect of language is one of the cornerstones of the argument for transformational grammar, for only such a grammar has available the "technical devices for expressing a system of recursive processes," and only with such devices can the creative aspect be formulated explicitly.[21] The only way to handle the fact that language has an infinite set of sentences and that it is used by people with a finite time for learning is to postulate a system of rules. The task of the grammarian is to find the best statement of the form of these rules. Knowing a language is a matter of having mastered these (as yet incompletely specified) rules; the ability to handle new sentences is evidence of knowing the rules that are needed to generate them.

It is important at this juncture that we make a clear distinction between two pairs of terms that are often confused, *competence* and *performance,* and *comprehension* and *production.* The following passage discusses competence and performance.

> The speaker produces a signal with a certain intended meaning; the hearer receives a signal and attempts to determine what was said and what was intended. The performance of the speaker or hearer is a complex matter that involves many factors. One fundamental factor involved in the speaker-hearer's performance is his knowledge of the grammar that determines an intrinsic connection of sound and meaning for each sentence. We refer to this knowledge—for the most part, obviously, unconscious knowledge—as the speaker-hearer's "competence." Competence, in this sense, is not to be confused with performance. Performance, that is, what the speaker-hearer actually does, is based not only on his knowledge of the language, but on many other factors as well—factors such as memory restrictions, inattention, distraction, nonlinguistic knowledge and beliefs, and so on. We may, if we

---

[20]Lado's suggestion that contrastive analysis precede language testing is a recognition of this problem.

[21]Chomsky (1965), p. 8.

like, think of the study of competence as the study of the potential performance of an idealized speaker-hearer who is unaffected by such grammatically irrelevant factors.[22]

The grammar of a language, then, is a description of competence; it may be compared, to use an analogy first suggested by Saussure, to the score of a musical work. The score necessarily underlies any performance, but does not account for all the features of any single performance. A moment's thought makes clear that linguistic performance may be either active or passive, that both the speaker and the hearer are in fact performing. The implication of this for language learning is extremely important, for it suggests that one may learn a language just as well by listening as by speaking. The implication for language testing is equally important, for it suggests that we can find out about "knowledge of a language," which is the same as underlying linguistic competence, equally well when we test passive and active skills.

This last does not of course mean that an individual's performance as a speaker is the same as his performance as a listener; such a claim would clearly be ridiculous, for it would be tantamount to saying that anyone who could read a Shakespeare play could also write it. All that it does claim is that the same linguistic competence, the same knowledge of rules, underlies both kinds of performance.

Knowledge of rules is also the principal factor in the understanding of messages with reduced redundancy. Miller and Isard (1963) have shown that the intelligibility of a sentence depends on whether it follows syntactic and semantic rules. Sentences which break semantic constraints (e.g., "A witness appraised the shocking company dragon") prove more difficult to understand and repeat than those that do not, and ungrammatical sentences (e.g., "A diamond shocking the prevented dragon witness") prove even more difficult. This effect became even clearer when they studied the resistance of sentences to masking by added noise; grammatical sentences proved to be far more resistant than ungrammatical ones. Thus, they showed that the "knowledge of the language" providing the listener with help in handling sentences with reduced redundancy was a knowledge of rules, of the grammar of the language.[23]

If we accept that "knowledge of a language," "linguistic competence," is a matter of knowledge of rules, what implications

---

[22]Chomsky and Halle (1968), p. 3.

[23]An alternative explanation in terms of a Markovian model is possible, but has been shown to be inadequate on other grounds. See Chomsky (1956).

does this have for language testing? First, we must keep clear the various reasons for which language tests are designed; we are concerned here with proficiency tests, or what Lewis has called "summative assessment"[24] and not with diagnostic tests. Further, we are concerned with a test that is independent of a specific set of materials and of the language analysis that lies behind it. In searching for a test of overall proficiency[25], then, we must try to find some way to get beyond the limitation of testing a sample of surface features, and seek rather to tap underlying linguistic competence. This can only be done with any degree of certainty if we can be sure that we are presenting the subject with novel utterances, or calling on him to produce utterances that he has not heard before. The simplest way to do this is to set up an interview situation calling for normal language functioning; this method however is both difficult to score reliably and prohibitively expensive to administer. A long-term solution to this problem is to use such interviewing techniques as a method of validating other measures.[26] Until this is done, another worthwhile approach appears to be to make use of the principle of redundancy, and test a subject's ability to function with a second language when noise is added or when portions of a text are masked.

REFERENCES

Carroll, J. B. *Testing*. Washington, D.C.: Center for Applied Linguistics, 1961.

Chomsky, N. "Current Issues in Linguistic Theory." *The Structure of Language*. J. A. Fodor and J. J. Katz (eds.). Englewood Cliffs: Prentice-Hall, 1964.

———. *Aspects of the Theory of Syntax*. Cambridge, Mass.: MIT Press, 1965.

———. *Cartesian Linguistics*. New York: Harper & Row, 1966.

Chomsky, N. and M. Halle. *The Sound Pattern of English*. New York: Harper & Row, 1968.

Fries, C. C. *Teaching and Learning English as a Second Language*. Michigan: University Press, 1945.

Godel, R. "F. de Saussure's Theory of Language." *Current Trends in Linguistics*, Volume III. ed. T. A. Sebeok. The Hague: Mouton, 1966.

---

[24] Lewis (1968).

[25] The lack of such a test invalidates most attempts to compare the effectiveness of various teaching materials, for the selection of specific language elements for the test will bias it in favor of the materials using the most similar selection.

[26] See Spolsky (1968).

Lado, R. *Language Testing*. London: Longmans, 1961.

Lewis, E. G. "International Education Assessment: English as a Foreign Language." *Problems in Foreign Language Testing, Language Learning,* Special Issue Number 3 (1968), 125-45.

Shannon, C. E. and W. Weaver. *The Mathematical Theory of Communication.* Urbana: University of Illinois Press, 1949 (1963).

Skinner, B. F. *Verbal Behavior*. New York: Appleton-Century-Crofts, 1957.

Spolsky, B. "A Psycholinguistic Critique of Programmed Foreign Language Instruction. *International Review of Applied Linguistics*, 4 (1962) 487-96.

———. "Language Testing—The Problem of Validation." *TESOL Quarterly*, 2 (1968) 88-94.

Spolsky, B. *et al.* "Preliminary Studies in the Development of Techniques for Testing Overall Second Language Proficiency. *Problems in Foreign Language Testing, Language Learning,* Special Issue No. 3 (1968), 79-101.

Upshur, J. A. "Language Proficiency Testing and the Contrastive Analysis Dilemma." *Language Learning*, 12 (1962), 123-8.

PRODUCTIVE COMMUNICATION TESTING: PROGRESS REPORT

John A. Upshur

Trends in second language testing tend to follow trends in second language teaching. And in the United States—at least in recent times—trends in second-language teaching have tended to follow trends in linguistics.

I don't have to remind the reader that foreign language instruction has been offered from time to time for many different purposes including, for example, the wish to increase students' appreciation for their own language or to provide training in "logical thinking." Today we hear much more about learning foreign languages in order to communicate with speakers of those languages and to participate in their cultures. Courses which reflect this view have communication as their goal and language as their contents. And for those courses advertised as "linguistically based," the contents are language as it is defined and described by linguists.[1]

By the early 1940's structural linguistics had achieved an advanced state of knowledge about the surface facts of language; discrete units at the linguistic levels of phonology, lexis, and grammar provided the "linguistic base" for the new foreign language courses, and this discrete-point approach is the major one in language teaching and language testing today (Jakobovits, 1970).

When the purpose for testing is control of instruction (as exemplified in the better programmed courses), and when instructional possibilities are limited by a discrete-point approach, it is reasonable that discrete-point tests be used (Upshur, 1969*b*). But discrete-point teaching has not met with complete success in producing competent communicators (Jakobovits, 1970). And it does not seem to be the case that discrete-point teaching provides an adequate foundation for language learners; use of language for communication should be included in language courses from the outset (see Roeming, 1968). As courses change to include communicative use of language so must language tests.

---

[1] I do recognize that linguists differ in their conceptions and that the claims for some courses may be quite empty. I recognize also that the successes and failures of any course must be due also to the contributions of other disciplines such as psychology and pedagogy.

There is, however, a more compelling reason to go beyond discrete-point testing. Each year many thousands of people take English language proficiency tests, the results of which affect the careers of those who take them, even though the validity of these tests is quite low. A proficiency test score may be crucial for an applicant in obtaining a job or a university admission. Visas are granted or withheld; pay and promotion are determined; programs of study for young children are set—all on the basis of foreign language proficiency test scores.

The adequacy of discrete-point proficiency testing has been challenged on both empirical and theoretical grounds. Most empirical validation studies have been conducted with university students as subjects and grades in academic courses as criterion measures. Results of these studies have shown that correlations between proficiency test scores and academic grade averages are low or nil (Educational Testing Service, 1968); that discrete-point tests predict less well than work-sample tests (Holtzman and Spencer, 1964); and that prediction by proficiency tests differs according to communication requirements of different courses (Upshur, 1967). Theoretical challenges to the discrete-point approach have come from linguistics (Chomsky, 1959, 1965; Fillmore, 1969), from psycholinguistics (Jakobovits, 1970) and sociolinguistics (Cooper, 1968), from psychology and information processing (Quillian, 1967; Reitman, 1965), and from information theory (Spolsky, 1968).

I have argued elsewhere (Upshur, 1969a) that a major reason for the stagnant state of foreign language proficiency testing has been the absence of an adequate model of language creativity, or the communicative use of language. Jakobovits has warned, however, that "because of the practical concerns involved in language testing one [should] not postpone the task of developing [new] language tests until such time as adequate theoretical models become available" (Jakobovits, 1969, p. 69). And it is encouraging to be able to report that his warning is being heeded. Recognizing that functional load of discrete items is indeterminate and that natural language redundancy runs from approximately 60% to more than 90% (Garner, 1962), Bernard Spolsky (1968) has developed proficiency tests to determine the ability of an examinee to utilize this redundancy when he listens to English spoken through white noise. Ted Plaister (1967) has rejected the popular view that a listening test should be made up of a collection of items each designed to test a discrete point (Lado, 1961). He has developed a work sample test of aural comprehension for university students; the early results of his work look promising.

It is less encouraging for me to have to report a lag in the development of proficiency tests in which the examinee is the sender rather than the receiver of information. During the past year I have been working with several colleagues[2] on the problem of productive communication testing, but I must report here only on progress; I cannot announce a solution.

Let me note first that we are interested in communication and communication tasks, and that in this work we explicitly reject the discrete-point approach. We do not, in other words, accept the notion that a linguistic description of a language can specify a set of items, the knowledge of which will assure unimpeded ability to be understood.

Productive communication may be roughly defined as follows: as a result of some action by a speaker (or writer) his audience creates a *new* concept.[3] Successful communication implies a correspondence between the intentions of a speaker and the concept created by his audience.[4] I am using the term *communication tasks* to refer to constraints imposed by different sources of information which may be available to an audience, and which may be utilized by a speaker. For example, I may hold up a red pen and say, "This will give you an idea about the state of my bank balance." If you were not able to see the pen, I would instead have to say something like, "I've spent all my money." Thus, the perceptions available to an audience constitute one source of information, and are a communication task variable. Other communication task variables include, for example, what the audience already has been told, and even the language or languages which the audience knows.[5]

These ideas about communication and communication tasks have guided our test development efforts. As it turns out the procedure is a little different from a listening comprehension test; the main difference is a change in roles. In the comprehension test the examinee does not know what the examiner will say; he listens, forms a concept and somehow indicates what that new concept is. The examinee's new concept is compared with the examiner's

---

[2] Special credit should be given to Edith Loundon and Barbara Hockman for planning, to William Orzolek for experimental test administration, to John Peterson for developing electronic aids, and to Miho Sakakibara for art work.

[3] My use of *speaker* and *writer* obviously imply language mediated communication. For purposes of this paper, I wish to make this a restriction.

[4] A more complete explanation of the process and of the relation between *concepts* and *meaning* may be found in Upshur (1969a).

[5] Working hypotheses about the communicative performance of speakers may be found in Upshur (1969a). Essentially, communication involves discovering what an audience knows and how he processes information.

intentions. If the two agree, the examinee is given the credit for comprehending. In our productive communication tests the examiner doesn't know what the examinee will say; the examinee speaks (or writes) and the examiner listens, forms a concept and indicates what that concept is. The examiner's new concept is compared with the intentions of the examinee. If the two agree, the examinee is given the credit for communicating.

The first problem encountered in developing production tests of this type is determining the intentions of the examinee. The second problem is occasioned by the necessity for keeping the examiner unaware of what examinees intend while still having a standard measure for all examinees. One solution for these problems is as follows:

(1) The examinee is presented with four pictures differing significantly on one or two conceptual dimensions. These may represent, for example, a person performing four different "actions," or the four conjunctive possibilities of a man with or without a hat walking up or down a staircase.

(2) The examinee is instructed to provide a single sentence description to a visually remote audience of one picture which is randomly selected from the set.

(3) The audience—the examiner—makes a best guess as to which picture is being described.

(4) The examinee's directed intentions are compared with the examiner's guesses.

A number of variations of this basic technique have been employed, with examinees producing both written and oral English, but the general findings I shall report here do not require a discussion of those variations.

Before presenting results, however, I should like to review George Perren's (1967) excellent summary of problems in testing the spoken language. In addition to the often-reported low scorer reliability of speech production tests he lists four problems:

(1) Isolating and objectively scoring the constituent elements of speech;

(2) Establishing relative weights for these elements in a total score;

(3) Eliciting comparable speech samples; and

(4) Finding time for administration and scoring.

To a degree, all of these problems have been alleviated—even if not completely resolved. Scorer reliability is quite satisfactory (0.99 for a representative sample of students at the English Language Institute); and, as I have already indicated, scoring is objective. Because we are not using the discrete-point approach, isolating constituent elements of speech is not relevant; and because we are measuring success of communication, weightings of the elements which produce that success need not be established. Finally, the development of special electronic aids allows us to administer and score an oral production test to a dozen students in the same time as is required for a multiple-choice grammar recognition test of the same reliability.

The first finding I would like to report is based upon our earlier work in which written communication was required of examinees. We discovered that, for most tasks, students with only a limited command of English could communicate perfectly if they were given enough time. Individual differences in amount of communication began to appear as progressively more severe time constraints were imposed.[6] This finding led to our decision to use rate of communication as the primary measure in our subsequent development of oral communication tests.

Before reporting other general results I should mention that the tasks we use in our oral tests provide no problems when the examinee and audience both speak the same language—for native speakers of Arabic, English, Japanese, and Spanish, communication is perfect. With a four picture item such as I described earlier, response time is less than ten seconds.

I have already reported scorer reliability of 0.99; a preliminary determination of test-retest reliability for a 36-item experimental test was 0.92.

It has been relatively easy to show that oral communication testing of this form is feasible and reliable. The meaning of scores is not so easy to determine. Several findings do, however, suggest answers.

(1) For students with a wide range of proficiency as determined by discrete-point tests, amount of successful communication and time required are highly correleated; for students with a narrow range of proficiency, the correlation is low. These students are similar with respect to amount of successful communication but are different with respect to time.

(2) For students with a narrow range of proficiency there is zero intercorrelation among teachers who rate them on speaking ability.

---

[6] For the population we were working with, two minutes to describe a display containing thirty-six bits of information was found to be optimal.

(3) Correlations between rate of communication scores and discrete-point tests are quite high for examinees who have been studying English in the United States; the longer they have been in the United States the higher is the correlation.

(4) Correlations between oral communication scores are higher with composition ratings than with discrete-point tests, when raters are instructed to grade compositions according to the amount of unambiguous information the writer has been able to convey.

These findings have led to the following conclusions:

(1) That time required to communicate is a highly sensitive measure, but we do not yet know the extent to which this represents retrieval time for lexical items, language-processing time, or translation time;

(2) That scores (especially amount of communication) do reflect a general language proficiency factor; and

(3) That the test does provide information not available from discrete-point tests.

In conclusion I will just note that the arguments about the inadequacy of discrete-point testing are convincing enough, and our preliminary work with communication testing is encouraging enough that we will continue our work directed towards the development of generally usable test instruments.

REFERENCES

Chomsky, N. *Aspects of the Theory of Syntax* Cambridge, Mass.: MIT Press, 1965.

———. "Review of B. F. Skinner's *Verbal Behavior.*" *Language,* 35 (1959), 26-58.

Cooper, R. L. "An Elaborated Language Testing Model." *Problems in Foreign Language Testing, Language Learning,* Special Issue No. 3, 1968.

Educational Testing Service, *Test of English as a Foreign Language: Interpretive Information.* Princeton: E.T.S., 1968.

Fillmore, C. J., "Types of Lexical Information." *Research Report,* The Ohio State University, Computer and Information Science Research Center, 1969. pp. 65-103.

Garner, W. R. *Uncertainty and Structure as Psychological Concepts.* New York: Wiley, 1962.

Holtzman, P. D. and R. E. Spencer, "It's Composition—But Is It Reliable?" *Research Report No. 32,* University Park, The Pennsylvania State University Office of Examination Services, 1964.

Jakobovits, L. A. "A Functional Approach to the Assessment of Language Skills." *Journal of English as a Second Language* IV, 2 (1969), 63-76.

———. *Foreign Language Learning,* Rowley, Mass: Newbury House, 1970.

Lado, R. *Language Testing* London: Longmans, 1961.

Perren, G. "Testing Ability in English as a Second Language: 3. Spoken Language." *English Language Teaching,* 22 I (1967), 22-29.

Plaister, T. H. "Testing Aural Comprehension: A Culture Fair Approach." *TESOL Quarterly*, I, 3 (1967), 17-19.

Quillian, R. "Word Concepts: A Theory and Simulation of Some Basic Semantic Capabilities." *Behavioral Science*, 12 (1967), 410-30.

Reitman, W. R. *Cognition and Thought*. New York: Wiley, 1965.

Roeming, R. F. "Foreign Language Teaching in the Creative Mode." *Modern Language Journal*, 52, 4 (1968), 216-19.

Spolsky, B. This volume, pp. 164-75.

Upshur, J. A. "English Language Tests and Prediction of Academic Success." *Selected Conference Papers of the Association of Teachers of English as a Second Language*. National Association for Foreign Student Affairs, 1967.

———. "Measurement of Oral Communication." *IFS Dokumentation, Leistungmessung im Sprachunterricht,* H. Schrand (ed.) Marburg/Lahn: Informationzentrum für Fremdsprachenforschung, 1969*a*, Pp. 53-80.

———. "TEST Is a Four-Letter word." Paper presented to the EPDA Institute, University of Illinois, 1969*b* .

DISCRETE-POINT TESTS VERSUS TESTS OF INTEGRATIVE SKILLS*

John W. Oller, Jr.

Agnosticism concerning the testability of language skills, though common among linguists, cannot be shared by the classroom teacher. The teacher cannot wait for the linguists, psychologists, sociologists, psycholinguists, sociolinguists, etc., to resolve all of the controversies about theories of language and learning. The teacher must do something even if it is wrong. The purpose of this paper is to review several testing techniques and to discuss their applicability to specific aspects of language competence. Some of the arguments for and against certain types of teacher-made tests will also be presented.

To begin with, I would like to define a few technical and nontechnical terms. I will use the term "test" to refer to any observable activity a student is asked to perform under controlled conditions in order to determine his capacity to perform similar activities under less rigid controls. The technical terms "reliability" and "validity" will be used according to the following nontechnical definitions: a *reliable* test is one that produces the same results under the same conditions on different occasions; and a *valid* test is one that faithfully simulates the conditions and activities of the skills it seeks to measure. On the basis of these definitions we may establish the axiom that a *good* test is one that not only provides valid and reliable information about the effectiveness of the student's learning and the teacher's instruction, but also functions as an integral part of the teaching-learning process by focusing attention on, and giving practice in useful language skills.

With the above definitions and the axiom just stated in mind, I would like to consider two overlapping but, I think, significantly different viewpoints on language teaching and testing. The first is based primarily on structural linguistics. It emphasizes knowledge of the forms and structures of language. The second stems from a

*This paper is a revised version of an invited lecture originally presented at the TESOL Convention, New Orleans, 1971, in the pre-convention workshop on testing. I am grateful to Lois McIntosh (the pre-convention Chairman), William Slager, David Ewing, and several of my colleagues at UCLA for their useful comments and suggestions concerning the content of this paper. In addition, I would like to thank the participants of the workshop for their stimulating comments and questions. Any errors, of course, are my own. I also gratefully acknowledge permission to quote from David Harris's book (1969).

variety of pragmatic theories. It was aptly expounded as early as 1904 by Otto Jespersen when he cogently argued that to teach a language is to teach a student to communicate in real-life situations. One could easily maintain that these two schools of thought are not mutually exclusive, and I would agree. Nevertheless, the teaching methods which derive from these viewpoints are distinct in crucial respects. Also, they lead to two essentially different types of language tests. Following Carroll (1972), we will refer to them as *discrete-point tests* and *tests of integrative skills*. I believe that the former derive from structural linguistics, while the latter are based on the school of thought of which Jespersen is representative.

I. DISCRETE-POINT TESTS

A. Tests Based on Contrastive Analysis

According to Robert Lado (1961) in his widely-used book on language testing, traditional linguistics suggests an analysis of language into three levels: (*a*) phonology—which includes sounds, stresses, and pitches; (*b*) syntax; and (*c*) semantics—which Lado identifies with lexicon. We must note that these divisions are not always clear-cut and are certainly not universally agreed upon by linguists or psycholinguists (Oller, in press). Nevertheless, they are frequently proposed as a basis for distinct types of discrete-point test items.

Lado (1961, pp. 212-13) gives several examples of items aimed at testing the auditory comprehension of Spanish speakers who are learning English. In one item type suggested, the student hears a sentence and must identify the one of three pictures that it best describes. For instance, Lado suggests that the student might hear the sentence "It's a sheep." He has in front of him the pictures of a ship, a sheep, and a baby asleep. He must select one of them. This supposedly tests the phonological contrasts within English between "a ship," "a sheep," and "asleep." The motivation for the item in terms of the contrastive analysis of Spanish and English is that Spanish lacks the /i/ and /iy/ distinction found in the words "ship" and "sheep." Of course, this kind of justification for the item will not work in many cases if the learners are from language backgrounds other than Spanish.

In order to test control of stress contrasts in English, Lado suggests a picture item which shows a boy looking (*a*) directly at a brick wall, (*b*) over a brick wall, and (*c*) at a soccer goal. The student hears the sentence (1) "²Hè loôked òver the ³wáll¹." Since this contrasts with the sentence (2) "[2]Hè loóked ôver the [3]wáll[1]" and with (3) "He looked over the goal" (and, of course, stress is irrelevant for this last sentence), Lado assumes that this item yields information about the student's skill in using English stress patterns. The difficulty is that many native speakers of English might use sentence (1) to refer either to situation (a) or (b). Hence, the item is indeterminate. This is often a problem in the construction of multiple-choice items.

To measure skill in handling intonation contours, Lado proposes an example which shows (a) two boys, one standing and one sitting, (b) a girl sitting, and a boy standing, (c) two boys standing, one of them slightly taller than the other. The student hears "[2]The [4]bóy[2], [2]who stoòd úp[1], [2]was [3]táll[1]." Because of the heavy stress on "bóy" and the clause "who stood up," Lado claims that the native speaker will prefer choice (b). However, it seems to me that the sentence could also go with (a). The only way to make the choices unambiguous would be to provide more context.

To test word order, Lado offers an example of a picture item showing (a) a dog house, (b) a dog, (c) a dog bone on a plate. The student hears the sentence "Have you seen our new house dog?" The rationale for choice (c) escapes me, but there is a possibility that speakers of certain languages (especially Spanish) might confuse "house dog" with "dog house." Again, the use of contrastive analysis looms large.

As a final case of this type Lado suggests a vocabulary item. The student sees (a) an explosion (a crash?), (b) a trash can, and (c) an ash tray. He hears "Do you want an ash tray?" The mind reels at the prospect of attempting to rationalize and construct items of this type. When even *post hoc* analysis of an exemplary item fails to suggest a rationale, should not the theory be drawn into question? It is difficult to recommend the contrastive analysis method as a basis for construction of discrete-point items. Of course, items based on the contrastive method are a small subset of possible discrete-point test items. It is possible for discrete-point items to relate somewhat more directly to the kinds of skills that people have to utilize in order to communicate.

B. Other Types of Discrete-Point Items

Not all of the test professionals have followed the kind of language testing theory espoused by Lado. In his book *Testing English as a Second Language*, Harris (1969) places little emphasis on contrastive analysis. He deals both with discrete-point items and with tests of integrative skills, but he devotes more space to the former than to the latter. The book includes numerous practical pointers on the construction of multiple-choice items and provides an excellent discussion of many other significant testing techniques. The bulk of the text is concerned with multiple-choice tests. Brief discussions of translation and dictation are included. There is a somewhat more extensive review of composition and oral interview techniques.

Typically, multiple-choice tests are broken down into several types intended to measure various components in language skills. Harris (1969, p. 11) gives the following breakdown which I have elaborated slightly in order to differentiate discrete-point and integrative skills tests.

Components	Language Skills			
	Listening	Speaking	Reading	Writing
Phonology/ Orthography				
Structure	DISCRETE-POINT TESTS			
Vocabulary				
Rate and General Fluency	INTEGRATIVE SKILLS TESTS			

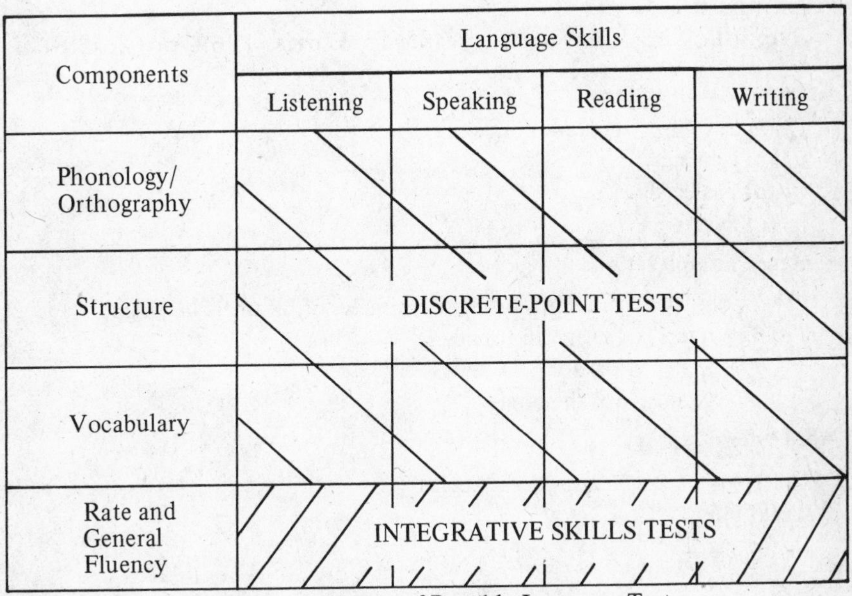

Figure 1.   A Matrix of Possible Language Tests (cf. Harris, 1969, p. 11).

The figure suggests a division of language skills into listening, speaking, reading, and writing (across the top of the chart), and into various components of these skills on the left side of the chart, reading down. Generally speaking, emphasis on the first three components, that is, phonology/orthography, structure, or vocabulary will lead to discrete-point types of tests, whereas emphasis on the last component, rate and general fluency, will yield integrative skills tests. Most of Harris's book is devoted to multiple-choice items which test the first three components listed.

Multiple-choice items can of course be presented in various ways: The test questions and alternatives may be presented orally or in writing, and they may be responded to orally or in writing depending on the purposes of the test. Some examples follow.

As a test of auditory discrimination (from Harris, 1969, p. 32), the student may hear the words:

(1)   (a) cot   (b) caught   (c) cot[1]

The task is to determine whether all are the same or whether one is different from the other two and if so, which one is different. There are, of course, many variations on this type of auditory discrimination item.

The following items are suggested by Harris (1969, pp. 26-28):

Grammatical structure

(2) Mary _____ in New York since 1960.
   (a) is living
   (b) has lived
   (c) lives

Sentence interpretation

(3) An old friend of John's brought *him* news of his uncle last night.
   Him refers to (a) an old friend
                    (b) John
                    (c) the uncle

Word order

(4) When _____ _____ _____ _____ ?
   (a) plan
   (b) you
   (c) to go
   (d) do

Vocabulary (Harris, 1969, p. 52)

(5) A brief, light sleep
   (a) yawn
   (b) nap
   (c) struggle
   (d) hug

---

[1]Notice that in some dialects of American English, this contrast no longer exists. Hence, this is a questionable item by most test standards.

(6) The old woman was too _____ to push open the door.

   (a) harsh
   (b) deaf
   (c) sincere
   (d) feeble

Other discrete-point items, typical of those found in the *Test of English as a Foreign Language* (TOEFL produced by Educational Testing Service; Princeton, New Jersey), are designed to test specific writing skills. The following items are from Harris (1969, pp. 71-72).

Subject verb agreement

(7) The design of the two new bridges (are/is) very unusual.

Structural parallelism

(8) She enjoyed sewing, reading, and just (to sit/sitting) on the porch watching the people go by.

Case of pronouns

(9) To my little brother and (I/me), Uncle John was the most wonderful friend.

Comparison of adjectives

(10) The afternoon rush hour is the (worse/worst) part of the day.

Formation of adverbs

(11) The man tipped his hat and spoke very (polite/politely) to the ladies.

Formation of irregular verbs

(12) Neither of the children would tell us who had (broke/broken) the window.

In terms of the definition of a good test given at the outset of this paper, the most serious disadvantage of discrete-point tests in general is that they fail (in most cases) to faithfully reflect actual language usage. Usually they require the student to perform highly artificial tasks and on the basis of his performance attempt to infer his level of competence for a different sort of task altogether. A second disadvantage is that they do not usually fit smoothly into a total program for language instruction. That is, they often fail to provide the student with practice in useful language skills. Also, they may serve to confuse rather than to instruct the student concerning the points tested. A third disadvantage is one that applies to all tests of the multiple-choice type. They require substantial skill on the part of the person who prepares them, and this skill may not be applicable to anything but item writing. They demand considerable expenditure of time and effort in writing, proofing, pretesting, revising, and sometimes recycling the whole procedure, before they are ready for use.

On the other hand, there are some advantages to the discrete-point approach. If one assumes that teaching of the target language can be discrete-point oriented, such tests provide diagnostic information not available from multiple-choice tests that require integrative skills. (We shall see below, however, that other types of integrative skills tests provide very finely detailed diagnostic information.) Some of the advantages which might be listed for discrete-point tests are also applicable to all multiple-choice tests, for example, ease of administration and scoring. Especially in cases where large numbers of students must be tested in a relatively short period of time, the amount of care and time required for the preparation of a multiple-choice test may be justified. (It does not necessarily follow that the test must be based on the discrete-point philosophy which argues for the testing of one and only one point of the language at a time.) Moreover, reliability in scoring with such tests is nearly perfect. This, of course, does not guarantee that the test on the whole will be reliable. For example, if a large percentage of the students have a tendency to answer items differently on different occasions, no matter how reliable the scoring, the test may still be unreliable.

II. TESTS OF INTEGRATIVE SKILLS

Perhaps the best way to distinguish integrative skills tests from discrete-point tests is to define the latter and to suggest that the former includes every test which is not an instance of the latter. Actually, the differences between them are not so much of type as of degree. We might speak in terms of a continuum ranging from discrete-point items at one end to full-scale language use at the other. At any rate, discrete-point items generally aim at testing one and only one point of grammar, phonology, vocabulary, or whatever, at a time. It is rarely necessary for a student to understand whole sentences in order to answer discrete-point items correctly, and it is probably accurate to state that it is never necessary for a student to understand a context longer than a sentence in order to answer a discrete-point item. In fact, if it were necessary, the item would violate the cardinal principle of the discrete-point approach.

It is important to realize that all multiple-choice tests are not discrete-point tests. In the test types considered in this section, several multiple-choice examples are given. In those instances, however, it is impossible to state precisely where the student went wrong if he answers incorrectly. This means two things. First, such items do not conform to the discrete-point mandate. Second, if anything more specific than a global measure of proficiency is required, multiple choice items which measure integrative skills are proably not the best approach. Some of the other tests of integrative skills, however, such as dictations and cloze tests, as we will see below, do provide useful diagnostic information.

A. Reading Skills

The following examples from tests of reading skills were actually written for foreign students at the University of California, Los Angeles. They require the student to select the appropriate paraphrase for a given sentence. In working through them the reader will see that it is necessary for the student to understand abstract relationships between subjects, verbs, and objects, among a great many other things which probably will not be explicitly characterized in theories of language for some time to come. It would be impossible at the present time to say precisely what points of language usage are involved, and this puts the items clearly in the domain of integrative skills.[2]

(1) Reading Comprehension
Directions: Choose the sentence which **best** expresses the meaning of the given sentence. *More than one answer may be possible, so be sure that you pick the best one.*

1. Helen's brother got married when she was eighteen years old.
   (a) Helen's brother got married at the age of eighteen.
   (b) Helen's brother was eighteen years old when she got married.
   (c) When Helen was eighteen, her brother got married.
   (d) When Helen's brother was eighteen, he got married.
   (e) Just eighteen years before Helen, her brother got married.

2. Sitting on the floor, Janet watched her husband paint the chair.
   (a) While Janet sat on the floor, her husband watched her.
   (b) While Janet painted the chair, she watched her husband.
   (c) While she was sitting on the floor, Janet watched her husband painting the chair.
   (d) Janet watched the floor while her husband was painting the chair she was sitting in.
   (e) Janet watched her husband paint the chair which was on the floor.

3. The more fully mechanized factory has undoubtedly strengthened the long-term drift of women into paid occupations.

---

[2]Of course, this limits the possibility of using this test as a diagnostic device. This is a disadvantage, however, only for integrative skills tests that consist of multiple choice items. See below the discussion of dictation and cloze tests.

(a) Mechanization helped management gain more control over female labor over the years.

(b) Mechanization helped the steady increase of women in employment outside of factories.

(c) Mechanization helped add to the steady increase of the female labor force.

(d) Mechanization helped the steady increase of women's salaries in industry.

(e) Mechanization helped speed up the inclusion of women in the labor force.

Another item type which we found useful for placement of foreign students in English as a Second Language classes at UCLA requires that the student select from several alternatives the sentence that best expresses the main idea of a given paragraph. Again, this item type is clearly in the domain of integrative tasks.

(2) Reading: Understanding the Main Idea of a Paragraph

Directions: Read the paragraph and then choose the statement that **best** expresses the central idea.

> The obvious method of discovering whether the class has studied its work, and of prodding them on to study in the future, is to ask questions. Written questions with written answers are "tests," "quizzes," or "examinations." Horrible words. My soul sickens at their very sound. I sat through so many hundreds of them . . . yet I have never been able to think of a substitute and have yet to meet anyone else who has.

(a) Hundreds of examinations have been given in the past.

(b) Written questions are the best type of examination.

(c) It is obvious that the class has not studied its lesson.

(d) Tests are horrible, but no one has found a substitute.

(e) Students must be prodded to answer the questions on a test.

B. Cloze Tests

One of the most promising types of integrative skills tests which has been proposed for measuring either achievement or proficiency in foreign language or second language situations is the cloze test. This method was first used with *native* speakers by Taylor (1953) to determine the difficulty of reading materials. The cloze technique of test construction simply deletes every nth word (5th, 6th, or 7th usually) from a passage of prose. The student is then required to replace the missing words or to restore the passage by placing other contextually acceptable words in the blanks.

There has been some discussion about the best way to score a test of this type. With native speakers it has been shown that it makes little difference whether only the exact words restored to the passage are counted as correct, or whether other acceptable substitutes are allowed.[3] In a recent study at UCLA, we discovered that the best of five scoring methods for use with *nonnative* speakers was to count any word that fit the context as correct. Other scoring systems which were more elaborate yielded no more information. Also, by allowing acceptable substitutes as well as the exact words, a significant increase in correlation with the *UCLA ESL Placement Examination* was achieved (Oller, 1972*b*).

Below, an example of a cloze test is included. To get some idea of what skills the student must employ in order to restore the missing words, the reader may wish to work through the passage. Surprisingly, cloze test scores seem to correlate best with other tasks which require skill in listening comprehension (Darnell, 1968; Oller and Conrad, 1971; and Oller, 1972*b*).

Directions: (1) Read the whole passage through. (2) Then, go back and fill in the blanks with the words you think are missing. (3) Use only one word for each blank. (4) Contractions like "don't," "can't," "he's," "you're," and "we'll" can be used to fill in a blank. (5) Try to fill in every blank.

I did not have the pleasure of knowing Mr. Ravel in the days when he was still struggling with the first principles of the English language. Like everyone else, of course, I __(1)__ heard of him, and had smiled __(2)__ his difficulties with the idiosyncracies of __(3)__ tongue, as reported in the newspapers __(4)__ the time. You will recall, for __(5)__ , his remarks in excited and broken English __(6)__ the absurdities of the word "fast." __(7)__ horse was fast when he was __(8)__ to a hitching post. The same __(9)__ was also fast under exactly diametric circumstances __(10)__ he was running away. A woman __(11')__ fast if she smoked cigarettes. A __(12)__ was fast if it didn't fade. __(13)__ fast was to go without food. Et cetera. __(14)__ a language!

Today, M. Ravel speaks English __(15)__ only the faintest of French accents, __(16)__ what he has to say is __(17)__ salted with Gallic gestures and mannerisms. __(18)__ other evening, after listening with polite incredulity __(19)__ an account of my own present difficulties __(20)__ the French language, he shrugged his __(21)__ .

"Perhaps. But when you have mastered __(22)__ , you will understand. Like everything __(23)__ French, our language is always logical, __(24)__ see. But this English! Ah! I __(25)__ it; but I do not understand __(26)__ ." "Logical" is the last adjective I __(27)__ use in describing the French language. __(28)__ I had no chance to say __(29)__ .

"Listen!" said Mr. Ravel. "Last winter I __(30)__ a very bad cold. A friend __(31)__ to me, 'Jules, your voice is __(32)__ husky.' Husky? As an adjective I

---

[3]Sometimes the misleading term "synonym" has been used. This would suggest that when the subject does not restore the original word to the test that he usually replaces it with some synonym, in fact this is often not the case.

  (33)   not know the word. As a noun   (34)   is an Eskimo. What does this
  (35) , my voice is husky? I consulted   (36)   dictionary. 'Husky,'
adjective . . . Ah! To be   (37)   ! 'Powerful, strong, burly.' Like an Eskimo.
Logical   (38) . Very neat! . . . Then, to myself, I frown suddenly. Husky?
  (39)   is my voice my friend was   (40)   of. And that—most positively—is
  (41)   husky! It is not strong. It   (42)   not powerful. With my cold, it
  (43)   so weak I can hardly use   (44) . Is this some American humor my
  (45)   employs? I look in the dictionary   (46) . Ah! I discover a second
meaning: 'dry, harsh, hoarse.' So!   (47)   see what my friend means. He
  (48)   my voice is husky. He means   (49) ` voice is hoarse."
    Mr. Ravel shook his   (50) .
(From Brown, 1956, p. 115.)

C. Dictation

Another form of test, one which has been extremely popular
among language teachers for many years, is dictation. Professional
test writers and evaluators, however, have regarded dictation as
somewhat uneconomical and uninformative as a testing device.
Valette (1967) is a refreshing exception to the trend, but Robert
Lado (1961, p. 34) has argued that dictation is not a good measure
of listening comprehension or phonological discrimination because
the sounds are often given away by the context. He has also
remarked that dictation is not a good test of word order since the
word order is given and it cannot be a test of vocabulary because the
vocabulary is given. In several recent studies of the *UCLA ESL
Placement Examination* it has been demonstrated that dictation is an
extremely useful measure of overall proficiency in English as a
second language (Oller, 1972*a*, and Oller, 1972*c*). The two passages
given below are examples selected for the fall examination of 1970.
The second passage, which is obviously more complex in structure
and vocabulary, yielded better discrimination among subjects and
higher correlation with other parts of the entrance examination.[4]

I

John was a pleasant looking young man./ Anna was a pretty young girl./
She had a small turned-up nose./ Together they walked down to the river./
They sat on the grass near the water./ It was a pretty place./ There were trees

---

[4]The slash marks in the examples of dictations indicate the location of the pauses.
Obviously, other positions for the pauses could have been selected. The important thing to
remember is that the length of sequences between pauses should challenge the short-term
memory of the nonnative speaker. Also these sequences should be spoken at conversational
speed.

all around./ They were alone./ No one could see them./ They had their fishing poles with them./ They had brought sandwiches to eat./ They began to fish./
(From Dixon, 1950, p. 69.)

II

Joe is a freshman and he is having/ all the problems that most freshmen have./ As a matter of fact,/ his problems started before he even left home./ He had to do a lot of things/ that he didn't like to do/ just because he was going away to college./ He had his eyes examined/ and he had his cavities filled/ although he hates to go to a dentist,/ and he had his watch fixed by a neighborhood jeweler./
(From Praninskas, 1959, p. 217.)

The average score for the first passage was 23.7 out of 30 points. The average for the second passage was 20.6 out of 30. The standard deviation was greater for the more difficult passage. Also, it yielded more discriminating information. The two passages, however, correlated at nearly .80.

The administration procedure is important to the success of dictation as a testing technique. The most important factor is rate of speaking. If the dictation is to be a test of skill in handling the spoken word, it must be spoken (or read, in this case) at a fairly fast clip. Reading dictation at a snail's pace is probably not much of a test of anything but spelling. At UCLA, we follow the method used by Lois McIntosh (which is also used, I am told, on the New York State Regents examinations). First a passage is read once through at conversational speed. The second time it is read with pauses at convenient phrase or clause boundaries while the students write down what they hear. Marks of punctuation are given. The third time the passage is read again at normal speed with occasional pauses to allow students to make corrections.

To show that dictation is not, as Lado and other professional testers have suggested (cf. Oller, 1972a), an uneconomical and imprecise writing exercise, consider the following errors made in dictations by college-level foreign students at UCLA. Also, notice the diagnostic implications of these errors.

Errors from Dictations

(On the left side of the arrow, the original phrasing is given; to the right side appears the student's rendering.)

(1) best described as exponential. ——> best described as <u>an exponential period</u>
(2) from the beginning of time ——> from the <u>beginig at time</u>

(3) the new has barely a chance to become familiar ——> the new has <u>early to change</u> to become familiar

(4) that the famous generation gap ——> that <u>famous</u> generation gap

(5) science and technology have created ——> <u>sceince</u> and <u>technolege</u> <u>has</u> created

(6) this ocean and its ways ——> this ocean and its <u>waves</u>

(7) riches ——> <u>richness</u>

(8) than the early sailors ever dreamed of ——> than the early sailors <u>never</u> dreamed of

(9) an accelerated rate ——> <u>on</u> <u>un</u>accelerated rate

(10) knowledge of ——> knowledge <u>for</u>

(11) of being consigned ——> of <u>bean</u> consigned

(12) too many changes for comfort ——> <u>to</u> many changes for <u>confort</u> (Spanish spk.)

(13) promises ——> <u>promesses</u> (Spanish spk.)

(14) riches ——> <u>reaches</u> (Spanish spk.)

(15) today's search ——> tod<u>ay search</u>

(16) at both ends of the spectrum ——> at both __ of <u>espactroms</u> (Persian)

(17) the result is ——> the <u>reasult</u> (Persian, possibly an analogy with reason)

(18) this ocean and its ways ——> this <u>ocine</u> and <u>this</u> ways

(19) change has been the law of life from the beginning of time ——> <u>change the lite off there</u>, from <u>begining time</u> (Japanese)

(20) to become familiar before it is replaced by something even newer ——> to become <u>for million befor es</u> replaced by something even new __ (Arabic)

(21) something new has been added ——> something new has been <u>had it</u> (Italian)

(22) as change continues to ——> as change continue<u> to</u> (Italian)

(23) for at least five thousand years ——> for <u>adlist 20,000</u> years (Bulgarian)

(24) to find practical means of feeding people better and means of helping them avoid the terrible damage of wind storms. ——> to find <u>partical man living</u> better and <u>mean help man and boy tellable damag store</u>. (Chinese)

(25) avoid the terrible damage of windstorms ——> <u>the boy</u> terrible damage of <u>ministers</u> (Japanese)

However problematic dictation may be in terms of scoring or administration, it clearly does provide a tremendous wealth of information about how well the student understands the language. It certainly is naive to suggest (as some "experts" have, see my discussion on this, 1972a) that in taking a dictation all the student needs to know is how to spell English words. It is clear even from a cursory examination of these few errors, that the student is not simply copying down words, but is involved in an active and complex process of analysis-by-synthesis. Also, the diagnostic implications of the errors in many cases are much more transparent than in more "objective" tests.

D. Composition

Another popular form of examination, which has been used both as a measure of achievement and of proficiency, is the traditional composition. The major difficulty with using composition as a testing device is correction. It is frequently impossible to determine precisely what it was that the student was trying to say. The following examples illustrate this problem. The material in normal type is what the student actually wrote. The cross-outs are words that the student crossed out. The material in italics written above the line is my estimation of what the student might have been trying to say. Note that in some cases it is very difficult to determine what the student had in mind. For this and other reasons, scoring compositions by most methods is somewhat unreliable.

Examples of compositions written by foreign students at the college level

(1) Topic: "When I Was a Child"

There is one impression of my childhood which stands
There is one ~~souvenir~~ impression of my childhood which persists
out among the others and which I will talk about here.
among others and which ~~is related to~~ concerns this souvenir.
It seems as if I have been using the expression
"When I was a Child"—It seems as ~~if I had said it~~ if I have
"When I was a Child" for the best part of my life.
been saying it for most of my life. It must have been very soon
The first time I used it was not long after I had
after I learned to talk, the first time that I could vocally
begun to learn to talk and to grow up.
express that I was already grown up.
Robert and I were about the same size, so it was
Robert and I were about the same strength and energy, so that it
usually a fair fight. I can vividly remember
~~sometimes~~ was a "fair" fighting. I can vividly remember wrestling
wrestling with him, and how my mother had to
with him, and my mother having to separate us for hours.
separate us for hours.

(2) Topic: "When I Was a Child"

I started school when I was six years old. My parents
I attend the school when I was six years old. And my parents

died the following year. I made good grades in
passed away on next year. In the school I had good grade
elementary school. Since I was a child I have enjoyed
through elementary school. From I am a child. I like to
Chinese boxing as exercise. This is why I have a healthy body
exercise Chinese boxing. That is the reason. Why I have a
today. I also like several other exercises, for example,
healthy body today. I also like several other exercise.
playing basketball, ping-pong, swimming, and mountaineering.
Example, play basketball, ping-pong, swimming, and mountaineering.

Conclusion

Many other types of tests deserve mention, but for lack of time I must omit them. The above examples are intended to give a picture of various types of discrete-item tests, particularly of the multiple-choice type, and also to review some of the major types of integrative skills tests. In spite of the fact that some of the integrative skills tests seem to have little in common, and regardless of the fact that they may seem to be unreliable as far as scoring is concerned, repeated studies show that scores on tests of integrative skills tend to correlate better with teacher judgments, better among themselves, and better with other measures of language skills than do any of the discrete-point types because they more nearly reflect what people actually do when they use language.

Practices in language testing stem from theories of language learning and teaching (Upshur, 1971). The discrete-point test is a reflection of the notion from teaching theory that if you get across 50,000 (or some other magic number of) structural items, you will have taught the language.[5] The trouble with this is that 50,000 structural patterns isolated from the meaningful contexts of communication do not constitute language competence; nor does a sampling of those 50,000 discrete-points of grammar constitute an adequate test of language competence. The question of language testing is not so much whether the student knows such-and-such a pattern in a manipulative or abstract sense, but rather, whether he can use it effectively in communication. To answer the latter question, tests of integrative skills are imperative. This does not mean that discrete-point items should never be used but that when they are used, it should be with an adequate appreciation of their practical limitations.

------

[5]For criticism of this viewpoint see Belasco (1971), and Oller (1971).

REFERENCES

Allen, H. B., and Campbell, R. N. (eds.). *Teaching English as a Second Language: A Book of Readings*. New York: McGraw Hill, 1972.

Belasco, S. "The Feasibility of Learning a Second Language in an Artificial Unicultural Situation." Pimsleur and Quinn (1971).

Brown, J. I. *Efficient Reading*. Boston: Heath, 1956.

Carroll, J. B. "Fundamental Considerations in Testing for English Language Proficiency of Foreign Students." In Allen and Campbell (1972). Pp. 313-20.

Dixon, R. *Elementary Reader in English*. New York: Regents, 1950.

Harris, D. P. *Testing English as a Second Language*. New York: McGraw-Hill, 1969.

Jespersen, O. *How to Teach a Foreign Language*. London: Allen and Unwin, 1904. Reprinted in 1956.

Lado, R. *Language Testing*. New York: McGraw-Hill, 1961.

Oller, J. W., Jr. "Dictation as a Test of ESL Proficiency." In Allen and Campbell (1972). Pp. 346-54. *(a)*

———. "On the Relation Between Syntax, Semantics, and Pragmatics." In Makkai, A., et al (eds.). *Linguistics at the Crossroads: Proceedings of the 11th International Congress of Linguists, Bologna, Italy*. The Hague, Mouton, in press.

———. "Scoring Methods and Difficulty Levels for Cloze Tests of ESL Proficiency." *Modern Language Journal*, 56 (1972), 151-8. *(b)*

———. "Language Communication and Second Language Learning." Pimsleur and Quinn (1971). Pp. 171-79.

. "Assessing Competence in ESL: Reading." *TESOL Quarterly* 6 (1972), 313-24. *(c)*

Oller, J. and C. Conrad. "The Cloze Procedure and ESL Proficiency." *Language Learning*, 21 (1971), 183-96.

Pimsleur, P. and Quinn, T. (eds.). *The Psychology of Second Language Learning*. Cambridge, England: Cambridge University Press, 1971.

Praninskas, J. *Rapid Review of English Grammar*. Englewood Cliffs, N. J.: Prentice-Hall, 1959.

Taylor, W. L. "Cloze Procedure: a New Task for Measuring Readability." *Journalism Quarterly*, 33 (1953), 42-8.

Upshur, J. A. "Productive Communication Testing: Progress Report." G. Perren and J. L. M. Trim (eds.). *Applications of Linguistics*. Cambridge, England: Cambridge University Press, 1971. Pp. 435-42. Reprinted in this volume, pp. 175-183.

Valette, R. M. *Modern Language Testing: A Handbook*. New York: Harcourt, Brace, 1967.

CONTEXT FOR LANGUAGE TESTING*

John A. Upshur

While I was still trying to choose a title for this paper, I heard at a recent conference on second language teaching, a talk which began and ended with the same sentence, "Language like every other blessing derives its value from its use alone."[1] The theme of that paper was that we can never fully understand the nature of language until we consider its use; the fundamental fact of language is that it is a tool for communicating something to somebody. I am convinced that the same can be said of testing. We are here because we recognize the value of testing; we should also realize that a test like every other blessing derives its value from its use alone. We can never fully understand the nature of testing until we consider its use; the fundamental fact of testing is that it is a tool for communicating something to somebody. The context for language testing that I will discuss is the communication environment of teaching and learning a second language in an educational program.

An educational program can be viewed as an information processing system. There are certainly many ways of conceptualizing educational programs—or anything else. All these ways of analyzing are simplifications. An educational program is so complex that we can't think about it in all its rich detail without constantly losing sight of basic parts. Some kind of simplification is, therefore, necessary. I've decided to look at an educational program as an information processing system because I think this view will best allow us to focus upon the place of testing in education.

I should at this point make clear what I mean by an information processing system. By *system* I refer to a set of related or connected parts which form some kind of functional unity. We are accustomed to talking about languages as systems although some speak of form classes which occur in "slots" of sentence patterns, while others speak of "strings" related to other "strings" by "transformational rules."

The game of pocket billiards (or pool) can also be thought of as a system in which there are players, cue sticks, balls, and a table with

---

*This paper was made possible thanks to travel funds granted to the author by the University of Pittsburgh Bangkok Project.

[1]John W. Oller, Jr., "Linguistics and the Pragmatics of Communication," paper delivered to the TESOL annual convention, San Francisco, California, 1970.

pockets. One player strikes the cue ball with his cue stick setting it in motion. It strikes another ball which moves in a direction determined by the angle at which the cue ball strikes it. That ball may in turn strike still other balls to set them in motion. Pocket billiards can be seen, therefore, as a mechanical system in which the parts—the balls—affect one another by the forces they apply to each other. In an information processing system the parts interact by giving and getting information rather than mechanical force.

Last December my wife and I decided to leave the ice and snow of the Michigan winter for a two-week vacation on a tropical beach. En route we stopped for a few days in a city where I became quite suddenly aware of sensations all too common to travelers abroad. I said to my wife, "I don't feel very well. I think I've caught it." She went to the hotel lobby and explained the situation to the clerk who called a doctor from a nearby clinic. He came to my room within the hour, gave me an injection, some pills, and some reassuring words. By afternoon I felt fine and was on the plane headed for the beach.

I haven't recounted this episode to gain sympathy, but only to show how parts of a system can interact by giving and getting information. My wife's behavior depended upon the information she got from me. The clerk gave information to the doctor because he got information from my wife. Because communication in the system was good, the doctor arrived, I got well and enjoyed my vacation.

Let me now describe an educational program as an information processing system. I've chosen the flowchart as a means of representation because it is easy to follow visually, and it allows one to talk in more or less detail. It is especially well suited to discussion of systems; and as I hope to demonstrate, tests are necessary parts of dynamic information processing systems.

A flowchart has three figures: rectangles, diamonds, and trapezoids which are connected to one another by arrows. The rectangles contain statements about procedures to be followed; the diamonds contain questions and represent the need for making decisions; the trapezoids contain initial or final statements; and the arrows indicate the hierarchical or chronological relationships among the statements and questions.

Figure 1 shows a rather common and extremely simple educational program. In this sytem the student enters, we give him instruction, and he leaves. We don't even ask how much he has learned. At least, if we ask, it doesn't affect the way the system works.

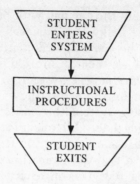

Figure 1. A Very Simple Educational Program

Figure 2 is a flowchart of an educational program in which one continues to provide instruction for a student until he meets the criteria for success in the program. That is, we continue to teach him until he learns.

The student enters the course; we instruct him (in English as a second language for example); then we test him according to the goals of the course; we next ask whether he has met our performance criteria; if he has, we graduate him; if not we send him back for further instruction and continue as the arrows indicate.

Before I go on, I want to make an observation. The program of Figure 2 includes a question, it requires someone to make a decision. Information is needed in order to make the decision, and a test is the means for communicating information about the student to the decision maker. In an educational program, or in any other system, tests will generally preceed any anticipated decision points.

The program of Figure 2 has two serious flaws in its design. We teach any student who comes to us regardless of whether he needs instruction or not, and we have no way of getting rid of him if he does not learn. Figure 3 shows a somewhat more sophisticated program in which we test to see whether a student is qualified, that is, whether he will learn, and we test him also in order to determine whether he already knows those things we are planning to teach him.

I'm quite sure that the three programs I've just described do exist somewhere, but I want to describe to you a language teaching program I know of, which includes rather extensive, formal testing procedures. It is located at a reputable American educational institution. I won't name the school, however, because it probably is not unique.

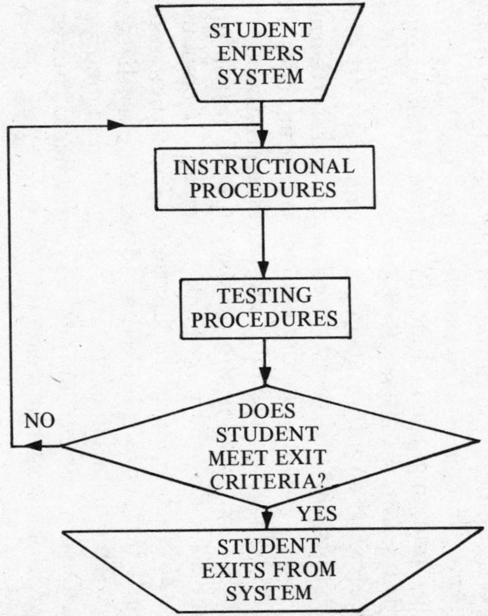

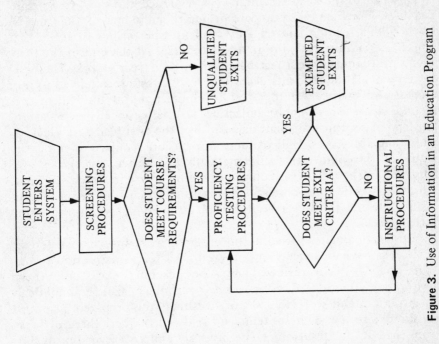

Figure 3. Use of Information in an Education Program

Figure 2. A Simple Educational System

This institution offers a three-year sequence in a modern foreign language. The first two years are primarily audio-lingual, the third is essentially a reading course. Any student who wishes to study the language is admitted to the first year course. At the end of the first year the students take a test based upon their year's work. The best 50 percent of the students according to this test are admitted to the second-year course. Another test is administered at the end of the second year. This highly objective test is designed to measure mastery of second year material, and like the first-year test yields a wide range of scores. Half of these students are required to end their study at this point; the students with the better test scores are admitted to the third-year course—a reading course in which students select the works in the foreign language that they wish to read. These highly selected third-year students all receive very good grades for this course.

The two major tests used in this program are soundly constructed. Each year's syllabus was first analyzed by a test construction team. This analysis was reviewed by the teaching staff and then appropriately modified. For each vocabulary list, grammatical construction, and so forth a set of five items was prepared. A group of teachers reviewed these items and selected the best three or four from each set for pretesting. The pre-test results were analyzed, and one item was taken from each set for the final test form. Selection of those items was made according to standard procedures in order to yield an instrument which would give the widest possible distribution of scores.

I have given only an outline of the considerable, painstaking effort that went into test construction for this language program, and perhaps one might conclude that here is an example of a highly effective testing program. If, however, we evaluate this program in the context of an information processing system, I think we will have to conclude that it is grossly inefficient, and, furthermore, it tends to inhibit good teaching in the course, and it impedes the development of a better language teaching and learning program.

First of all, what is the primary use of test information for the system? The flowchart in Figure 4 makes it obvious. The students enter the first course, are instructed, and then tested. Then each student's test score is looked at to see if he has been a high achiever or not. The high achievers are sent to the second year course. The low achievers are sent on their way elsewhere. The same procedure is followed for the second year.

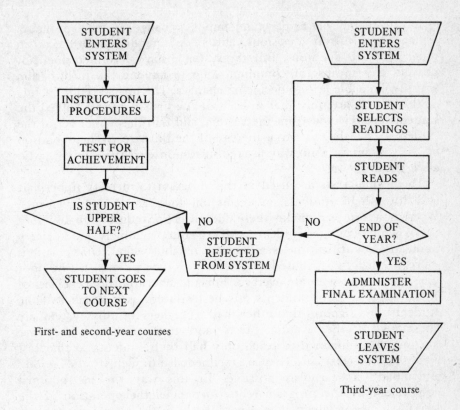

Figure 4. Use of Final Examination Information

The test procedure does give information about a student's attainment, but when we consider its *use* we note that the information is used only to determine a student's aptitude for further study. How much better it would have been to administer a foreign language aptitude test at the start of the course and not have students waste a year, or even two years, in the course before they are rejected. Perhaps it is not so bad to use a student's ability to learn in a first-year audio-lingual class to predict his ability to learn in a second-year audio-lingual class. Less defensible is using a measure of a student's ability in an audio-lingual course to determine his ability to *read* in a second language; yet this is the basis for selection of third year students in this program.

I made two other objections to the use of tests in this program; that they impede the development of a better program, and that they inhibit good teaching.

Improvement of a program implies change in the program. Changes result from decisions, and people require information in order to reach decisions. But the system I have described does not provide any means for communicating to anyone the information which will enable him to decide on changes. The formal requirements of the system are only that in each of the first two years half of the students are rejected from the system, and that the remainder of the students leave the system at the end of the third year. The operation of the system is in no way altered in response to the students who enter the program.

The formal tests are used in this program to identify upper-half and lower-half students in terms of their year's achievements. Whereas a test can make these identifications quite reliably in a group which contains students who are either genuinely good or very poor, the identification is much less reliable when achievement is more normally distributed: a few very good students, a few poor ones, and many who are average. For a teacher to produce a class of either good or poor students, his best strategy is to teach half the students and ignore the other half. Teachers in this system are conscious of the eventual tests and their use, and they are unconsciously inclined to teach only half their students so that test results will be clear cut. They are inclined also to identify the "good" and "bad" as early as possible. In this way the instructional component of the program tends to parallel the operation of the larger system of which it is a part. Early in the course the teacher performs the same function that the entire course will ultimately perform, that is, identifying the "good" and the "bad" and rejecting the latter. At this point, the "bad" are not formally removed from the program; the teacher just ignores them. Creative teaching is unnecessary since the goal of the program is already accomplished. Almost anything the teacher does will result in the "good" achieving more in the year than the "bad" do.

Here we have a double example of the self-fulfilling prophecy: the teacher's early judgements are confirmed by the final test results; and the program's designers are pleased to have confirmation of their hypothesis that only half the students in any year learn enough to continue. The system has been justified.

I have tried to show how a poor system can tend to produce poor teaching. But we know that good teaching does exist. Can this good teaching be used as a model for good systems, for good educational programs? I think that it can; and I think further that the way it can do so is by showing how and when to test.

Figure 5 is a generalized flowchart of a teaching-learning situation in which the teacher has already decided (or learned) what to teach and in which some kind of feedback from the teacher is necessary for learning. In essence, this system consists of two overlapping tests.

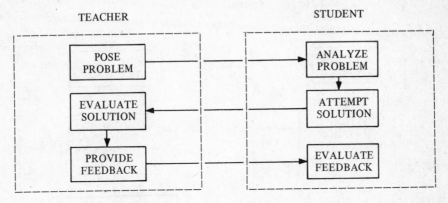

Figure 5. Teaching-Learning Model

The problem posed by the teacher may be as simple as, "Repeat after me: /hæt/." He listens to the student response; was it /hat/ or /hæt/?, and judges the student's ability to hear and produce a particular English vowel contrast. This is one test.

The student says /hæt/ or /hat/ in order to have the teacher say "OK," or "No, try it again." This is the other test. In the teaching-learning situation, the teacher uses test information in order to know what kind of feedback to provide. The student uses his test information in order to know whether his performance is acceptable, or whether it must be altered in some way.

This simple scheme brings into focus two related facts: the teacher knows what is "correct" or "appropriate," whereas the student does not yet know; the related fact is that the student is using test information to change his own behavior, but the teacher is not changing. In summary, the teaching-learning situation is one in which two people are testing each other in order that one of them can change; the one who changes we have termed "student."

I suggested earlier that good teaching does exist and that it can be taken as a model for educational and testing programs. But we know that good teachers are constantly learning and improving; the good teacher is most often characterized as creative. Learning, improving, creating, all imply change. Thus the good teacher is also a "student." This is illustrated in Figure 6. Here the student begins by posing the problem. His presence in class says, in effect, "Teach me." The teacher analyzes that instructional problem and attempts a solution. He then observes the student's response to his instruction. If it is not satisfactory he changes his analysis of the teaching problem or his attempted solution. He has become the student.

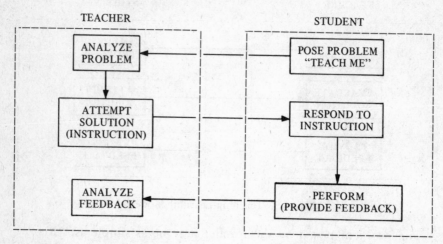

Figure 6. The Teacher as Student

The good teacher model is, therefore, a *dynamic* information processing system in which each participant tests the other in order that the teacher may learn what and how to teach, and the student may learn that which is being taught. In Figure 7 I've attempted to indicate some of the dynamics of the system.

When he begins, the teacher's first task is to select what is to be learned (1) and present an appropriate task for the student (2). The student then attempts to analyze the problem in order to determine what is required of him (3) and then to devise a way of doing it (4). If he fails to understand the problem or to see a possible solution, he may inform the teacher who will then produce a more appropriate task (2 again). If the student is able to understand the problem and generate a solution, he produces some behavior (5) which the teacher can observe and compare with a criterion for adequate performance (6). If the student's performance is satisfactory, the teacher lets him know. The student accepts this as confirmation of his solution; he adopts the hypothesis by which he derived the solution. If, however, his performance is not satisfactory the teacher must try to decide what went wrong (7). He may decide to select a simpler problem to

TEACHER   STUDENT

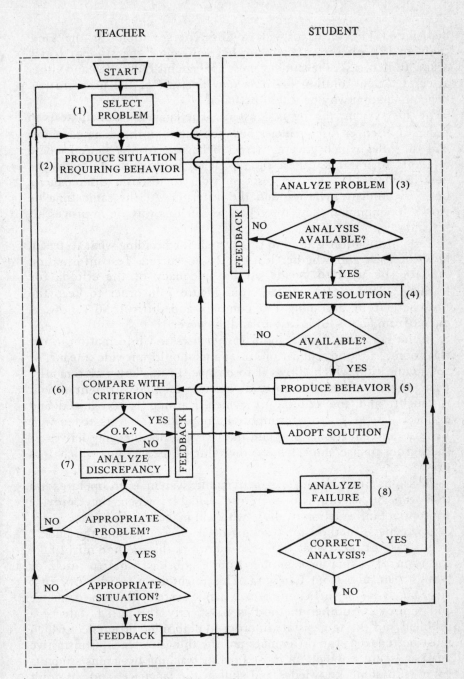

Figure 7. Dynamic Teaching-Learning (Testing) System

be learned (1), or to provide a different situation for the same problem (2); on the other hand, he may signal the student to try again. In that case, the student must analyze his failure (8) and either attempt a new solution (4) or a new analysis of the problem (3), depending upon why he thinks he failed.

In this system, testing is constant. The language student tests in order to discover discrepancies between the hypotheses he generates and the rules which govern correct behavior. At the same time he attempts to minimize these discrepancies. In this way he learns the new language. The teacher tests in order to discover discrepancies between student behavior and the criterion. At the same time he works to minimize these discrepancies. In this way he improves his teaching.

Test information is used in this system for deciding what to teach, how to teach and whether learning has occurred. Test information can also be used to decide on the adequacy of the criteria for learning. (This use is omitted from Figure 7 in order to keep the flowchart from becoming too complex and difficult to follow. A circuit from (7) to (6) is easy to add, however.)

In the same way that a good teacher uses test information in the classroom, a good education program should provide means of communication which allows it to change. In this larger system also, tests provide information to guide changes in what is taught, how it is taught, and the criteria by which learning is recognized and defined. There is another important question for tests to answer. Because an educational program like every other blessing derives its value from its use alone, what is the value of the learning which does occur?

Decisions must be made if a dynamic system is to operate, and tests can be useful, and therefore valuable, when they provide appropriate information to those who will make the decisions.

One general method for reaching decisions is "passing the buck." In the case of the "what to teach" question, this method might take the form of asking an examiner from Cambridge what to teach, or asking a linguist from Canberra. This might be a satisfactory first step, but it is not sufficient for a dynamic system which is to change and improve. Another method is to specify the initial state of a problem and the target state in order to determine differences which must be reduced; the differences are the things to teach. Contrastive analysis is not enough. In most English teaching programs students enter with some knowledge and skill in the language, and we don't want to waste time and effort teaching things that students already know. A test can tell us what these things are. A test can tell us also what the students want to know. We are never able to teach our students much that they don't wish to learn. The test itself can be quite simple: ask the students what they want—and ask again next week and the week after, because just as their knowledge can change, so can their aspirations. There is another test which will help us decide what to teach. In a program which is constrained by time, we cannot expect to teach everything, but we *can* expect to teach more to some students than to others. A language aptitude test can help us to decide what to teach to whom.

I should mention one test which is *not* taken by the students. We noted earlier that the teacher is defined as the one who knows what the student is to learn. Deciding on what to teach must depend upon what the teacher knows. Testing the teacher can give this information. I realize that I am offering an unpopular suggestion; but remember that we are considering dynamic systems. Teachers also change. They can learn things which can then be included among those things that their students are to learn.

Let me offer a suggestion also for answering the question of how to teach. A useful method is to decide on techniques or operations which have proved effective in "similar" situations in the past. How do we know when techniques are successful? Tests give us measures of success. But how do we decide when situations are "similar"? There is certainly similarity between two situations in which students are comparable with respect to what they already know, what they want to learn, and their aptitudes for learning; and we have already seen that testing can give us that information.

Tests can also give us information about reasonable criteria of learning. Statements about what to teach are often made in linguistic terms: for example, comprehension of questions of the form, "Isn't it in Bangkok that we're meeting?" A reply of "yes" can be interpreted as an indication of comprehension, but this reply is not adequate. If we are to conclude that the student has indeed learned, how much time do we give him to think, to decode, or to translate? Should he respond in five seconds? Three? One? Many battles have been waged over questions like this, but I wish to talk only about the use of tests in establishing criteria of learning.

In this example of comprehension teaching, a teacher may first accept from a student a reply of "yes" at any time after the question was posed. He can then adopt as a criterion of learning that the student respond more quickly than before. Accordingly, so long as the student increases his speed, learning is occurring. When the student's performance stabilizes, the teacher concludes that a criterion of greater speed would not be reasonable for the student, given the techniques and materials available. At that point he goes on to teach something else.

Before continuing I want to make clear what a criterion is. First of all, it is not the same thing as a program goal. It is only a standard to which test behavior can be compared. When behavior will be judged as either "satisfactory" or "unsatisfactory" the criterion which will yield the most test information is the one which will be satisfactorily met about half of the time.

Just as tests can be used in the classroom to recognize a student's increasing ability to understand English, tests can be used to recognize an educational program's increasing capacity to teach English. Tests to determine what the program is able to teach at any point in time establish reasonable criteria for evaluating in-service teacher training, the addition of language laboratories, changes in instructional techniques, or almost any other change which can be made in the program.

When we have decided what to teach, how to teach, and what the criteria of learning are, there are no problems in discovering when learning has occurred. A test to provide this information has been completely specified.

There is one more general method for making decisions that I will discuss. This is called "planning." In planning, a simplified description of a complex problem is constructed, and means are devised for solving that simplified problem. One hopes that its solution will result in the solution of the complex problem. The complex problem which English teaching programs attempt to solve is producing students who can communicate with English speakers by means of the English language. This complex problem is often simplified to teaching a knowledge of English. We have what is known as a linguistically oriented program when "knowledge of English" is characterized as the ability to decode and construct sentences which conform to the rules of English grammar as set forth by linguists.

It is certainly possible to solve simple problems while complex problems remain. Tests of achievement in our courses and of proficiency in communication can show us how valuable our programs are. When we find that students who attain more in the program do not become correspondingly better communicators, we must be prepared to revise our plans.

I've been talking about language testing and change. The context I chose is the system which includes within itself the capacity to grow and improve. Tests have value in this system because of their use; in a dynamic educational program we can do more for our students tomorrow than we were able to do today.

CROSS-CULTURAL BIASES IN LANGUAGE TESTING

Eugène Brière

Throughout the United States, as well as in many other countries in the world, various standardized tests have been developed to permit test users to make important inferences concerning the populations being tested. This paper will restrict the discussion to those standardized instruments used by schools and, furthermore, limit the discussion of the inferences made about the students to two basic types—linguistic and/or instrumental inferences.

The main purpose of this paper is to show that a majority of these standardized tests contain either linguistically biased or socioculturally biased factors which invalidate *any* linguistic or instrumental inference made about many of the populations being tested. More specifically, it is my contention that: (*a*), linguistic and sociocultural testing factors are frequently inseparable (Ervin-Tripp, 1964; Gumperz, 1970; Ulibarri, 1972); therefore, the contamination of one set affects the other; and (*b*), most standardized tests are culturally biased for any group which does not come from the same sociocultural background as that of the group used as the basis for standardizing the test, i.e., the *modal* group (Arvizo, 1972; Mercer, 1971*b*, 1972; Ulibarri, 1972).

In the United States, the modal group most frequently used consists of middle-class, white, native speakers of English. This very factor obviously represents a cultural bias for any group which does not come from a middle-class, Anglo background. The groups most criminally affected by these cultural biases are the American Indians living on reservations, the ghetto-dwelling Blacks and speakers of Spanish. The ghetto-dwelling Spanish speakers consist of two basic groups—Mexican-Americans and Chicanos. For the purpose of this paper, Mexican-Americans are defined as immigrants from Mexico, the majority of whom are primarily monolingual speakers of Spanish. The Chicano is a person born in the United States whose language dominance may range from monolingual Spanish, through bilingual Spanish and English to monolingual English. Soberanis (1971) describes the Chicano as a person who "Has become aware of his cultural heritage and the beauty and sophistication of being bilingual and bicultural." "Chicano" was once considered a pejorative term but is now used with pride by the group. Although the

Mexican-American and Chicano groups differ in some respects, there are enough similarities of cultural and linguistic heritage, along with the similarities of problems confronted by both groups when taking standardized tests in school, to make me feel justified in referring to both groups in this paper as Chicanos.

In order to explain my previous statement that American Indians, Blacks, and Chicanos are the groups "most *criminally* affected by the cultural biases" of standardized tests, I should first define what I mean by *linguistic* as opposed to *instrumental inferences*.

Quite simply, *linguistic inferences* involves decisions concerning a person's language ability. One kind of linguistic inference that is frequently made involves a measure of an aspect of a student's language proficiency, i.e., linguistic competence, in a specific target language which is not native to the student. TOEFL is an excellent example of a standardized test specifically designed to measure proficiency in English for nonnative speakers. TOEFL contains multiple-choice sections intended to measure a student's knowledge of English structure, his vocabulary, and reading, writing, and listening abilities. On the basis of these tests, inferences are made about the level of a student's proficiency in English (including, by implication, his proficiency in oral production which is *not* tested) by comparing the student's scores to a set of "norms" established with other groups.

Another type of *linguistic inference* which is frequently made concerns the verbal ability of a student, presumably in his native language. This type of inference is frequently made on the basis of scores received on subtests in larger test batteries specifically designed to measure things other than verbal or language ability *per se*. For example, a most common occurrence in public schools in the United States is to make linguistic inferences based on the verbal ability sections of such tests as the CAT, the CTMM or the Stanford-Binet which were designed to measure total scholastic achievement, general knowledge, and mental maturity and I.Q. respectively. Obviously, since the tests were not designed to measure specific language abilities, I feel the validity of language inferences made on the basis of subsections of such tests are extremely questionable.

Instrumental inference, perhaps not the happiest choice of terminology, I define as the kinds of decisions made on the basis of a student's scores on a standardized test which affect his grade placement in school, the kind of curriculum to which he will be exposed, and, frequently, the role he will be expected to fulfill in the dominant culture. In short, I feel that instrumental inferences, or decisions concerning the student, are school and societal decisions.

As I stated above, the linguistic and cultural factors in tests are essentially inseparable. Consequently, linguistic inferences are frequently made on the basis of cultural data and instrumental inferences are made on the basis of linguistic data. When the cultural and linguistic data are accurate, reliable, and reasonable for the *particular* student being tested, we will probably not err too greatly in making linguistic or instrumental inferences or both. Unfortunately, this is rarely the case in standardized testing situations. The following chart is an attempt to synthesize the different kinds of testing situations we most frequently encounter.

QUALITY OF TEST FACTORS

		Linguistic Factors	Sociocultural Factors
	I.	+	+
	II.	+	-
	III.	-	+
	IV.	-	-

QUALITY OF INFERENCES

In this chart it is assumed that linguistic and instrumental inferences can be made from essentially the same data. The two basic factors of standardized tests mentioned previously are linguistic and sociocultural and may be present in directions and items as well as in testing techniques and procedures. The quality of the factors is shown by the pluses and minuses in the cells. A plus (+) in a cell indicates that the factor in the test labeled at the head of the column is ideal for the particular student or group being tested. A minus (-) in a cell indicates that the testing factors are contaminated, unrealistic, or totally inappropriate for the particular student or group being tested.

The quality of the linguistic or instrumental inferences can be determined by reading across the rows. Any combination which includes a minus (-) detrimentally affects the quality of the inference made. In short, a minus in any cell indicates that the test is culturally or linguistically biased, or both. Consequently *any* inference made about a student on the basis of such an instrument is invalid.

Roman numeral I represents that extremely rare occasion in which a standardized test contains no linguistic or sociocultural bias for the particular student being tested. For most standardized tests in the United States, the student would have to be a native speaker of standard English, come from a middle-class (preferably White) home and have shared the sociocultural experiences of the modal group. The language of the test itself, and that used by the test administrator, would be appropriate for the student's maturational level (Kennedy, 1970) and would not involve any instructions which would exceed the short-term memory of the student (Jones, 1970).

In spite of the inherent difficulties (see the discussion by Mercer, 1970) involved in achieving valid linguistic and cultural factors both at once, the linguistic and/or instrumental inferences made on the basis of scores from such tests should be fairly accurate. Unfortunately, this is the only condition which would permit decisions to be made with any degree of confidence. All other possible combinations of linguistic and sociocultural factors involve biases.

Roman numeral II is a fairly frequent situation encountered by speakers of standard English who come from cultural backgrounds different from those of the modal group. It is interesting to note that not only ethnic minority groups are involved in this situation but also lower-middle-class Whites. In other words, the language used in the directions and items on the test *may* be understood perfectly well by the students taking the tests, but a cultural bias may be contained in specific items in the test, or in the testing procedures, or both. The poverty-stricken White from many parts of the country, many American Indians, Blacks, and Chicanos may well understand the standard English used in the test from the standpoint of linguistic competence but be completely unable to determine what the "best" answer to a question is if the item or procedures are completely foreign to their individual cultures. Perhaps a few examples will help clarify the situations which occur under the conditions of Roman numeral II.

A typical example of a linguistically acceptable but culturally biased item is one which appears on the frequently used CTMM (California Test of Mental Maturity) in order to make both linguistic and instrumental inferences. The stem states, "Bananas are _____ ," and the choices are, "(a) brown, (b) green, and (c) yellow." "Yellow" is considered the only correct answer. But why is this the only correct answer? For the Chicano, living in a Mexican culture at home, the use of green bananas for cooking is more prevalent than yellow bananas. For the American Indian on the reservation, or for the Black in the ghetto, brown bananas may be the most prevalent. It is a well-known fact that the remote trading posts on the reservation and the corner grocery stores in the ghetto do not have the facilities for keeping fruit and vegetables in the condition that middle-class Whites consider optimal. Consequently, my guess is that "brown" would be an excellent choice for American Indians or urban Blacks.

Whereas the first example is factually *wrong* for some cultures, the following examples are factually *correct* but culturally irrelevant for many groups. Two kinds of culturally irrelevant items are found in vocabulary and usage sections of many standardized tests. An example of such a vocabulary item in one form of the MAT (Metropolitan Achievement Test) is the word "escutcheon" used as a stem with five choices given to define it. Even if a child happens to get the right answer, and most will not, of what possible use is this word to minority groups in the United States? It is a "school" word never used in the ghettos, the reservations, or the shanty towns. The way in which this makes no sense to many minority group members is dramatized by the Dove "Chitlin' Test of Intelligence." This test is written in Black English Vernacular (BEV) and is designed to dramatize the cultural irrelevance of BEV vocabulary to middle-class Whites. Most Black ghetto dwellers would have no difficulty with an item such as: "A gas head is a person who has a _____ . (a) staple of lace; (b) fast car; (c) process; (d) stealing habit; (e) drug habit." They would know that the answer is (c), "process" (i.e., an abbreviation for a hair-straightening process). Few Anglos, by contrast, would know the answer because we simply do not know enough about Black ghetto culture.

Examples of culturally biased "usage" items found in so many standardized tests are contained in the CAT (California Achievement Tests). In these types of items "correct" answers involve making the "proper" distinctions between "who" and "whom", "can" and "may", and "lie" and "lay". In short, these items measure distinctions which are rarely made by anyone in spoken speech and are only used by "old-lady-school-teachers," primarily in writing.

Pursuing the "old-lady-school-teacher" syndrome (a term I owe to Labov, 1970), I would like to give an example of a culturally biased item which depends on a moral judgement that matches the morality of the modal group. Such an item in the general intelligence section of WISC (Wechsler Intelligence Scale for Children) is "Why is it better to give money to a charity than to a beggar?" To receive full credit the child's response must contain two of the following ideas: charities are in a better position to investigate the merits of the case; giving to a charity is a more orderly way of making a contribution, etc. He receives no points at all if he says "a beggar is liable to keep it himself," or "charity takes care of beggars." What is wrong with those answers? They are only "wrong" by Anglo, middle-class standards (i.e., according to people who deduct charitable contributions from their income taxes).

Culturally biased items are obviously important in that they increase the difficulty of basing any kind of valid inference on tests that contain them. What is even *more* frightening to me are the culturally biased testing procedures.

The procedures of the Wepman Auditory Discrimination Test seem to be appropriate for most groups, but as a part Mohawk Indian, I have been trained never to trust a stranger behind my back in a small room. This sort of thing is frequently true of American Indians, Blacks, and Chicanos. Since the test administrator (tall, big, authoritative, and threatening) stands *behind* the children during the test (presumably to avoid lip cues), I wonder how valid the results are with groups who have been culturally trained *not* to allow a threatening figure to get behind them?

According to Kluckhohn (1962), religiously "the Navajo fears final completion so that a 'spirit outlet' must always be left in the design." Obviously, for any Navajo child who has been trained in this religious concept, the techniques used in the Goodenough Draw a Man (or Drawing Competition Test) would be completely invalid from the standpoint of making any inferences about his I.Q.

Chicanos and Navajos are trained to lower their eyes in the presence of authority as a sign of respect. Blacks are trained at a very early age that the less one says to "the man" (meaning any White man) the less trouble he will get into. What then is the possible reason for a test administrator asking innumerable questions with obvious answers and insisting that the child "look at him while he talks"? (For fuller discussions of culturally biased testing procedures used with minority groups, see the following: for American Indians, Brière, 1968 and 1969; for Blacks, see Labov, 1970 and 1971; and for Chicanos, see Ramirez, 1972.)

We have spent a great deal of time on Roman numeral II (+ language, − cultural) because it is so prevalent, subtle, and deadly. It is deadly because many of the instrumental inferences made about minority children based on such tests are erroneous and cause irreparable harm to the child. It is astounding to many of us who have worked on the reservations and in the ghettos that such people as Bereiter and Engleman (1966), Deutsch, Katz, and Jensen (1968) and Hernnstein (1971) have failed to understand (or even detect in any sense) the cultural biases involved in the very instruments which they use to label Blacks as linguistically and culturally deprived or deficient, and as having low I.Q.'s due to hereditary factors. Since their pseudoscientific methods add an air of credibility to their claims,they are still influencing a great number of our teachers at home—to the obvious detriment of the children.

Roman numeral III involves a situation in which the cultural factors in the test are appropriate for the population but the language is not. The language of the instructions and items that are used by the test administrator, could be inappropriate for the student's maturational level (Kennedy, 1970). The language can be biased by difficult or unusual syntax, unusual lexical items, ambiguous statements, or interference in the form of excess verbiage that adds nothing to the understanding of the task. In short, not only may the language be linguistically inappropriate for the particular maturational level, but it may also add unnecessarily to the short-term memory load of the student (Jones, 1970). Jones and Kennedy (1970) have written excellent reports concerning the language of tests and have spelled out some of the difficulties in achieving appropriate directions from the standpoint of linguistic factors as well as psychological appropriateness in terms of short-term memory load. They cite many examples of some of our "best" standardized tests in the United States as having failed in this category. This type of situation could also affect speakers of BEV who are aware and comfortable with the cultural content of the test but speak a dialect that is completely different from the test language. I have never seen a test which is minus-linguistic, plus-culture that has anything remotely to do with American Indians and Chicanos. Once again, as soon as a minus appears, all confidence in any type of inference is removed. If a child cannot understand the directions or the items, no matter how culturally appropriate the test is, he will not be able to "play the game." Consequently, his scores should be treated as having occurred at chance levels.

Roman numeral IV represents the tests which should be **burned** rather than administered. They affect adversely everyone taking them. For the Spanish-speaking Chicano, the Black who speaks BEV, and the American Indian who speaks his ancestral language, almost *any* standardized test used in school falls into this category. Clearly, any decisions made in the minus-language, minus-culture situation are invalid. Yet many American Indians, Chicanos, and Blacks are placed in mentally retarded (MR) classes on the basis of the results of such tests (Mercer, 1971*a*). At this point the self-fulfilling prophecy takes over. The bright child who has been erroneously labeled MR, resents it and soon drops out of school to fulfill the role he has been placed in by a criminal misuse of invalid tests.

The Black psychologists of the American Psychological Association realize that Roman numeral I (plus-language, plus-culture) never exists for Black groups, and they have called for a moratorium on testing. Chicanos are beginning to voice their long-felt concern about the inappropriateness of our current testing procedures, and they too are calling for a moratorium on testing. American Indian tribal council members, parents, and members of the Bureau of Indian Affairs (BIA) are beginning to make the same demands. The need for new tests relevant to minority groups is painfully obvious.

One of the most difficult problems in achieving sociocultural appropriateness for any group is the all too frequent assumption made by many educators and test designers that groups are monolithic in structure (or that they ought to be). This produces the kinds of norming procedures in testing, and curriculum development by educators, that depend upon samplings from the dominant socioeconomic class of any group or, in the more unfortunate cases, simply rely on the stereotypes of certain groups. Nothing could be more misleading. Middle-class Whites do not represent the same sociocultural values held by Whites at a lower place on the socioeconomic scale. All American Indians, Blacks, or Chicanos are not the same, yet, in spite of a great deal of publication concerning the dangers of treating a particular group as monolithic in structure, the differences are frequently ignored (Arvizu, 1972; Carter, 1970; and Palomares, 1972). The recent work of Jane Mercer in the United States is an interesting and refreshing departure from the "monolithic-structure" assumption.

Mercer (1971*b*, and 1972) asserts that I.Q. tests are Anglocentric and are consequently biased for non-Anglo groups. She identified many of the sociocultural characteristics of the modal group and then chose eighteen of them as a basis for studying Black and Chicano groups. The eighteen sociocultural characteristics were dichotomized so that one category corresponded to the modal sociocultural configuration of the community, and the other category was nonmodal. I.Q. was used as the dependent variable, and the sociocultural characteristics were the independent variables. The multiple correlation coefficient was significant at the .001 level. Twenty-five percent of the variance in I.Q.'s could be accounted for by sociocultural differences of Black and Chicano groups combined.

When she separated the Chicano groups from the Black groups she was able to determine, through a stepwise multiple regression, five of the most significant social characteristics as predictors for each group. For the Chicanos, the most important characteristics were: (1) occupation of head of household; (2) whether head of household was reared in an urban environment in the United States; (3) size of family; (4) buying own home; (5) English spoken at home.

For Blacks, the five best indicators were: (1) having a mother reared in the North; (2) occupation of head of household; (3) male head of household; (4) living in an intact family; and (5) buying own home.

Thus she found that the more the family was like the modal social configuration of the community, the higher the I.Q.'s of the Black and Chicano children. The fewer sociocultural characteristics of the modal group existing in minority groups, the lower the I.Q. scores received by the children. A glance at the extremely informative figures furnished by Mercer (1971b) helps to dramatize the problem.

Although the testing situations I have described are bleak and somewhat frightening there are some reasonable answers. The first thing which *must* be done is to isolate and describe the sociocultural characteristics of each group, realizing that no group is monolithic in structure. Second for the time being, we could use Mercer's pluralistic, sociocultural perspective to evaluate each child in terms of two frameworks simultaneously—the standardized norms for the test and the norms for the sociocultural group to which he belongs. The first would be a prediction of performance in school as it is now structured, and the second would give a more realistic assessment of the child's potential for learning. Third, we can admit the sociocultural differences which exist and start working on new curricula in schools which are relevant to each of the various groups. Fourth, new tests can be developed which take into account all of the factors in steps one through three.

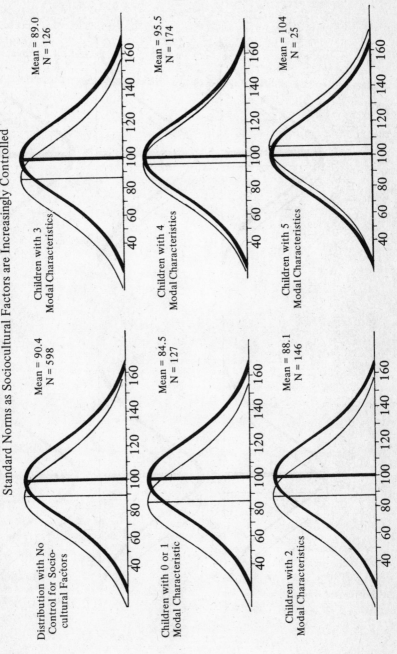

Figure 1

Convergence of the Average I.Q. Test Scores of Chicano Children with the Standard Norms as Sociocultural Factors are Increasingly Controlled

Distribution with No Control for Socio-cultural Factors

Mean = 90.4
N = 598

Children with 0 or 1 Modal Characteristic

Mean = 84.5
N = 127

Children with 2 Modal Characteristics

Mean = 88.1
N = 146

Children with 3 Modal Characteristics

Mean = 89.0
N = 126

Children with 4 Modal Characteristics

Mean = 95.5
N = 174

Children with 5 Modal Characteristics

Mean = 104
N = 25

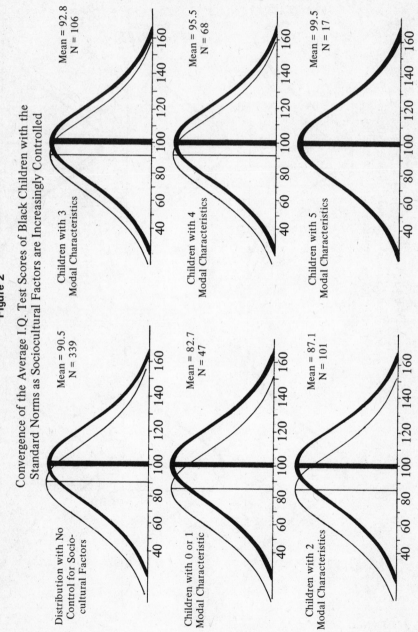

Figure 2

Convergence of the Average I.Q. Test Scores of Black Children with the Standard Norms as Sociocultural Factors are Increasingly Controlled

Distribution with No Control for Socio-cultural Factors — Mean = 90.5, N = 339

Children with 0 or 1 Modal Characteristic — Mean = 82.7, N = 47

Children with 2 Modal Characteristics — Mean = 87.1, N = 101

Children with 3 Modal Characteristics — Mean = 92.8, N = 106

Children with 4 Modal Characteristics — Mean = 95.5, N = 68

Children with 5 Modal Characteristics — Mean = 99.5, N = 17

Right now, the important thing is to stop talking and start doing. We simply cannot allow the mislabeling of children to continue through the use of linguistically and culturally biased standardized tests.

In spite of the urgent need for "doing," one final word of caution *must* be given. Some people who have become aware of the linguistic biases in testing have decided to do something about it by translating existing standardized tests into other languages. For example, there is some work going on in California to translate the Stanford-Binet into Chinese and Spanish. I find this kind of attempt at solving a serious problem naively useless.

In the first place, everyone should know that certain words connoting specific concepts in one culture have no direct translation equivalent in the language of another culture. If an item has to be paraphrased in another language, the statistical analyses of the item are then clearly invalid since it is a different item to be used with a different group. Secondly, all of the cultural biases of one test are translated into another instrument which is then even more invalid than the first.

Translation of existing standardized tests into other languages is, to me, one of the most foolish practices occurring today and should be stopped completely, since the end result places the minority-group child at the mercy of an instrument which is minus-linguistic and minus-cultural.

REFERENCES

Arvizo, S. F. "Anthropological Implications in the Education of the Mexican American." Mazon (1972).

Baratz, J. C. "Teaching Reading in an Urban Negro School System." *Language and Poverty*, F. Williams (ed.). Chicago: Markham, 1970.

Bereiter, C. and S. Engelmann, *Teaching Disadvantaged Children in the Preschool*, Englewood Cliffs, N.J.: Prentice-Hall, 1966.

Brière, E. J. "Teaching ESL among Navajo Children." *Problems in Foreign Language Testing.* J. A. Upshur (ed.). *Language Learning*, Special Issue No. 3, 1968.

―――. "Testing ESL Skills among American Indian Children." *Monograph Series on Languages and Linguistics*, J. E. Alatis (ed.). Washington D.C.: Georgetown University Press, 1970.

―――. "Are We Really Measuring Proficiency with Our Foreign Language Tests?" *Foreign Language Annals*, May, 1971.

Buros, O. K. *Tests in Print*, Highland Park, N.J.: The Gryphon Press, 1961.
———. (ed.). *The Sixth Mental Measurements Yearbook*, Highland Park, N.J.: The Gryphon Press, 1965.
Carter, T. P. *Mexican Americans in School: A History of Educational Neglect*, New York College Entrance Examination Board, 1970.
Deutsch, M. and associates. *The Disadvantaged Child*, New York: Basic Books, 1967.
Deutsch, M., I. Katz, and A. R. Jensen (eds.), *Social Class, Race, and Psychological Development*, New York: Holt, Rinehart & Winston, 1968.
Di Stefano, J. J. "Interpersonal Perceptions of Field Independent and Dependent Teachers and Students." *Working Paper Series*, No. 43, London, Canada: University of Western Ontario, Nov., 1970.
Ervin-Tripp, S. "An Analysis of the Intersection of Language, Topic and Listener." *American Anthropologist*, 66 (1964), 86-102.
Kagan, S. and M. C. Madsen, "Mexican American and Anglo American Children of Two Different Ages under Four Institutional Sets." *Developmental Psychology*, 1971.
Gumperz, J. "Lectures on Social and Linguistic Interaction in the Classroom." Unpublished. Berkeley: University of California, Fall, 1970.
Hernnstein, R. J. "I.Q." *Atlantic Monthly*, Sept., 1971.
Jones, M. H. *The Unintentional Mental Load in Tests for Young Children*. Los Angeles, California: Center for the Study of Evaluation, UCLA Graduate School of Education, CSE Report No. 57, May, 1970.
Kennedy, G. D. *The Language of Tests for Young Children*. Los Angeles, California: Center for the Study of Evaluation, UCLA Graduate School of Education, CSE Working Paper No. 7, Feb., 1970.
Kluckhohn, C., and D. Leighton. *The Navajo*. Garden City, N.Y.: Doubleday (in cooperation with the American Museum of Natural History), revised, 1962.
Labov, W. *et al. The Study of Non-Standard English*. Washington, D.C.: U.S. Office of Education, 1969.
———. *Systematically Misleading Data from Test Questions*. Transcript of the Colloquium sponsored by the University of Michigan: School of Social Work and Department of Linguistics, April 1, 1970.
———. "Academic Ignorance and Black Intelligence." *Atlantic Monthly*, June, 1972.
Mazon, M. R. (ed). *Adelante: An Emerging Design for Mexican American Education*. Austin, Texas: Center for Communication Research, The University of Texas at Austin, 1972.
Mercer, J. R. "Sociological Perspectives on Mild Mental Retardation." *Social-Cultural Aspects of Mental Retardation: Proceedings of the Peabody-NIMH Conference*. New York: Appleton-Century-Crofts, 1970.
———. "Sociocultural Factors in Labeling Mental Retardates." *Peabody Journal of Education*, 48, No. 3, April, 1971 (*a*).
———. "Pluralistic Diagnosis in the Evaluation of Black and Chicano Children: A Procedure for Taking Sociocultural Variables into Account in Clinical

Assessment." Report presented at the Meetings of the American Psychological Association, Washington, D.C., 1971(*b*).

———. "Sociocultural Factors in the Educational Evaluation of Black and Chicano Children." Report presented at the 10th Annual Conference on Civil and Human Rights of Educators and Students, Washington, D.C., National Education Association, 1972.

Natalicio, D. S. and F. Williams. "What Characteristics Can 'Experts' Reliably Evaluate in the Speech of Black and Mexican American Children?" *TESOL Quarterly*, 6, No. 2 (1972), 121-7.

Palomares, U. "The Psychology of the Mexican American." Mazon (1972).

Peal, E., and W. E. Lambert. "The Relation of Bilingualism to Intelligence." American Psychological Association, Washington, D.C., 1962.

Ramirez, M. "Current Educational Research: The Basis for a New Philosophy for Educating Mexican Americans." Mazon (1972).

Soberanis, M. "On the Chicano." Unpublished article. Sacramento State College, Sept., 1971.

Ulibarri, M.-L. "Toward a Philosophy of Education for the Chicano: Bilingualism and Intellectual Development." Mazon (1972).

TESTS CITED

Auditory Discrimination Test. Joseph M. Wepman; Language Research Associates. Chicago, Ill., 1951, 1956.

California Achievement Tests (CAT). Ernest W. Tiegs, Willis W. Clark; California Test Bureau. Monterey, California, 1957, 1964.

California Test of Mental Maturities (CTMM).

Culture Fair Intelligence Test, Raymond B. Cattell, A. K. S. Cattell; Institute for Personality and Ability Testing. Champaign, Ill. 1933, 1963.

Dove Counterbalance Intelligence "Chitling" Test. Adrian Dove; Mimeographed. Los Angeles, California, no date.

Drawing Completion Test. G. Marianne Kinget; Grune & Stratton, Inc. New York, 1952.

Goodenough Draw A Man Test (also titled Goodenough Intelligence Test). Florence L. Goodenough;New York: Harcourt, Brace, World, 1926. (1963 Revision entitled "Goodenough-Harris Drawing Test," F. L. Goodenough, D. B. Harris; New York: Harcourt, Brace, World, 1963).

Metropolitan Achievement Test. Walter N. Durost, *et al.*; New York: Harcourt, Brace, World, 1964.

Stanford-Binet Intelligence Scale, S. Pinneau, L. M. Terman, M. A. Merrill; Boston, Mass.: Houghton Mifflin Co., 1916, 1960.

Test of English as a Foreign Language (TOEFL). David Harris, Leslie Palmer; Educational Testing Service. Princeton, N. J.

Wechsler Intelligence Scale for Children (WISC). David Wechsler; Psychological Corporation. New York, 1949.

PART IV: DISCUSSION QUESTIONS

1. Compare the testing technique of sampling knowledge of a few of the items in a list by virtue of a discrete-point test with the technique of measuring a range of creative skills on an integrative test. Can a statistical model apply to both? Are the tasks set the learner similar?

2. "What does it mean when we say that someone knows a language" (Spolsky, p. 164)? Does the distinction between competence and performance help in answering this question? How does one distinguish between the knowledge of physics and the ability to understand a lecture on physics? Can the competence-performance distinction help here? Can linguistic competence be separated distinctly from other types of competence as is implied in the quote on pp. 173-74?

3. What are the applications to teaching of the observation that students should be tested with novel utterances (Spolsky, p. 173)?

4. Upshur suggests that correlations between proficiency tests of the discrete-point type and "academic grade averages are low or nil" (p. 178). Does this necessarily imply that the tests used are deficient? In what ways? Consider the case of a student majoring in engineering as compared with a political science major.

5. If as Spolsky states, "we can find out about 'knowledge of a language' . . . equally well when we test passive and active skills" (p. 174), should Upshur be concerned at all with "productive communication testing" (p. 179)? What experimental results might justify using a test of so-called passive skills as a basis for estimating active abilities? Recall the remark by Stern (p. 17) that *all* language skills are active.

6. It is reported by Upshur that for nonnative speakers individual differences in ability to communicate seemed to appear only "as progressively more severe time constraints were imposed" (p. 181). This seems to indicate that limitations on memory and speed of processing verbal information are an aspect of communicative competence (that is, the underlying capacity rather than the act of performance itself). However, Chomsky and Halle (as cited by Spolsky, p. 173-74) relegate memory factors to performance. Is the "knowledge of a language," equated by Spolsky to "underlying linguistic competence" (p. 174), therefore less than the ability to use language for communicative purposes?

7. Examine the testing techniques used in several language programs. Is the emphasis on discrete-point test items or integrative skills? Are there items which seem to fit both categories?

8. Suggest tests of integrative skills other than those discussed by Oller. Or consider variations in the mode of presentation. Similarly, for discrete-point items.

9. By the definitions on p. 185, can a test be reliable without being valid? Valid without being reliable? More importantly, can a test be valid and reliable without being a "good" test according to the "axiom" proposed by Oller (p. 185)? Do you agree or disagree with the "axiom"? Under what circumstances might a teacher be forced to use a test not "focusing attention on and giving practice in useful language skills"?

10. Try giving the same dictation to one or more classes of second language students. Examine the errors and attempt to identify those that can be attributed to intralanguage confusions versus those that can be accounted for by interlanguage interference. What other sorts of errors occur? (Refer to Richards, pp. 195-196.)

11. Repeat Question 10, only this time use a cloze test.

12. Why should it be more difficult to score compositions than dictations or cloze tests? In what ways might the composition tests be better controlled to make them easier to score? Refer to the technique Upshur used for "productive communication testing" (pp. 177-83).

13. In his second paper in this section, Upshur suggests that teaching and testing are really two sides of the same coin; that testing is a constant, on-going part of teaching. What are some of the ways that information from good tests can help to improve teaching, and conversely, what are some of the ways that good teaching can help to improve testing? How can diagnostic tests of the type discussed on p. 211 be used to increase the efficiency of instruction? What are some of the difficulties involved in the diagnosis of specific problems? Recall the remarks by Spolsky concerning the difficulty of determining the necessity or lack of it for particular points of grammar and the indeterminacy of functional load.

14. If language proficiency tests fail to reveal improvement in the ability of students to communicate after a period of course work in the language, what are some of the possible explanations? How might the alternative explanations be narrowed down by appropriate experimental research?

15. Upshur observes that "the complex problem which English teaching programs attempt to solve is producing students who can communicate with English speakers by means of the English language. This complex problem is often simplified to teaching a knowledge of English. We have what is known as a linguistically oriented program when 'knowledge of English' is characterized as the ability to decode and construct sentences which conform to the rules of English grammar as set forth by linguists" (p. 212). Compare this statement with Spolsky's suggestion that "knowledge of a language . . . is the same as underlying competence" (p. 174) which is defined as "knowledge of rules" (p. 173). In what ways might the apparent disagreement concerning the relevance of the linguist's definition of competence be resolved? In what ways might it be reflected in practice, either in testing or in teaching?

16. How might the term "cultural bias" be defined? Is it possible to avoid a definition which would label any test whatsoever as "culturally biased"? Are different definitions required for tests created for different purposes?

17. Can language tests, which are constructed explicitly to discriminate between individuals of varying levels of skills, be "culturally biased"? Is the case different when we are considering tests which presume to measure skills other than language-related ones?

18. Cultural bias in tests is an explosive issue, particularly in American society today. Consider the "criminality" of the "melting-pot" myth. How would you characterize the view that it is the function of schools to eradicate "deviations" in children who differ from the dominant White middle class? Why is such a view potentially damaging?

19. Brière's observations pertain primarily to testing, but could they be extended to teaching in general? Consider ways in which messages expressed in the form of subtle, relationship-defining attitudes may affect student performance. (Part V discusses this issue in greater detail.)

PART V

SOCIOCULTURAL AND MOTIVATIONAL FACTORS

INTRODUCTION

There is more to learning a second language than is sometimes indicated in discussions of the topic. In addition to the content aspect and coding operations that are often the center of linguistic considerations, there is also a relationship aspect of human communication which may have tremendous effects on language learning. In an excellent book, entitled *Pragmatics of Human Communication* (New York: Norton, 1967), Watzlawick, *et al.* demonstrated clearly that a pragmatic approach to interpersonal relationships is required. They show that in many interactional patterns it is quite impossible to offer an adequate explanation of observed facts unless the context of interactions is taken into account. This observation is applicable not only to interpersonal interactions, but is also true of intergroup interactions across cultural boundaries.

Attitudes and resultant motivations may well be more important sources of data for theories of second language learning than are formal characteristics of language. Attitudes of people about people are expressed in messages to the effect: "This is how I see you . . . This is how I see you seeing me . . . This is how I see you seeing me seeing you . . . " (Watzlawick, *et al.* p. 52), and the like. It is in this realm—the domain of interpersonal and intercultural relationships—that attitudes have their being and that socio-cultural motivations are spawned.

The first paper in this section, by Gardner, leaves no doubt about the fact that the degree of success achieved by a learner is influenced greatly by his view of the people who use the target language. In fact, the paramount importance of such considerations leads Tucker and Lambert, in the second paper of this section, to the hypothesis that methods of language teaching might well be modified to introduce the target language "almost incidentally" into the learning situation.

It is maintained by Gardner, as well as by Tucker and Lambert, that there are two "independent sources" of variability in successful foreign language study: first, there is "linguistic ability", a factor closely related to I.Q., and second, there is an "attitudinal factor" which has to do with the learner's orientation toward the people who use the language. From a pragmatic viewpoint there seems to be a parallelism, between content-level coding operations and linguistic ability on the one hand, and between relationship-level messages and attitudes on the other. Further, the emphasis of Tucker and Lambert on the importance of "how, when, and under what circumstances it is appropriate to communicate as well as what should be said" asserts the importance of a pragmatic approach to teaching in the sense of Oller's paper in Part I. An adequate theory of second language learning must consider not only the contexts of messages on the content-level but also contexts on the relationship-level. The learner must become able to cope with both.

The last paper in this section, by O'Doherty, considers some of the broader implications of intercultural, relationships as mediated by languages. He is actually reporting on the result of a recent UNESCO conference where a team of researchers examined socioeconomic and political factors which might help determine policies concerning second languages and the effects such policies might have on the learning of those languages.

ATTITUDES AND MOTIVATION: THEIR ROLE IN SECOND LANGUAGE ACQUISITION

R. C. Gardner

My intent in this paper is to review some of the research we have conducted which indicates just how dynamic and potent the role of the parent might be in the language learning situation. I think it is meaningful to distinguish two roles of the parent which are relevant to his child's success in a second language program. For want of better labels, I'm going to refer to them as the *active* and *passive* roles, even though these labels are not completely descriptive. By the *active role* I mean that role whereby the parent actively and consciously encourages the student to learn the language. In the active role, the parent monitors the child's language learning performance, and to the extent that he plays this role he attempts to promote success. That is, the parent watches over the child and makes sure he does his homework, encourages him to do well, and in general reinforces his successes. I believe it is safe to assume that differences in the extent to which parents vary in this encouragement function would have some influence on the child's performance in any learning situation.

The other type of role, the *passive role*, is more subtle, and I think more important, primarily because the parent would probably be unaware of it. By the subtle role, I mean the attitudes of the parent toward the community whose language the child is learning. These attitudes are important, I believe, because they influence the child's attitudes, and it is my thesis (and I'll try to convince you of its validity) that the child's attitudes toward the other language community are influential in motivating him to acquire the second language.

To contrast these roles, let me suggest one possible example. An English-speaking parent might actively encourage a child to learn French. He may stress the importance of doing well in that course, and might see that the child does his homework, and so forth. To himself, and to any observer, he might be perceived as actually helping the child. This is the active role. This same parent might hold positive or negative attitudes toward the French community. To the extent that he holds negative attitudes, he may be undermining his active role, by transferring to the child negative attitudes about the French community and thus reducing the child's motivation to learn the language. This is the passive role. By his own attitudes the parḛ. may develop in the child doubts concerning the real need for the language (particularly in the case where the parent does not speak that language). If the child fails an exam in French, he might anticipate some anger from his parent (who after all, is encouraging him to succeed), but he can always salve his own conscience by rationalizing that it is not really necessary to learn the language, as is evidenced by the fact that his parent gets along well enough without it. A negative attitude in the home can support this rationalization and thus possibly defeat the active role. Although my example is with reference to an English-speaking child involved in learning French, I think the same description might be applicable to the Puerto Rican child in New York, or the Navajo child in Arizona, who is attempting to learn English.

I have emphasized the role of attitudes in second language acquisition because we have conducted a number of studies (Feenstra, 1967; Gardner, 1960; Gardner and Lambert, 1959; Lambert, *et al.* 1960; also see Gardner, 1968) which have demonstrated that the student's attitudes are related to second language achievement. Rather than describe each study, let me outline the general approach in all of them. The design of a typical study involves testing a large group of students who are studying French as a second language. Measures are obtained on each student's language aptitude (Carroll and Sapon, 1959), his attitudes toward the French-speaking community and outgroups in general, his reason (orientation) for studying French, the degree of effort expended in learning French, and finally his skill in various aspects of French achievement. Generally, there is a total of thirty to forty measures obtained on each child. The relationships among these measures are investigated by means of a statistical procedure known as factor analysis. This technique allows one to mathematically investigate the interrelations (given in terms of correlation coefficients) of all the measures to determine which of the measures form separate clusters (i.e., factors). If, for example, the language aptitude measures and the measures of French achievement were positively associated in the same cluster, this would indicate that students who have language aptitude do better on measures of French achievement than do students with less language aptitude. On the basis of such a relationship one might assume that achievement in French is dependent upon an aptitude for languages.

The actual results of these studies indicated that in fact language aptitude is related to French achievement, and moreover that a complex of attitudinal-motivational variables are also related to French achievement. That is, two major clusters are generally obtained, one a language aptitude—French achievement cluster, and the other an attitudinal-motivational—French achievement cluster. These two clusters, or factors, are independent of each other, and furthermore they seem to involve different aspects of second language skills which are stressed in the schoolroom situation, while the attitudinal motivational cluster tends to involve those second language skills which would be developed outside the classroom in interaction with the other language community. In summary, it appears that differences in language aptitude result in differences in the extent to which the student can acquire second language skills dependent upon active instruction, whereas motivational differences influence the extent to which the student acquires skills which can be used in communicational situations.

This generalization is based on results of studies conducted in Montreal and London, Canada, as well as in Maine, Louisiana, and Connecticut. In each of these areas the results clearly indicate that a particular pattern of attitudinal-motivational components facilitated second language acquisition. Students who emphasized that learning the second language would permit them to interact with the French-speaking community, tended to have positive attitudes toward the French, or a favorable orientation toward outgroups in general. Furthermore, they were more motivated to learn French in that they worked harder. Such students were more successful in acquiring French. Because the major characteristic of this configuration appeared to describe an interest in acquiring French for purposes of integrating with the French-speaking community, we referred to this configuration as an integrative motive.

The concept of the integrative motive implies that successful second language acquisition depends upon a willingness (or desire) to be like valued members of the "other" language community. The acquisition of a new language involves more than just the acquisition of a new set of verbal habits. The language student must adopt various features of behavior which characterize another linguistic community. The new words, grammatical rules, pronunciations, and sounds, have a meaning over and above that which the teacher is trying to present. They are representations of another cultural group—and as such, the student's orientation toward that group should be expected to influence the extent to which the student can incorporate these verbal habits. Whereas the ability-oriented psychologist stresses the fact that second language learning involves the acquisition of new verbal habits, and hence prior verbal skills will facilitate their acquisition, the orientation emphasized here is that these new verbal habits also are representations of another linguistic group, and that suitable social attitudes will also facilitate their acquisition.

Although the integrative motive appears to promote the successful acquisition of a second language, there remains the question of how the integrative motive develops. In their cross-cultural study of children's views of foreign peoples, Lambert and Klineberg (1967) demonstrated in a number of different countries that the child's parents play a major role in the development of attitudes about other ethnic groups. Research in our own laboratory similarly demonstrates that children's attitudes toward both English and French Canadians are highly related to the attitudes of their parents, and it seems reasonable to assume that the child reflects the attitudinal atmosphere of his home.

In two of the studies on the motivational variables underlying second language achievement, we had the opportunity to obtain information from the parents. In one of the Montreal studies (Gardner, 1960) we interviewed the students' parents and compared the responses of parents of children who were integratively oriented with those of children who were instrumentally oriented. The results demonstrated that in contrast to the students who professed an instrumental orientation, integratively-oriented students tended to come from homes where the parents also professed an integrative orientation and where the parents had definite pro-French attitudes. (In short, the students were apparently reflecting the parents' attitudes in their choice of orientations.) Interestingly, however, there did not appear to be any relation between the student's orientation and the number of French friends the parents had or the degree of French proficiency that the parents expressed. Parents of the integratively-oriented students did, however, think that their children had more French-speaking friends than did the parents of instrumentally-oriented students. Whether this was a statement of fact (i.e., that the integratively-oriented students did have more French-speaking friends) could not be ascertained from the data gathered. It is equally possible that because of their own favorable attitudes towards the French-Canadian community, the parents of the integratively-oriented students were willing to ascribe a number of French friends to their children, while parents of the instrumentally-oriented students with their comparatively unfavorable attitudes would not admit that their children associated with many French-Canadian children.

These relationships between the parents' attitudes and the students' orientations suggest that the student's orientation grows out of a family-wide orientation and consequently that to some extent the degree of skill which the student attains in a second language will be dependent upon the attitudinal atmosphere in the home concerning the other linguistic group. Thus it is possible that parents who have favorable attitudes toward the French community and who feel that learning the language is valuable because it allows one to learn more about the group and meet more of its members actually encourage their children to study French, whereas the parents with the unfavorable attitudes and the instrumental orientation do not effect the same degree of encouragement.

In a more recent study, Feenstra (1967) systematically investigated the role of parental attitudes, by including ten measures obtained from the parents, in the factor analysis. Thus rather than determining how a few parental attitudes related to the child's orientation, he was able to study how parental attitudes clustered with respect to the children's language aptitude, motivation, and French achievement. Of major concern to this discussion were his findings that parents who emphasized the integrative orientation and who held positive attitudes toward French Canadians, encouraged their children to study French and actually had children who were skilled in some aspects of French achievement. In short, he found evidence that there is an association between what I have termed here the *active* and *passive* roles of the parent, and that these roles are related to French achievement. Furthermore, he also found that parents who were favorably oriented toward outgroups in general appeared to transmit this orientation to their children, and that this attitudinal disposition was also related to French achievement. Both of these findings support the conclusion that the child's integrative attitudinal orientation is fostered in the home, and that this accepting home environment has a direct association with second language achievement.

In summary, all of our findings to date support the conclusion that second language achievement is facilitated by an integrative motive, and that the development of such a motive is dependent upon a particular attitudinal atmosphere in the home.

The studies that we have conducted were concerned with English-speaking children learning French as a second language. At one time I thought that because of this, our data might not be relevant to the sort of situation with which TESOL is concerned. Recently, however, I was involved in a research project with the Center for Applied Linguistics in Washington which was concerned with the American Indian child learning English as a second language. I believe now that the relationships that we have obtained for the acquisition of French as a second language would probably also be obtained in that situation. Rather than emphasizing the language which is being acquired, I think it might be more meaningful to emphasize the usefulness of the language which is being acquired. Rather than isolating studies which are concerned with the acquisition of French or English or German, I think it may be more useful to look at the potential usefulness of the second language. Our studies on the acquisition of French as a second language have been conducted in a number of different geographical settings. In some of these French could be classified as a "high use" language. One can and does live in this environment and function extremely well by using French alone. In other words, French is a highly active language in that community, and proficiency in the language permits one to communicate in a situation where otherwise he couldn't. This contrasts with other geographical areas in which we have worked where French is a "low use" language. That is, an individual may be able to use the language in some communicational situations, but by and large he could communicate reasonably well without it. I think I should add that differentiating between high use and low use languages assumes that there are some other avenues available to the communicator, so that whereas Montreal would be classified as a geographical setting in which French is a "high use" language, the individual can, nonetheless, make use of English as an alternative if he so desires. A geographical setting like Hartford, Connecticut, might be classified as a "low use" area or at least lower than Montreal. It is probably true that in Hartford, one could make use of French if one desired, but it is not as important for communication, and the individual can function almost completely in English. It seems to me that in many areas where ESL programs would be offered, English is probably a "high use" language but that the child has other avenues that he can use. The Navajo living in a border town, can undoubtedly make good use of English, or alternatively, he would if necessary use the other avenue of limiting most of his communications to his native language and possibly learning only a very limited amount of English for highly specific purposes. From the point of view of the student, this situation appears to be highly analogous to that of the English-speaking individual living in Montreal.

We recently obtained some data suggesting that the foregoing analysis is relevant to students learning English as a second language (Gardner, 1968). These data were obtained from 300 educators of American Indian children in the U.S.A., and although the children themselves were not tested, the reactions of the teachers suggest that attitudinal variables are operative in this group. One analysis involved teachers' views of Indian students, non-Indian students, and Indian adults. This analysis suggested that the teachers perceive the Indian student as similar to, yet different from, both the non-Indian students and Indian adults. The comparative reactions indicate that the Indian student is perceived as possessing some traits in common with elders of his own cultural group, some in common with students from the non-Indian culture, and others which are truly midway between both groups. In short, the teachers, at least, are indicating that the Indian students seem to be taking on some characteristics of the non-Indian community. These, of course, are reactions of the teachers, and consequently it might be argued that there is little reason to assume that the Indian student is in fact integrating with the non-Indian community. However, further analyses of these reactions indicate that the teachers of the older students perceive Indian students more similarly to the non-Indian student community. That is, with increased age and contact with the educational system, it might be hypothesized that the Indian children appear to be becoming more like the non-Indian community. At least, these appear to be the feelings of the teachers involved.

The graphs presented in Figures 1-3 similarly indicate the role that social factors play in motivating children to learn a second language. These data are also based on the attitudes of the teachers of American Indian children. These three graphs illustrate the mean attitude scores for different teachers in different grades. Each graph consists of four points, the mean for teachers of grades 1-2, the mean for teachers of grades 3-4, for 5-7, and for 8-12. Each mean is based on the attitude test scores of approximately sixty teachers. Figure 1 demonstrates that the teachers of grades 1-2 feel that Indian students are more motivated to learn English than do teachers of grades 3-4, and that these teachers rate their students as more motivated than do teachers of grades 5-7. Teachers of grades 8-12, on the other hand, indicate that there is an increase in motivation for their students.

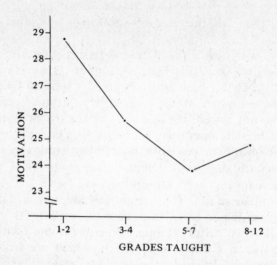

Figure 1.   Educators' attitudes concerning students' motivation to learn English as a function of grade taught.

There are, of course, many ways in which these results can be interpreted, but one parsimonious interpretation is that these attitudes of the teachers reflect the motivational characteristics of the students in their classes. This interpretation would suggest that there is a decrease in motivation to learn English to grade 7, and from there on the motivation tends to increase. You can almost see this as indicating the inquisitive exuberance of the young child, the gradual apathy of the older child in an educational atmosphere that may not appear meaningful to him, and then the awakening of the possible importance of the program to the maturing individual.

Figure 2 is also based on the teacher's attitudes, but this illustrates their attitudes about the amount of pressure from the peer groups to avoid the use of English. Applying the same logic to these data suggests that the younger child experiences relatively little pressure from his peer group to avoid using English, but that this increases to a peak at grades 5-7, and then falls off slightly. The pattern parallels that for the measure of motivation and suggests possibly that from grades 1-7 there is a decline in motivation to learn English and that consequently children pressure others to avoid using English which in turn decreases the motivation to learn English. After grade 7, with the development of an appreciation of the usefulness of English, the pressure from the group appears to fall off.

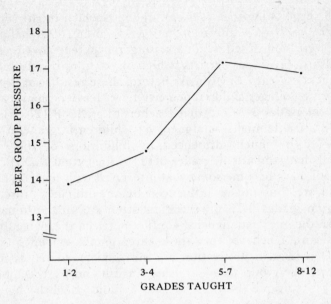

Figure 2.   Educators' attitudes concerning the amount of peer group pressure to avoid using English as a function of grade taught.

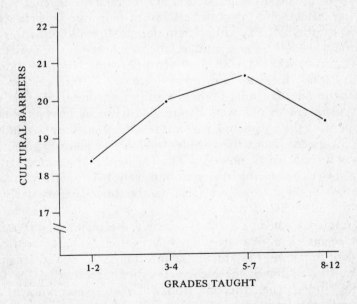

Figure 3.   Educators' attitudes concerning the influence of cultural barriers in impeding English acquisition as a function of grade taught.

Figure 3 suggests another social component which might serve to influence the students' motivation to learn English. Items making up this scale were concerned with assessing the extent to which the Indian culture provided barriers which make it difficult for the Indian student to learn English. As before, these results suggest that teachers of the younger children perceive fewer barriers than teachers of children in grades 5-7, and that teachers of grades 8-12 see less of a cultural barrier. It might be argued that children in grades 1-2 are too young to be much influenced by inhibitions of the Indian culture, and that students in grades 8-12, to the extent that they are still in school, have become somewhat integrated with the non-Indian culture and are thus not as influenced by the Indian culture. The children from grades 3-7, however, are often still in the home and possibly are the ones experiencing conflict between the two cultures. It is significant, I believe, that these three graphs evidence similar patterns. Decreases in motivation are mirrored by increases in the pressure from the group to avoid using English and by the apparent presence of cultural barriers which inhibit English language acquisition.

The results presented in Figures 1-3 represent significant variability in the means as a function of the grade the teacher taught. That these effects are possibly real rather than due to artifacts is suggested by the fact that other attitude measures did not show any effect due to grade. For example, the teachers also completed a questionnaire concerned with their attitudes about Indian students' ability to learn English, and there were no differences on this questionnaire due to grade. If these results were due to the fact that teachers from grades 3-7 were dissatisfied with the level of English achievement of their students, it seems possible that they would have expressed concern about their students' ability to learn English. This result was not obtained, however. The teachers of the various grades seem to be experiencing different motivational qualities in their students which seem to reflect social factors operating passively but significantly on the students.

To summarize then, I'd like to review the major points raised. First, it seems clear that attitudinal-motivational characteristics of the student are important in the acquisition of a second language. Secondly, the nature of these characteristics suggests that the truly successful student (i.e., the one who will acquire communicational facility with the language) is motivated to become integrated with the other language community. Thirdly, this integrative motive appears to derive from the attitudinal characteristics in the home and must be fostered by an accepting attitude, by the parents, concerning the other language group. And finally, the process of second language acquisition involves taking on behavioral characteristics of the other language community and the fact that the child will experience resistance from himself and pressures from his own cultural community.

REFERENCES

Carroll, J. B., and S. M. Sapon. *Modern Language Aptitude Test* (MLAT). New York: Psychological Corporation, 1959.

Feenstra, H. J. "Aptitude, Attitude and Motivation in Second Language Acquisition." Unpublished dissertation. University of Western Ontario, 1967.

Gardner, R. C. "Motivational Variables in Second-Language Acquisition." Unpublished dissertation. McGill University, 1960.

———. "Motivational Variables in Second-Language Learning." *International Journal of American Linguistics,* 32 (1966), 24-44.

———. *A Survey of Attitudes of Educators of American Indian Children.* Research Bulletin No. 66, University of Western Ontario, 1968.

Gardner, R. C., and W. E. Lambert. "Motivational Variables in Second-Language Acquisition." *Canadian Journal of Psychology,* 13 (1959), 266-72.

Lambert, W. E., *et al.* "A Study of the Roles of Attitudes and Motivation in Second-Language Learning." Mimeographed. McGill University. 1960.

Lambert, W. E., and O. Klineberg. *Children's Views of Foreign Peoples.* New York: Appleton-Century-Crofts, 1967.

SOCIOCULTURAL ASPECTS OF LANGUAGE STUDY

G. R. Tucker and W. E. Lambert

The development of "communicative competence" in a foreign language (FL) involves much more than the mastery of a surface linguistic code. It also involves the development of an awareness of and sensitivity toward the values and traditions of the people whose language is being studied. Unfortunately, these sociocultural aspects of the target language (TL) are often completely neglected or, at best, poorly transmitted.

Paradoxically it is these sociocultural aspects of the TL which are likely to attract the interest of the FL student more than the purely linguistic aspects. In fact, much of the recent disenchantment with FL study may derive directly from the mindless and seemingly unending flood of repetition and pattern practice drills with which both beginning and intermediate students are confronted. With the widespread elimination of required FL courses, students who elect FL study are now more motivated by a desire to learn about other peoples and their way of life and by a desire to be able to interact with these people. This intense desire on their part suggests that we consider seriously, as an alternative to traditional FL teaching, the possibility of teaching FL's by moving from the sociocultural aspects to the linguistic with language *qua* language being introduced almost incidentally.

This duality is also reflected in the fact that two demonstrably *independent* sources of influence are important in successful FL study: (1) linguistic ability (e.g., a language-oriented talent such as I.Q.); and (2) attitudes and motivational orientation toward the other group and their culture (e.g., an interest in sociocultural matters, apart from language). Jakobovits (1970), Nelson, *et al.* (1970), and Lambert and Gardner (1971) all discuss, in detail, and from slightly different perspectives, the relative contribution these variables make to FL mastery.

The attitudinal component manifests itself in at least two forms, an instrumental in contrast to an integrative orientation; and it is crucial for the FL teacher to realize that sociocultural factors can and do affect this attitudinal component. For example, the student's interest will certainly be affected by his perception of the utility of acquiring a particular FL. English speaking students living in the Province of Quebec today must learn French if they want to earn a living in the occupation of their choice; students in other Canadian provinces or in the U.S. face no such demands, either explicit or implicit. Even this situation in America may change, however, with the widespread development of bilingual education programs in diverse parts of North America (cf., Andersson and Boyer, 1970), and an accompanying reduction of the heat under the "ethnic melting pot" (cf., Fishman, *et al.* 1966). That is to say, in time American students may eventually see more value in FL's and may even encounter social pressures to learn them. Students may also become more motivated in the study of any FL as an intermediate objective, i.e., seeing the successful mastery of any second language as an automatic preparation for acquiring a third, fourth, or subsequent language.

A student's integrative orientation to FL study may be even more dramatically influenced by various sociocultural factors. In the first place, the student will be affected by the ethnolinguistic composition of the larger linguistic community of which he is a member. Joshua Fishman and his colleagues (1966) have pointed out that there are significant forces operating within the country to maintain various immigrant languages—each of which becomes a potential target for FL study. Particularly in urban areas, the minority group's language coincides with one of the foreign languages available to middle-class students for FL study at school. It is quite common, for example, to offer French as the language in Vermont or New Hampshire, Spanish in California or New Mexico, Portuguese in Rhode Island, etc. However, the community-wide stereotypes in these areas are usually characterized by a downgrading of the group's representatives and by a lack of desire to identify with that group. Unfortunately, members of these groups often have a relatively low socioeconomic status, and the stereotypes which characterize lower-class behavior and thoughts are attributed to their language and its study. In these situations, the attitudinal component acts as a detriment or negative motivating force for both student and teacher.

Also, we know that parental attitudes can and do affect children's orientations and hence success in FL study (cf., Feenstra, 1969). When the parents accept the minority group members as peers because of positive interpersonal contacts established on the job or in the neighborhood, the children are less likely to develop unfavorable stereotypes of the other group's members.

Of even more importance than parental or community-wide attitudes are the attitudes and expectations teachers develop. Recent investigations have directed the attention of educators to the relationship between teachers' subjective biases and their evaluations of pupils (e.g., Frender, Brown, and Lambert, 1970; Rosenthal and Jacobson, 1968; Seligman, Tucker and Lambert, 1971; and Williams, 1971). The findings of these studies suggest that the teacher who is insensitive to local varieties of important world languages may show her personal bias by denigrating the local variety actually used by certain of her pupils. The results also raise another type of question: Will a teacher with a nativelike command of the phonological system of the TL be more responsive to students who themselves possess better command, or will she react with equal tolerance toward all students during the beginning stages of FL study?

Although an understanding of each of the above factors is very important for predicting success in FL study, the crucial question may well be whether the FL training program prepares the student to communicate with members of the target group, whether he learns how, when, and under what circumstances it is appropriate to communicate as well as what should be said.

How might we take better advantage of the attitudinal component in FL teaching? The results of recent social psychological investigations (Lambert and Klineberg, 1967) suggest that cultural and linguistic training should be started early, preferably by ten years of age. It is at this stage that foreigners are most likely to appear "different but interesting" while later they will be perceived as "different and bad." These findings suggest that teachers should start at very early age levels to present sympathetic culture contrasts that lead to a recognition of the basic similarities of mankind. Furthermore, a FL teacher will likely be more successful in her work if she can capitalize on the feelings of today's young people who no longer feel that their own society (be it France, the U.S., Russia, or China) is the best of all possible worlds and who are instead searching for a better world, open and receptive to foreign peoples and their ideas.

To what extent can the attitudinal component be modified once the student has acquired the prevailing stereotypes or expectations of his parents and his community? Two alternative strategies are available: (1) intensive study of the TL; and (2) vicarious preparation. The first might take the form of an immersion program of instruction totally via the FL. There is good reason to believe (cf., Lambert, Just, and Segalowitz, 1970; d'Anglejan and Tucker, 1971; Lambert and Tucker, 1971) that English Canadian children following a "home-school language switch" program of French instruction learn to read, write, speak, and understand English as well as carefully selected English counterparts who are schooled via English.

In addition, at no apparent cost, they learn to read, write, speak, and understand French to a remarkable degree. They also develop more positive outlooks toward French Canadians than do their peers in the community who have not had the benefit of this exciting educational innovation.

The second alternative, that of vicarious preparation, could take the form of a systematic introduction to the other culture, its people and values, before any formal language training is started. The potential of such programs is immense, and it is about time educational researchers put the idea to a careful test. One should, however, recognize the types of risks one runs in setting up "vicarious preparation" programs. Two negative types of reaction come to mind: "secondary anomie" and the "echh reaction." The term "secondary anomie" is used to characterize a student's dissatisfaction when, having thoroughly prepared himself to study a language by a prior vicarious immersion in the other culture, he finds that he lacks even the most rudimentary skills needed for communication with members of the target group. For those planning FL programs, there is a delicate balance involved; the inability to express himself may become a strong motivating force for one student while for another it may result in a sense of despair and rejection of FL study.

The "echh reaction" is a term that helps describe a student's disgust or shock when exposed to certain novel values, traditions, or customs associated with a foreign people. For example, a group of elementary students studying French in the U.S. exchanged letters, tape recordings, and slides with another group of French-speaking youngsters in Upper Volta. They learned through this exchange that many of the Africans ate and enjoyed eating grasshoppers; they also saw that the African youngsters typically had dirty feet. Their first reactions were negative not only toward these people whose language they were studying, but also, interestingly, to Blacks here in North America. In this example, American eating customs and values of cleanliness threw the attitudinal switch. It takes a gifted teacher tc capitalize on such incidents and use them to her advantage.

In summary, we are asking this question: Is it possible to teach the strictly linguistic code of a FL without teaching a sensitivity to the other culture and its people? Our belief is that any attempt to do so is likely to turn the student off, and he will reject the code itself and the people represented by the code. On the other hand, helping children develop cultural sensitivity as they develop language skills capitalizes on a natural interest and motivation to learn about other people, including minority groups at home and foreign people from abroad, and provides a basis for learning the other group's language.

REFERENCES

Andersson, T. and M. Boyer. *Bilingual Schooling in the United States.* Washington, D.C.: U.S. Government Printing Office, 1970.

d'Anglejan, A., and G. R. Tucker. "The St. Lambert Program of Home-School Language Switch. *Modern Language Journal* 55 (1971), 99-101.

Feenstra, H. J. "Parent and Teacher Attitudes: Their Role in Second-Language Acquisition." *Canadian Modern Language Review* 26 (1969), 5-13.

Fishman, J. A., *et al. Language Loyalty in the United States.* The Hague: Mouton, 1966.

Frender, R. W., B. Brown, and W. E. Lambert. "The Role of Speech Characteristics in Scholastic Success." *Canadian Journal of Behavioral Science,* 2 (1970), 299-306.

Jakobovits, L. A. *Foreign Language Learning.* Rowley, Mass.: Newbury House, 1970.

Lambert, W. E., and R. C. Gardner. *Attitudes and Motivation in Second Language Learning.* Rowley, Mass.: Newbury House, 1972.

Lambert, W. E., M. Just, and N. Segalowitz. "Some Cognitive Consequences of Following the Curricula of the Early School Grades in a Foreign Language." *Monograph Series on Language and Linguistics.* J. E. Alatis (ed.). Washington, D. C.: Georgetown University Press, 1970.

Lambert, W. E., and O. Klineberg, *Children's Views of Foreign Peoples.* New York: Appleton-Century-Crofts, 1967.

Lambert, W. E., and G. R. Tucker. *Bilingual Education of Children.* Rowley, Mass.: Newbury House, 1972.

Nelson, R. J. *et al.* "Motivation in Foreign Language Learning." J. A. Tursi (ed.). *Foreign Language and the "New" Student. Northeast Conference on the Teaching of Foreign Languages.* New York; Modern Language Association, 1970.

Rosenthal, R., and L. Jacobson. "Teacher Expectations for the Disadvantaged." *Scientific American,* 218 (1968), 19-23.

Seligman, C. R., G. R. Tucker, and W. E. Lambert. "The Effects of Speech Style and Other Attributes on Teachers' Attitudes toward Pupils." *Language in Society,* (in press).

Williams, F. "Psychological Correlates of Speech Characteristics: On Sounding Disadvantaged." *Journal of Speech and Hearing Research,* 13 (1970), 472-88.

SOCIAL FACTORS AND SECOND LANGUAGE POLICIES

E. F. O'Doherty

There is a sense in which everything one does, with the possible exceptions of idiosyncrasies and simple sensory responses, will be affected by the social setting. It is inevitable that a social institution of such importance as language will be dependent on the social setting perhaps even more than on individual personality factors. Language can be thought of primarily as a device for interpersonal communication. It is thus the social institution *par excellence.* For although organisms other than man can certainly communicate with one another, they do not do so by patterned sets of conventional signs. The language of a group is an integral component of its culture. In terms of the concept of culture patterns, which are thought of as forming living wholes of interralated parts, a change in the language of the group will entail far-reaching consequences for the people whose culture it is. This is fairly obvious in the case of a change from one language to another (e.g., the replacement of Irish by English in Ireland over several centuries), but is not so obvious when the replacement is not complete, and where the two languages coexist within the same culture. This is the case in perhaps a majority of nation states in the world today and is a consequence of the phenomenon noted in the report of the first Hamburg meeting: "Bilingualism . . . may be almost as essential as literacy" (Stern, 1967, p. 7).

THE CHOICE OF A SECOND LANGUAGE

The rapid increase of contacts between politically separate entities since the Second World War, together with a reduction in the potency of the concept of sovereignty of the individual nation, has resulted in the unprecedented growth of second language teaching and learning, and of interest in the problems it produces. It is clear that the choice of the second or third language which a social group may make will be determined by a variety of social criteria which will vary with the particular group concerned. Some of the social criteria moreover will affect the individual motivations involved in second language learning. One might therefore attempt a schematic presentation of the motivations involved in the problem of second language teaching and learning as follows (see Figure 1).

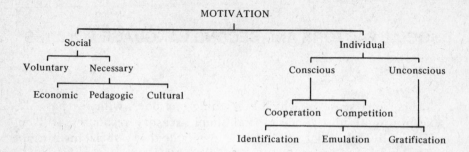

Figure 1.   Motivations in second language teaching and learning

In the past, one can easily find examples of voluntary social motivations determining the choice of second language learning. French in Russia, Poland, and Prussia in the eighteenth and nineteenth centuries is a good example. Choice of this kind is perhaps usually bound up with cultural-prestige factors, rather than with socioeconomic factors. Thus, a low-prestige culture may adopt the language of a high-prestige culture as a deliberate act of choice. In this case the adopted language will be seen to fulfil a function other than that of communication: it becomes a symbol in its own right—a symbol of civilization, culture, social class, perhaps of privilege. In such circumstances, another phenomenon may rapidly appear: the *first* language of the group may acquire a new symbolic significance. It may come to symbolize the traditional values, perhaps even the cultural identity and political unity of the group. This has happened in Europe many times, and may be reasonably expected to happen in Africa fairly soon.

But in general, one may say that the choice of a second language is now much less a matter of cultural prestige than of economic necessity.

Economic factors

This is probably the most obvious of the necessary social motivations leading to the adoption of a second language. The point is made in several conference papers.[1]

Technological factors

The necessity of a second language for purposes of higher education has been recognized in some countries for a comparatively long time. Apart from considerations of higher education, however,

---

[1] E.g., Gineste (cp.) and Lahlou (cp.).

the need for a second language of wide diffusion and high technological achievement has become apparent in many countries at much lower levels on the educational scale. In some of the new nations of Africa and Asia, which are undergoing rapid technological change, this very change itself demands a thorough grounding in a second language (English or French as the case may be) even at primary school level.

It is clear that many other factors, cultural, religious, and political, may enter into the determination of the precise second language chosen in a given society (Lewis, 1965, pp. 87-137). Some of the sociocultural aspects of second language learning—attitudes of one group to another, and the changes in such attitudes consequent upon the learning of the language of the second group (Lambert, 1965, pp. 44-55), social and cultural consequences for the individual child (Lewis, 1965, pp. 150-5)—have been dealt with in former reports. A valuable brief overview of work in this area will be found in Titone (1964, pp. 21, ff.). According to Titone, these "external factors" of a sociocultural kind "are easily reducible to the motivational category." Thus, a favorable attitude to the group whose language one is learning will *ceteris paribus* facilitate the learning process; and again, those who have already learned a second language will show more favorable attitudes to the group whose language it is than those who do not know the second language in question. Similar results have been found, e.g., by Riestra and Johnson (1962). The social value, prestige, or status of the second language is, as one might expect, found to be related to the ease or difficulty of learning it. Culture conflict can arise if the learner of a second language feels that his own native culture is threatened by the spread of the second language. Haugen (1956) underlines the importance of such culture conflicts. Problems of personality adjustment among bilinguals are due to their "bicultural position" in the first instance, and only secondarily to internal personality factors. On the other hand, it is recognized that a second language can the more readily be learned in its own distinct cultural context. It would seem then that culture conflict of some kind is the price one has to pay for the inestimable benefits of genuine bilingualism.

SOCIAL CONSEQUENCES OF THE INTRODUCTION OF A SECOND LANGUAGE

The economic, technological, and cultural values resulting from the introduction of a second language into a society must be carefully weighed against the possible adverse social consequences.

The evidence from history, linguistics, and cultural anthropology must be taken into account.

History

It has perhaps been too easily taken for granted that the spread of a single *lingua franca*, or the adoption of a single national language throughout a nation state, would operate as a unifying factor for the community. But if this is done to the detriment of a local minority language, or even if it is experienced as a threat to the local language, such a policy may be divisive and lead to serious conflict. The experience of France in relation to Breton, Spain in relation to Catalan, Italy in relation to the German-speaking regions of the north must be taken into account. A minority linguistic group, experiencing its minority language under threat of extermination, will understandably stiffen its resistance to the spread of the majority language. Care must therefore be taken to see to it that such minority languages are preserved and their cultural human values respected, while the need for a language of wider diffusion is sympathetically brought home to the minority language group. Parallel considerations must be borne in mind where the second language, however necessary as a temporary measure for economic, technological, or educational reasons, is that of a foreign power or of a different ideology. In these circumstances, a point may be reached where the receiving culture becomes strong enough to be conscious of itself as a distinct national entity, with its native language as a symbol of its distinct identity. It is relatively easy for a language to become a symbol in its own right, as a bearer of traditional values, allegiances, and aspirations. Just as each word of a language is a symbol, or conventional sign, so the language system as a whole may become a higher-order symbol. It is commonly believed that the thought forms and attitudes of a people are molded by their language, so that it is easy to understand how a language change can be felt as a threat to identity. While there is in fact no evidence for the beliefs just mentioned, the fact that they are believed gives them functional significance for those who believe them, in accordance with a well-known sociological principle.

There is a further point to note here, which may have far-ranging consequences. It is the fact that a language may in a relatively short period of time attain high cultural and scientific status. The position of German would seem to be a case in point in the past. It is conceivable that other languages, not now of high international, scientific, or literary status, may rise rapidly in this way.

The conclusion to be drawn from these considerations is that those who are in charge of a second language policy in their communities must be ready at all times to keep the positions of both the first and second language under contant review and perhaps even learn to anticipate the points at which significant changes may be expected to occur.

Languages in contact

In terms of the known history of languages in proximity, borrowings, cross-fertilization, and interpretation of each by the other is probably to be anticipated. The history of the English language after the Norman Conquest illustrates the point. The version of the Irish language as spoken by nonnative speakers whose vernacular is English would repay study in this connection. France has taken measures to preserve the purity of French, but the growth of *franglais* again illustrates the phenomenon in a small way. It is possible that languages of wide diffusion and high cultural status can survive such cross-fertilization and interpretation, but the effects on lower-status minority languages should be reckoned with. Such languages, while standing in greater need of borrowings, neologisms, etc., may not be able to survive massive cross-fertilization. Research must be carried out by linguists and cultural anthropologists in this area.

Cultural anthropology

The closely related disciplines of cultural and social anthropology, sociology, and social psychology have their contribution to make. The function of language as a factor in a culture pattern has already been alluded to. The second Hamburg meeting drew particular attention to some of these problems. It noted in particular the phenomenon of social mobility in relation to the learning of second languages. Such mobility is of two kinds, horizontal and vertical. Horizontal mobility refers to the geographical displacement within a community, or between states, as when a minority language speaker or a dialect speaker moves for seasonal employment. Vertical mobility refers to the shift up or down the social scale within the community. It would seem that social mobility in this latter sense may be closely related to proficiency in a high-prestige second language. Within a given language, in a highly stratified society, there are "sub-languages" characteristic of a particular class. In a rapidly developing nation, a similar phenomenon may occur with regard to the second, or foreign, language. There have been examples in the fairly recent history of Europe.

Personality factors

There is a reciprocal relationship between culture and personality. The culture is itself a creation of human persons, which in its turn through all the modes of education at its disposal, formal and informal, molds the personalities of its members. Thus the radical changes in a culture which may result from the widespread diffusion of a second language may be expected to affect the personality of the members of the group. One cannot expect to introduce a process of change and at the same time avoid the consequences of the change one has introduced.

These principles have certain obvious consequences for the learning of second languages. The child learns very largely through the process of identification. It follows that the closer the identification with the culture of the second language, the easier will be the learning process. The second language must be given functional significance in the child's world before it can truly function as a language. Without this, it may remain at the level of a mere coding and decoding instrument. In order to give it functional significance, a "reward" mechanism directly related to language must be built in. Entertainment, reading, television programs, and other forms of play activity must be viable in the child's world if a language is to function for the child *as a language*. The effect of language as a control mechanism in relation to behavior, as a source of voluntary action, and as a reward mechanism in its own right, is well known to psychologists, especially as a result of the work of Luria and his colleagues in Moscow. In addition to availing of these insights in pedagogy, an adequate program of second language teaching must avail of them as sociological phenomena.

Language learning and the family

The consequences of second language learning for the family present a rich source of research for the sociologist and the psychologist. Do families in rapid social transition (mobility up the social scale) acquire proficiency in a second language, or even change their vernacular more readily than families in a relatively more static position on the social scale? Does the acquisition of a second language by the children, when this is not known to the parents, or when the parents are not fluent in it, affect the cohesion, unity, and stability of the family? Does the attempt by parents to use a second language, not their own vernacular, and not the language of ordinary social intercourse in their environment, have adverse effects on the children's linguistic competence, or does it have an impoverishing effect on their conceptual capacity? There is some impressionistic evidence that all these questions should get an affirmative answer. Probably the monoglot family is the statistical norm throughout the world. But the number of families wherein the parents are of widely differing linguistic origin and background would seem to be increasing. In the monoglot family, the child probably finds a certain security in the single-language communication system. What are the effects if any when the parents communicate with him in different systems?

RESEARCH PROPOSALS

Although language is such an obvious and important social phenomenon, relatively little is known about the social psychology of second language learning. It is a matter of common experience that a child who does not speak the language of his peer group at play, will very rapidly acquire some competence in the peer group's language. If this is so, the following questions can be asked:

1. What is the minimum, maximum, and optimum size of a group for purposes of the linguistic integration of a new incoming member? (If the number is too small, the group may not be able to integrate the new member, or may adopt his language to some extent, while if it is too large, the new member may remain a linguistic isolate.)

2. Within the peer group, what is the order of language acquisition by the new member, in terms of phonemes, words, formal structures, etc.?

It would appear that some children acquire a relatively high proficiency in a second language by means of a relatively brief stay in the second language environment. For example, a few months stay in France might bring the average British child to a level of active and passive mastery of French equivalent to several years of primary school teaching. In Ireland there is some evidence that a short sojourn of even one month or less in an exclusively Irish-speaking environment benefits the primary school learner of Irish as a second language more than the school itself can do in perhaps several years. We need to ask:

3. What are the relative merits of prolonged school instruction in the second language in the environment of the first language (e.g., three years), compared to short experience of the linguistically saturated environment of $L2$ (e.g., three months)?

4. What are the economics of the two situations indicated in research No. 3? In other words, if the aim of a second language

program is the facilitation of trade, or cultural studies, etc., across linguistic frontiers, as distinct from a second language program geared to the very survival of a community (e.g., Common Market countries' second language needs, as compared to the second language needs of the newly emergent African states), and if investigation should show that the percentage of school children exposed to a second language in the primary school who actually reach the stage of using the second language as a normal means of communication is relatively small, and if moreover it should emerge that a similar or greater proportion could reach a comparable level of mastery through a brief sojourn in the environment of the second language, the economics of this could have profound effects on second language policy.

The Report on the International Seminar held at Aberystwyth in 1960 (Lewis, 1965, p. 109) discusses the differences between individual and social bilingualism. Some countries seem to have as their express aim, a linguistic situation describable perhaps as social bilingualism, i.e., where the very society itself would live and function in two linguistic environments simultaneously, as distinct from, e.g., the Swiss situation, where each individual may be bilingual and the state be a multilingual state, but each social unit or linguistic community is socially monoglot. We need to know:

5. To what extent is social bilingualism possible? In other words, what happens when a society as such has at its disposal two distinct intrasocial communication systems? Has such a society ever existed? Is the result a mélange (Anglo-Norman-French), or the driving out of one language by the other (on the analogy of currency), or the division of the community into two linguistic groups, with possible detriment to the society as a whole? It seems clearly to be important that policy makers should understand the possible long-range effects of a language policy aimed on the one hand at producing many bilingual individuals, and on the other hand one aimed at producing a bilingual society.

In order to survive, a social institution must have functional significance for those for whom it is an institution. The functional significance of second language learning is fairly easily seen at university and secondary school levels (introduction to a new literature, a new culture, commerce, travel, etc.). It is not so clear that second language learning at primary school level has a functional significance for the child. We need to know:

6. What are the typical and significant attitudes of children at different age levels to their exposure to a second language? This

raises the question of motivation, reward, reality relationships, time and space orientation in the second language, play activities, and the causes of antipathy or negativism in respect of the second language.

While there is no doubt about the value of a second language as a cultural and technological instrument in the developing countries, the whole problem of the relationship of first and second languages in a community is complicated by very powerful emotional factors. The second language may carry emotional overtones of colonialism or occupation, while the first language may become a symbol in its own right (of liberation, or cultural identity, etc.). We need to know:

7. What factors lead up to the critical flashpoint when the second language is likely to be rejected in favor of the first language? Historial, social, anthropological studies are necessary here.

8. It is strongly recommended that experts in the social sciences (sociology, anthropology, psychology, history, and many others) who have shown an interest and a competence in language problems, focus their expertise on some of the above problems.

REFERENCES

Gineste, R. "Facteurs linguistiques pédagogiques et économiques." Paper presented at the Conference on Foreign Language Learning, Hamburg, 1966.

Haugen, E. *Bilingualism in the Americas: A Bibliography and Research Guide.* University, Alabama: University of Alabama Press, 1956.

Lahlou, A. "La seconde langue dans les communautés bilingues ou multilingues." Paper presented at the Conference on Foreign Language Learning, Hamburg, 1966.

Lambert, W. E. "Social and Psychological Aspects of Bilingualism." in Lewis (1965)..

Lewis, E. G. *Report on an International Seminar on Bilingualism in Education.* London: Her Majesty's Stationery Office, 1965.

Riestra, M. A., and L. E. Johnson. "Changes in Attitudes of Elementary School Pupils towards Foreign Speaking Peoples Resulting from the Study of a Foreign Language." Unpublished paper. University of Puerto Rico, 1962.

Stern, H. H. *Foreign Languages in Primary Education.* London: Oxford University Press, 2d revised ed., 1967.

Titone, R. *Studies in the Psychology of Second Language Learning.* Zurich: Pas-Verlag, 1964

PART V: DISCUSSION QUESTIONS

1. Gardner emphasizes "how dynamic and potent the role of the parent might be in the language learning situation" (p. 235). What are some of the sociocultural differences which may influence the effect of parent-attitudes? Also, how might other variables come into play, e.g., peer group attitudes?

2. Consider some of the ways in which parents may unknowingly express attitudes toward linguistically and culturally different groups. (Notice that messages in this realm are frequently coded quite unintentionally and nonverbally in terms of facial expressions, tone of voice, choice of terms which reflect connotative biases, etc.)

3. Discuss some of the ways in which sociocultural contexts may affect the spectrum of intercultural relationship messages to which a learner is exposed. How may these messages affect attitudes and motivations? In particular, consider the differences in contexts that may hinge on the distinction between "foreign" and "second" language learning.

4. Suppose that the attitude of a learner's parents toward a target language group is highly positive and integrative. How might this affect the expression of intercultural relationship messages? Will the parents be apt to express their attitudes "passively" or "actively" (see Gardner, pp. 235-45)? Contrast this with negatively oriented ("ethnocentric") attitudes. How might we expect the latter to be expressed?

5. How could the possible factor of "anomie" in a culturally strange educational system play a part in the data of Figures 1, 2, and 3 (Gardner, pp. 242-43)?

6. Discuss ways in which the visible facts of social order may work in tandem with (or against) attitudes expressed by parents to establish cultural stereotypes (or possibly to abolish them).

7. Linguistic and psycholinguistic theories discussed primarily in Part I seem more directly concerned with the factor described by Gardner, Tucker, and Lambert as "linguistic aptitude" whereas theories of sociocultural aspects of language use and language learning seem most concerned with the factor of attitudes and motivations. The first factor is comprised by the capability to handle content-level coding operations in the abstract and the second factor is embodied in value systems which are expressed in relationship-level messages between persons and groups within and across cultures. What sorts of pragmatic contexts are relevant to the two factors? Are there any parallels between them? Discuss the terms "linguistic" versus "socio-cultural" meaning suggested by Tucker and Lambert (p. 246).

8. In the light of the data provided by Gardner, and Tucker and Lambert, consider the matter of a possible "optimal age for second language learning." Compare arguments motivated by considerations of mental maturation ("linguistic aptitude") with those arguments motivated by attitudinal

considerations (especially, stereotypes, integrative vs. instrumental motivation, utility of the target language in the learner's world, etc.).

9. Is it possible to explain the results of "total immersion experiments" of the sort mentioned by Tucker and Lambert (pp. 248-49) on the basis of "innate ideas"? Some other basis? Compare the experimental method of Lambert, *et al.* with what happens in normal communication and with more formal classroom situations.

10. O'Doherty introduces the notion of horizontal (geographical) and vertical (social) mobility. How might these notions be important to considerations of instrumental and integrative motivation? Is a horizontal move apt to be brought about by instrumental or integrative motivation, or both? What about a vertical move? What effects can horizontal mobility be expected to have on the relative stability and prestige of coexisting languages? Vertical mobility? Are there examples of learners who are apt to need English for horizontal mobility? Vertical mobility? Is one group more likely to achieve "standard English"?

11. Several of the authors in this section, including O'Doherty, mention the importance of peer group influence. Consider ways in which different language policies may affect such influences and ultimately bring about wide-ranging changes in linguistic demography. Discuss specific situations with which you may have familiarity. Can similar observations be made concerning the status of varieties of the same language, e.g., Black English, and so-called "standard English" (an ill-defined term at best)?

12. In view of O'Doherty's remarks, how might official language policies and widespread group attitudes affect second language learning? The relative stability of language varieties? Note the close interrelationship between messages on the relationship level (i.e., the expression of attitudes of people toward themselves and others) and political matters in general. Discuss the merits of the proposition that learner attitudes are a sort of microcosm of a larger sociopolitical scene.

PART VI

ALTERNATIVES TO FORMAL LANGUAGE INSTRUCTION

INTRODUCTION

We have seen throughout this book that the planning of a language component in a school curriculum requires consideration of the nature of language and language learning. It is especially important to consider the language learner in terms of his sociocultural background. Some of the approaches to the linguistic and educational factors which shape school language policy are discussed in the papers of this section.

Educational responsibility for children of minority groups is a question of concern in communities around the world. Language plays such a crucial role in this process that it is not surprising that some linguists have assumed that language is the *sole* factor responsible for a child's success or failure. Spolsky argues, however, that linguistic difficulties are symptoms of social problems, rather than causes of them. One solution that has been proposed is bilingual education. It may be possible to enhance the opportunities of the minority group through increasing the use of its language in the school.

Another possible application of bilingual education may be to teach second languages. It may be possible to capitalize on the fact (observed by Tucker, Lambert, and others) that in many cases children appear to learn a second language easily and incidentally when it is used as a medium of instruction in the school.

Stern reviews some of the observed effects of bilingual education in North America. Many of them seem to reflect different historical patterns of settlement and assimilation in North America. He suggests that bilingual education may be useful not only as an attempt to provide equal opportunity to minority groups, but also to improve language learning for other purposes as well.

Another alternative to traditional formal instruction is offered by Dykstra and Nunes. Their language skills program, which is a component of a broader educational curriculum, tries to put the emphasis on the child as the initiator of the learning process. This approach is consonant with what we have seen of the nature of language learning; the learner actively tries out hypothesis and looks for meaning in and through language as Macnamara and Kennedy observed in Part II.

The alternative proposed by Dykstra and Nunes, along with bilingual education as a means of teaching languages, accords well with the pragmatic approach advocated by Oller in Part I. An important question is whether such strategies can be incorporated on a wide scale into language teaching. Unfortunately, the field still seems to be dominated by drills and excercises which tend to minimize communication as well as the opportunity for the individual learner to contribute to the learning process.

Although there is not room for details of the program that Dykstra and Nunes have developed, they emphasize a precise definition of an overall objective which helps to define its own method: communication is built into the learning tasks while the learner progresses by modular gradation at a pace determined at each successive stage by the effectiveness of his previous efforts.

In the fourth paper of this section, Hale and Budar return to the questions posed by Kennedy in Part II. What are the conditions for successful language learning? Are these conditions necessarily identifiable with good language teaching? They conclude that degree of success in learning English as a second language is related to three main factors: (1) the amount of exposure the learner has to English; (2) the extent of his associations out of school with English-speaking students; and (3) the attitudes toward the use of English that are expressed in the learner's home. Without the favorable influence of these factors, special classes do not seem to be of much value. What is probably *most* important is the integrative motivation which was discussed especially in Part V by Gardner, Tucker, and Lambert. Practical ways in which this sort of learner motivation might be exploited are suggested.

THE LIMITS OF LANGUAGE EDUCATION

Bernard Spolsky

When a scholar finds his field becoming relevant to the society in which he lives, he is easily tempted to assume he can cure all the ills he sees. Applied linguists are no exception; many have jumped from seeing how language education might help those who do not speak the standard language, to a belief that language problems are basic. Thus, in a recent article Garland Cannon (1971) speaks of the "original linguistic causes" of discrimination and seems to argue that the solution of "bilingual problems" will lead to a new millenium. Reading an article like this, one is reminded of the enthusiasm with which the new methods of language teaching were propounded in the 50's and early 60's: give us the money and the machines, we said, and the linguists will show you how to teach everyone a foreign language.

This belief in the existence of linguistic solutions explains linguists' disappointment when they find programs in English as a second language, or as a second dialect, or in bilingual education, being greeted with suspicion by the community for which they are intended. Serious-minded, honest, and well-intentioned applied linguists are discouraged when the NAACP condemns programs using Black English as part of an "insidious conspiracy" to cripple the black children ("Black Nonsense," editorial in *The Crisis* [1971]), or when ESL programs are characterized as arrogant linguistic imperialism (editorial in *El Grito* [1968]). How can we be wrong, we ask, both when we try to recognize and preserve the child's language (as in bilingual or "bidialectal" programs), and when we try to teach the standard one (as in ESL or ESOD programs)?

The difficulty has arisen, I suspect, because linguists and language teachers have seen their task as teaching language: they have not realized that it is teaching students to use language. Thus, they have often ignored the place of language in the wider curriculum of school and in society as a whole. Take the example of literacy. We argue for adult literacy in English as a means of getting jobs, ignoring (or probably not knowing) that unemployment patterns are not controlled by linguistic but by racial factors. A Mexican American is out of work not because he can't read, but because there is no work, or because the employers don't hire Mexicans.

It is important to distinguish between language as a reason and language as an excuse for discrimination. There are clearly cases in which someone's inability to use a language is a reason not to hire him; in such cases, teaching him the language will solve the problem. But there are many other cases in which language is used as an excuse, like race or skin color or sex, for not hiring someone. No amount of language training will change this, for the discrimination exists in the hearer and not the speaker. Blacks and Spanish Americans know this, but applied linguists and language teachers have often not noticed.

Exaggerated claims, then, are a part of the difficulty. But I do not suggest that applied linguists should, like some theoretical linguists, simply decide that their field has no immediate social relevance. It is important to see applied linguistics as one of the fields with a contribution to make, but, at the same time to recognize clearly its limitations. For linguistic problems are a reflection of social problems rather than a cause. There is a linguistic barrier to the education of many children, but it is not the only barrier to social and economic acceptance.

The potential relevance of educational linguistics becomes more apparent if we look at language and language learning as part of the general school curriculum. There can be many views of the purpose of an educational system, but a central aim must be to make it possible for its graduates to take their place in society. To do this they need to be able to control effectively the language of that society.

The society in which people live today is not a single entity. We all live in a great number of worlds: the world of our home, of our neighborhood, of our church group, of our occupations, of the culture that interests us. And it is often the case that these worlds or societies each have different languages or speech varieties. With the rapid expansion of scientific knowledge for example, whatever other language requirements an individual may have, he must have good control of one of the world's major languages if he wishes to keep up to date with modern physics. Again, however well he knows English, a child living in a New Mexican pueblo must be able to use the language of his people if he is to participate in the cultural and religious life of the kiva.

There are indeed people who live in a true monolingual situation and can attain complete self-realization in that language. Someone born in middle-class suburban America who, if he travels at all, does so as a tourist without understanding the culture he is visiting, and who is satisfied with the culture provided by the television set and the newspaper, will no doubt be able to conduct his whole life in one language. Whatever his limitations, the advantages such a person has from life are denied to those who do not from the beginning master middle-class American English. To the extent that we believe that all people should have access to these opportunities, teaching English to those who speak other languages becomes a central responsibility of the American educational system; and not just to those who speak other languages, but also, as is becoming increasingly clear, to those whose dialect is not acceptable.

This is not the time to enter into the question of the fundamental advantages or disadvantages of nonstandard dialects. Linguists seem reasonably convinced that no language or dialect is inherently inferior to any other, with the possible exception of pidgins. But we must also recognize political reality: there is no doubt that middle-class American culture assumes that its members will speak the standard language, and that it penalizes in various ways those who do not (Leibowitz, 1971). One of the first tasks of the educational system is to make it possible to overcome this disadvantage. This means that any American school must be aware of the language or dialect background of its students and make it possible for them to acquire the standard language as quickly as possible. There is good evidence to suggest that during this acquisition period other learning can take place in the child's first language. There is reason to believe for example that it is a wise strategy to teach a Spanish-speaking child to read in Spanish while he is busy acquiring English, or to teach a Navajo-speaking child to read in his own language first (Spolsky and Holm, 1971). This type of strategy leads to the sort of educational structure that William Mackey (1970), in his excellent typology, would classify as dual-medium bilingual education, which aims at acculturation and at shifting the students to the standard language gradually but as soon as possible.

But this so far assumes that everyone wishes, and should wish, to belong to a single, monolithic, English-speaking culture. This melting-pot hypothesis has now happily been replaced by an acceptance of cultural pluralism. In this case, the languages of the minorities must be recognized not just as something to be used during the transitional period, but as an integral part of the school curriculum.

But exactly what this part should be is still a matter for investigation. There are two basic strategies; to decide that each of the two languages concerned should have equal status throughout the curriculum, or to give them different status. The former strategy might well be considered in those cases where one is dealing with two languages each of which has a standard literature and each of which provides access to all aspects of culture, commerce, and science, e.g., French, English, Spanish. In the United States, this model has been proposed as the ideal by Gaarder (1970) and by other foreign language teachers, and its implementation is the goal for the Dade County experiment in Florida. It has a number of special qualities. It assumes entry to the school system by two sets of students, each controlling a different language. During the initial period, English for the speakers of the X language is paralleled by teaching the other language to the speakers of English. The natural advantages that speakers of English would have over speakers of X is thus taken away: all students need to spend a large portion of their time acquiring a second language. The curricular cost is clearly large: the time spent on the second language is not available for other activitites, but the presumed reward is a generation of educated bilinguals, equally at ease in two languages and cultures.

A great deal of attention has been paid to this model and particularly to the Dade County program. In Dade County, Florida, the bilingual program began in 1961 to deal with the influx of Cuban refugees. In its first approach, the program was transitional, paralleling teaching English as a second language with the use of Spanish-speaking Cuban teacher aides. In 1963, Coral Way Elementary School began a program in which all pupils, whether English- or Spanish-speaking, were taught half the day in each language. Since then, three more Dade County schools have followed the Coral Way pattern. Evaluation of Coral Way has been favorable, with data supporting the general conclusion that Cuban children are, by sixth grade, equally proficient in reading two languages. But no detailed evaluation has yet appeared. The major question that will need to be answered is the generalizability of the Coral Way experiment, with its Cuban middle-class children, its national spotlight, and its generous support, to situations where Spanish speakers are less advantaged.

One of the most thoroughly documented studies in bilingual education is another middle-class experiment. In the St. Lambert, Montreal experiment (Lambert, Just, and Segalowitz, 1970; Tucker, 1971), a group of English-speaking parents asked for their children to be taught in French. After four years of the experiment, it is clear that the children have not suffered in educational achievement: their

English measures are no worse than their peers taught only in English, and while they are not yet as good in French as native speakers, they do very well in it. Somewhat disappointingly however, these children taught in French have no more favorable attitude to French-Canadians than do other Montreal English-Canadians, suggesting that neither language teaching nor teaching in a language leads to a basic change in social attitude.

The second strategy for bilingual education is to regard the X language as a limited culture-carrying medium and treat English as the main language of instruction. In this approach, the X language speakers use their own language for learning about their culture. In the first grades, X is used in the transfer classes, as a medium for concept development and for learning to read. But even when the English as a second language program has reached its goal, and the student can carry on with the main part of the curriculum in English, the X language remains the medium for cultural studies. In this model, then, we might have Spanish-speaking children learning to read in Spanish while learning English: when they move to a regular curriculum in English, they will still take a subject called Hispanic Studies, taught in Spanish. It must be noted that this strategy is in fact one that maintains culture at the cost of maintaining isolation: the X speakers are the only ones capable of learning in the X language. This can presumably be overcome at the cost of having English-speaking children learn X. But note that we are then left with a monolithic, "melting-pot," bilingual community, rather than two separate communities. The difficulties with this become clear when we consider a school with English and several X languages: if it is decided that *all* students must learn *all* languages, there will be little time for anything else.

Almost all the programs funded under the Bilingual Education Program follow this strategy, as a result of the fact that they are almost all aimed at the first one or two grades of elementary school. Many proposals assume that the program will follow the present children through the system, but time will tell what comes of this. For it to happen, there will need to be major changes in teacher training and the preparation of a great deal of new instructional material.

Given present official concern for accountability, a great amount of evaluative data has been collected in the course of new programs. But so far, there has been no published work that permits objective assessment of the techniques and approaches. The two main studies of bilingual programs (Andersson and Boyer, 1970; John and Horner,

1971) were written too early to do much more than quote from evaluation proposals. It may be some time then before we have any clear evidence of the effectiveness of various approaches to teaching and using a language other than English in school.

What I have been saying about X languages also provides a model for dealing with X dialects. Even though a dialect may be nonstandard, it will still need recognition as a potentially viable medium during the phase when the standard dialect is being taught. The possibility of maintenance for cultural purposes is presumably available, but it is unlikely to be chosen simply because the nonstandard dialect is generally not regarded as a valuable culture transmitter.

The American situation then calls both for English as a second language and bilingual education. A child coming to school must be taught the standard language if he is to have access to the general culture and economy. At the same time, he has a right to be taught in his own language while he is learning enough English to handle the rest of the curriculum. Communities that wish to maintain their own cultures and language may opt for this, recognizing the values and costs: separateness, and less time for "marketable" education. Communities that wish for a new blend of cultures may choose this, paralleling the teaching of English as a second language with the teaching of the second language to the English speakers. Establishing a language education policy like this will not solve society's ills: it won't overcome racial prejudice or do away with economic and social injustice. But it will be a valuable step in this direction and a contribution of linguistics to society.

REFERENCES

Andersson, T. and M. Boyer. *Bilingual Schooling in the United States.* Washington, D.C.: U.S. Government Printing Office, 1970.

Cannon, G. "Bilingual Problems and Developments in the United States."*PMLA*, 86 (1971), 452-58.

Fishman, J. A. and J. Lovas. "Bilingual Education in Raciolinguistic Perspective." *TESOL Quarterly* 4, (1970), 215-22.

Gaarder, A. B. "The First Seventy-Six Bilingual Education Projects." *Monograph Series on Languages and Linguistics*, 23. J. E. Alatis (ed.). Washington, D. C.: Georgetown University Press, 1970.

John, V. P., and V. M. Horner. *Early Childhood Bilingual Education*. New York: Modern Language Association, 1971.

Lambert, W. E., M. Just, and N. Segalowitz. "Some Cognitive Consequences of Following the Curricula of the Early School Grades in a Foreign Language." *Monograph Series on Languages and Linguistics,* 23. J. E. Alatis (ed.). Washington, D. C.: Georgetown University Press, 1970.

Leibowitz, A. H. *Educational Policy and Political Acceptance*. ERIC Clearinghouse for Linguistics, 1971.

Mackey, W. F. "A Typology of Bilingual Education." *Foreign Language Annals,* 3 (1970), 596-608.

Spolsky, B. and W. Holm. "Literacy in the Vernacular: The Case of the Navajo." *Studies in Language and Linguistics* 1970-71. J. Ornstein and R. W. Ewton, Jr. (eds.). El Paso: Texas Western Press, 1971.

Tucker, G. R. "Cognitive and Attitudinal Consequences of Following the Curricula of the First Few Grades in a Second Language." Paper read at the Fifth Annual Convention of TESOL, New Orleans, La., 1971.

BILINGUAL SCHOOLING
AND SECOND LANGUAGE TEACHING: A REVIEW OF
RECENT NORTH AMERICAN EXPERIENCE

H. H. Stern

Language teachers tend to be ambivalent in their attitude to the phenomenon of bilingualism. Many emphatically reject the idea that the teaching of languages can claim to create bilinguals; and the occasional bilingual student in the language class is often considered more of an embarrassment or a nuisance than a help to his less fortunate fellow students.

The psychological and social advantages of bilingualism have been the subject of much debate. Bilingual education, i.e., the provision of education through the medium of two languages, is not new. But earlier studies of efforts to provide such dual-medium schooling, for example in Welsh and English in Wales, or in Irish and English in Ireland, did not invite much enthusiasm for these attempts (e.g., Macnamara, 1966). The findings of these investigations were very much in line with the general trend of studies on bilingualism since the twenties which, apart from a few exceptions, presented a gloomy picture of the educational merits of bilingualism.

From this rather negative approach to bilingual education, there has been in recent years a considerable shift to a much more positive outlook. Bilingual education has aroused renewed interest. There is an eagerness to make education in two languages much more widely available and, indeed, to regard such bilingual forms of schooling as educationally desirable and as a remedy for a number of social ills. It is claimed that this movement can have practical significance for education in bilingual and multilingual communities and for foreign language teaching, quite apart from the theoretical interest it may have for psychology and psycholinguistics.

What has brought about this change of outlook? To what extent have the earlier misgivings about bilingual education been allayed? In what respects are the recent North American experiences and research in this area of wider interest and applicability? This article attempts to sketch briefly the new developments in bilingual education in North America and to indicate implications for second language teaching.

The trend towards language diversification, a characteristic feature of recent decades throughout the world, is manifested in North America in two distinct movements—one in the U.S.A., and the other in Canada which have much in common in certain respects but differ in others.

In the U.S.A., the assimilation of all ethnic groups to the American (White, Anglo-Saxon) language and culture has been an ideal right up to the most recent times. It is now giving way to the acceptance of language diversity and cultural pluralism within the United States as assets to be cultivated. The older anomalous policy of the "melting pot" is characterized by this example. First, you train a Spanish-speaking immigrant child through the school system to learn English. You cause him to abandon his own language loyalty and to reject his ancestral culture. Once you have succeeded, you teach him Spanish as a foreign language in school, generally without much success. In other words, one of the great national American resources, language diversity, is being thoughtlessly squandered. To preserve and cultivate it is one important reason for the bilingual education policy of recent years. This policy is to some extent the result of a recognition of one of the facts of American life, namely the continued existence and value of language loyalties in the U.S.A. (Fishman, *et al.*, 1966). Politically, it is a belated attempt to do justice to the non-English-speaking minorities. It is, therefore, to some extent, an act of social reform and recognition of rights in line with desegregation and with the acceptance of Black English (Labov, 1969). It concerns the rights of Indians, Eskimos, Puerto Ricans, Cubans, as well as Jews, Italians, Chinese, and other minorities, to be themselves in school, and in society at large. The minorities themselves have become increasingly aware of their influence and power; politicians conscious of their voting public recognize this fact and, therefore, begin to champion the cause of minorities.

This change of heart has been expressed in two types of legislation: the Bilingual Education Act of 1968, empowering Congress to appropriate funds for bilingual education projects; and legal provision in the schools of some states legitimizing languages other than English as the language of instruction in schools (Kloss, 1971).

Curious revivals occur. For example, in the states of Louisiana, Maine, Vermont, and New Hampshire, French-speaking groups are rediscovering their French past and consider it worthwhile to make their family and neighborhood patois the basis for a French-English bilingual education. In other school systems, Spanish-speaking children of Cuban, Puerto Rican, or Mexican origin are beginning to be given the chance to maintain their mother tongue while also learning English.

Typical American bilingual education projects provide education in the vernacular in the initial stages of schooling, e.g., in Spanish, French, or Navaho, and introduce English by degrees. Thus, the prototype of bilingual education aims at the maintenance and development of the mother tongue and at the same time provides opportunities for learning English. In some instances, projects have been started in which the school offers parallel opportunities for English-speaking children to learn a second language, e.g., Spanish, and to be exposed to the minority culture in the school. However, at present bilingual education in the United States is still in an experimental stage, and in practice it affects only a small number of children of various ethnic origins. The development, current state, and problems of these bilingual projects have been described in a few excellent recent studies: Andersson and Boyer (1970); Gaarder (1970); John and Horner (1971). In addition, the whole issue of educating young children between the ages of 3 and 8 in two languages was discussed at a three-day conference on child language held in Chicago in November 1971, under the chairmanship of Professor Theodore Andersson of the University of Texas. The proceedings of this important meeting will be published in 1972 by the International Center for Research on Bilingualism at the University of Laval, Quebec, Canada.

In Canada the situation is different. For many years, Canadians have viewed their ethnic philosophy as a "mosaic" of different nationalities, in contrast with the older "melting pot" philosophy of the U.S.A. The most important difference from the situation in the U.S.A. is of course the "French fact." In other words, Canada as a nation was created by two founding races, French and English, which constitute fairly distinct cultural and linguistic entities. As a result, the melting-pot philosophy has never had the same hold in Canada as in the United States. Although, in effect, the dominance of the English "establishment" was, and perhaps still is, a fact of Canadian life, national groups such as Italians, Germans or Ukrainians—not to speak of Indians and Eskimos—have maintained an ethnic identity.

During the last ten years, Canada has tried to come to grips in a constructive way with its major problem as a national entity, namely, the interaction between the English and French national groups. The development of thought and policy on all the bilingual and bicultural issues involved in work, education, government, and culture is embodied in one of the most fascinating documents of our times on this question, the *Report of the Royal Commission on Bilingualism and Biculturalism* (1967-71). This six-volume study attempts to recognize the legitimacy of national development through the medium of English and French and to resolve areas of possible conflict and frustration. It has already resulted in one major piece of legislation, the Official Languages Act of 1969, and the creation of a new office—that of the Commissioner of Official Languages, a kind of ombudsman on language questions (Commissioner of Official Languages, 1971).

In the past, before this change of outlook, English-speaking Canadians had made relatively little effort to learn French beyond what was offered as part of the traditional French-as-a-second-language curriculum in secondary schools. On the other hand, French-speaking Canadians, by force of circumstance, had to make the effort to learn English to overcome their handicap in social and economic advancement. In the eyes of many French Canadians, bilingualism had become more and more a "dirty" word, suggesting the gradual erosion of French in Canada, the inferiority of the Francophone minority, and constant concessions on their part to the overwhelming dominance of the English-speaking majority. It was this climate of opinion that has brought about demands of separatism from militant factions, and the more moderate demand of a fairer deal for the Francophone population and their language, expressed in the *Report on Bilingualism and Biculturalism.*

One of the more immediate consequences of the ideology expressed in this Report has been a general tendency among English speakers to demand an improvement in the attainments in French as a second language in schools.

The interest among Anglophone parents to have their children taught effectively in French has enormously increased. Against this background a private French-medium school for English-speaking children, the Toronto French School, was established in the early sixties by an enterprising pioneer, W. H. Giles.

During the past ten years, several school boards have also attempted to reform their French programs with more or less success. Although considerable advances have been made, and expenditures have been increased on French as a second language, including the creation of a new teaching force for French at the primary stage, it may be said, even without formal evaluation, that most of the results are not commensurate with the demands and expectations expressed by the public. For example, the Commissioner for Official Languages in his first annual report (1971) says "in too many parts of Canada, second-language teaching, by its often rote-learned irrelevance to the facts of Canadian life, has dulled rather than refined the instruments of dialogue."

In Montreal, a group of English-speaking parents, because of their strong belief in the need for effective bilingualism for English-speaking children growing up in the Province of Quebec, addressed a proposal to the Ministry of Education of that Province in 1965, for the creation of a bilingual school in the City of St. Lambert (a suburb of Greater Montreal). This request led to the setting up of a bilingual program in the St. Lambert Elementary School, a program which has become world famous.

The philosophy of the St. Lambert program is different from that of American programs. In this Canadian experiment, English is simply ignored during the first two years of schooling, because it is argued that English is taken care of by informal education in the home and neighborhood. Thus, the program is based on the notion of the "home-school language switch." The kindergarten and grade 1 classes are boldly conducted entirely in French by French-speaking teachers, and English is gradually introduced and increased as a medium of instruction only after these first two years. This courageous venture has worked well in St. Lambert according to the findings of an evaluation associated with this experiment, carried out by Professor W. E. Lambert and the Language Study Group of the Department of Psychology of McGill University.

In previous studies, Lambert had made ingenious use of the diversity of linguistic and cultural groups in Montreal for important investigations on questions of sociopsychological interest. For example, in cooperation with one of his students, Elizabeth Peal, he had compared a group of 89 bilingual 10-year-old children with 74 monolingual 10-year-olds in six French-speaking schools in Montreal on intelligence, teachers' ratings, and attitudes. Contrary to many previous studies on the effects of bilingualism, this study found that "bilinguals performed significantly better than monolinguals on both verbal and non-verbal intelligence tests" (Peal and Lambert, 1962). This study has become a landmark in a more positive view of bilingualism.

Because of their interest in the effects of bilingualism, Lambert and his colleagues have, over the last five years, systematically compared the bilingually educated children at the St. Lambert School with children educated monolingually in French or English in the same area of Montreal. Annual reports of this experiment published between 1969 and 1971 have yielded very encouraging results for this bilingual education program. The children in this program appear "to be able after four or five years to read, write, speak, understand, and use English as well as youngsters instructed via English in the conventional manner. In addition, and at no cost, they can also read, write, speak, and understand French, in a way that English pupils who follow the traditional French as a second language program never do" (Tucker and D'Anglejan, 1972).

These promising developments in bilingual education in Montreal have led to an increase in experimentation in bilingual schooling in other parts of Canada, particularly in the neighboring Province of Ontario. For example, in the course of the past two years, three school boards in the Ottawa area (the Ottawa Board of Education, the Carleton Board of Education, and the Ottawa Roman Catholic Separate School Board) have instituted similar bilingual education programs for several hundred children at the kindergarten and grade 1 stage. These experiments also appear to yield very promising results. In a recent study comparing the Ottawa "immersion" group with a matched sample from a non-immersion program, the results of the St. Lambert study were largely confirmed (Edwards and Casserly, 1971). The Modern Language Center of the Ontario Institute for Studies in Education has established a project to study the wider application of these bilingual education programs on a long-term basis and to assist in curriculum development. One of the first tasks of this project was to conduct a stock-taking seminar. At this seminar, the Canadian and American approaches to bilingual education were reviewed by practitioners and research workers. Papers and discussions of this very fruitful meeting were recently published by the Ontario Institute for Studies in Education (Swain, 1972).

Bilingual education is still a relatively new development in the quest for the improvement of second language learning. But if results continue to confirm the positive findings obtained to date, it may have considerable implications for the solution of various other language problems. For example, it may be seen as a possible approach to the education of minority language groups (e.g., U.S.A.), or as an answer to educational problems in countries which seek the development of education in the vernacular as well as education through a medium of wider communication (e.g., Ghana). It may equally be of significance to education in multilingual communities (e.g., India). Bilingual education may, therefore, have something to offer in the solution of the language problems of countries as diverse as India, Ghana, Wales, or New Zealand (e.g., Bender, 1971, or Schools Council, 1971).

Lastly, bilingual education also has implications for second language teaching. One of the most intriguing problems of language teaching arises from the fact that it is difficult, if not impossible, to attend simultaneously to the formal properties of language and to the meaning to be conveyed in a given situation.

Students of language since Saussure have noted the distinction that must be made between a language as a formal system and language in action which has been varyingly expressed by the juxtaposition of such pairs of terms as: langue-parole; code-message; competence-performance.

This distinction is also of great importance in understanding the problems of second-language learning. It has frequently been noted by many observers and critics of language teaching that the learning of the formal features of a language does not readily transfer to functional use. Someone who has studied a language diligently for many years often finds to his disappointment that he cannot understand or express himself adequately in real-life situations. It is of no concern to us for the purposes of this discussion whether he is taught by the "audio-lingual," "cognitive," or any other method. All classroom methods are similar in that they basically convey to the learner the formal properties of a language.

Popularly, this failure to transfer the formal learning is expressed by such sayings as "You can't learn a language in the classroom; you learn it only in the country," or "The only way of learning a language is by using it when you need it." However, one cannot fail to notice that young children appear to acquire a language by use of the language in meaningful situations without any apparent attention to formal features.

One of the foremost critics of formal language learning, John Macnamara, has attributed the failure to learn a second language to a lack of communicative impulse.

> the child learns his mother tongue by determining independent of language what his mother is saying to him and using the meaning to unravel the code. I am reasonably sure that the manner in which a child learns a second language in the street is basically similar . . . . Sense is everything. In the classroom things are the other way about. Language is everything. The teacher has nothing important to say to the child, and the child has nothing important to say to the teacher. The whole design of the classroom runs against the grain of the *faculté de langage*, the natural device for learning a language (Macnamara, 1972, p. 9).

If we take together two propositions: (*a*) children learn a language effectively in communicative settings; (*b*) a language cannot be learned effectively by classroom methods alone, it can be argued that if we convert the school or classroom into a truly communicative setting, a language might well be learned more effectively than by conventional methods of classroom teaching. It is this argument that makes bilingual schooling relevant for language teaching as an alternative to formal instruction or as a possible addition, because one of the central problems of formal language instruction is that it offers inadequate opportunities for the use of the language in genuine acts of communication.

Bilingual education as a means of second language learning appears to owe its success to the fact that it offers the necessary opportunities for the application of the language being learned. It does not invalidate language teaching as such, but where languages are of great importance in education, as they are in Canada and the U.S.A., and as they are no doubt also in other countries, bilingual education may provide an alternative to language instruction *per se*. Where languages continue to be taught as curriculum subjects, as no doubt they always will be, bilingual education may offer to the language teacher of tomorrow welcome and constructive ideas on how to put language learning to use.

It is with these thoughts in mind that the writer would recommend to language teachers and other educators concerned with language questions to interest themselves in the development of bilingual education. The attached bibliography is likely to help them understand the background of this new development and current thought on it.

REFERENCES

Andersson, T., and M. Boyer. *Bilingual Schooling in the United States*. Washington, D.C.: U.S. Government Printing Office, 1970.

Bender, B. W. *Linguistic Factors in Maori Education*. Wellington: New Zealand Council for Educational Research, 1971.

Commissioner of Official Languages. *First Annual Report 1970-1971*. Ottawa: Information Canada, 1971.

Edwards, H. P., and Casserly, M. C. *Research and Evaluation of the French Program 1970-71: Annual Report*. Ottawa: English Schools, The Ottawa Roman Catholic Separate School Board, 1971.

Fishman, J. A. *et al. Language Loyalty in the United States*. The Hague: Mouton, 1966.

Gaarder, A. B. "The First Seventy-Six Bilingual Education Projects." *Monograph Series on Language and Linguistics,* 23. J. E. Alatis (ed.). Washington, D.C.: Georgetown University Press, 1970.

John, V. P., and V. M. Horner, *Early Childhood Bilingual Education.* New York: Modern Language Association, 1971.

Kloss, H. *Laws and Legal Documents Relating to Problems of Bilingual Education in the United States.* Washington, D.C.: ERIC Clearinghouse for Linguistics, 1971.

Labov, W., *et al. The Study of Non-Standard English.* Washington, D.C.: U.S. Office of Education, 1969.

Lambert, W. E., and G. R. Tucker, *Bilingual Education of Children: The St. Lambert Experiment.* Rowley, Mass.: Newbury House, 1972.

Lieberson, S. *Language and Ethnic Relations in Canada.* New York: Wiley, 1970.

Mackey, W. F. *Bilingual Education in a Binational School.* Rowley, Mass.: Newbury House, 1972.

Macnamara, J. *Bilingualism and Primary Education: A Study of Irish Experience.* Edinburgh: Edinburgh University Press, 1966.

———. "The Objectives of Bilingual Education in Canada from an English-speaking Perspective." Swain (1972).

Peal, E. and W. E. Lambert. "The Relation of Bilingualism to Intelligence," *Psychological Monograph, General and Applied,* No. 546, 1962.

Royal Commission on Bilingualism and Biculturalism. *Report of the Royal Commission on Bilingualism and Biculturalism,* Books I-VI, Ottawa: Queen's Printer, 1967-71.

Schools Council Committee for Wales. *Report of the Working Party on the Experimental Bilingual School.* Cardiff: Committee for Wales, 1971.

Swain, M. (ed.). *Bilingual Schooling: Some Experiences in Canada and the United States.* Toronto: Ontario Institute for Studies in Education, 1972.

Tucker, G. R., and A. d'Anglejan. "An Approach to Bilingual Education: The St. Lambert Experiment." Swain (1972).

THE LANGUAGE SKILLS PROGRAM OF THE ENGLISH PROJECT

Gerald Dykstra and Shiho S. Nunes

The Hawaii English Program nearing completion by the Hawaii Curriculum Center has three components: Language Skills, Language Systems, and Literature. In the school year 1970-71, the first increment of Skills and Literature was operational in approximately 13 per cent of K-3 classes in the state and was followed by the remainder of the curriculum in 1971-72.

ASSUMPTIONS OF THE LANGUAGE SKILLS PROGRAM

Several important assumptions underlie the development of the Language Skills Program. The first is that school children differ. They differ in scholastic aptitude, intelligence, or ability; in socioeconomic background; in interests; in ability to communicate and in meanings they attach to words and behaviors and things; in attendance and absence from class sessions; in energy and need for rest; in styles and rates of learning and levels at which learning plateaus are reached; in educational needs; in physical needs, including hunger, hurt, and moods; in needs for indications of success or approval; in needs for supervision; in needs for peer association and indications of peer acceptance; in needs for educational guidance and advice; in needs for participating in decisions affecting their own activities; and so on, *ad infinitum.* These differences imply that the route a child takes to skills development, the specific content of programs, the manner of presentation, and the rate of his progress must match as nearly as possible his specific needs, abilities, and interests. The first assumption can thus be said to lead to an individualized approach. The Skills Program is accordingly conceived as a bank of materials designed to facilitate development of individualized programs that will help children proceed from their individual entry levels to sixth grade ability levels in language skills.

Secondly, the Skills Program assumes that language is for use in communication, and therefore any program of skills should be developed and evaluated within a context of purposeful communication. The program assumes that if the long-range purpose of a school program is the laying of groundwork for ability in effective communication, then the immediate purpose for the child should be to succeed in a communication task at his appropriate level—a task more complex than one he has mastered before but less demanding than one he will master next. The entire program has been designed as a series of such tasks leading to the accomplishment of higher level goals for each child. Experiences in interaction aimed at achieving goals in communication are to be made available at a wide range of levels, but no child is required to enter any skills program unless he both needs it and can succeed in effecting the communication required.

Thirdly, it is assumed that people achieve better when they know quite precisely what it is they are to achieve and how their attempts are to be judged. It is further assumed that the goals of a skills program can be explicitly stated and that clear criteria for achievement of such goals can be established. It is yet further assumed that these goals can be analyzed into lower-level goals until there are, in many instances, moment-by-moment objectives, each with a clear criterion for successful achievement. Such objectives should constitute parts of, or successive approximations to, the higher level objectives and goals. Thus the entire Skills Program is organized into a hierarchy of goals and achievement criteria stated in explicit terms.

Fourthly, the program assumes that in an educationally useful responsive environment, the child is a decision maker, and that someone or something in his immediate environment responds to his decision. Such an environment may, on appropriate occasions, consist of a child working individually with paper and a pencil, with a book, with a phonograph, with a listening headset, with a recorder and playback instrument of the reel or card type, with a film loop, and so on. On other occasions, the responsive environment may include a child and a teacher working on a program. More often it may include two students, one teaching or presenting and the other learning or seeing for the first time with his peer or near-peer. It may include larger groups or even an entire class engaged in an activity appropriate to such groupings. The responsive environment changes as the child's needs change. This concept of the learning environment as a series of changing environments with which the child is constantly interacting implies a departure from the classroom in the conventional sense. It calls for a specifically organized learning environment which not only allows, but simultaneously requires and provides for the child to make decisions as he progresses toward his goals.

A fifth assumption is that the teacher's role in such an environment changes in the direction of higher professionalization. Observation, evaluation, guiding, and planning become more important for the teacher than lecturing, cueing, testing, correcting, and clerking. In the Skills Program, the essential tools are available to allow the teacher to begin coping with the individual requirements of every child and thus fulfill one appropriate professional role of the teacher. In broader perspective this role includes all matters of professional counseling, advising, guiding, and directing. Other roles include management of the learning environments and serving as a model of the teacher-scholar interested in education. This assumption, inasmuch as it deals with individual teachers, relates also to the first assumption. Teachers differ, and the ways they actualize the assumed or hypothesized move toward higher professionalization must be expected to differ.

A sixth major assumption involves the concept of systems. The entire Language Skills Program constitutes a system in which there is a constant and dynamic interplay among the elements that make up the system: goals drawn from communication systems and organized hierarchically; outcomes described as successful behaviors in communication; pupils and teachers who play particular roles; a full bank of materials which serves at once as a series of cues, as tests for both diagnosis and achievement, and as goals; and a learning environment organized in a particular way. The full bank of materials is a network made up of four subsystems (Aural, Oral, Reading, Writing), each with its own network, flowchart, and different entry and exit points for different children, but each connected with the other three subsystems as well. Participants in the system are those pupils who have available both the full bank of materials and the specified learning environment, which includes a qualified teacher and an ungraded group of students in which one-third has always had at least two years of experience in the system, one-third has had at least one year of such experience, and no more than one-third is totally new to the system and the materials. If the integrity of the system is maintained, it is expected that certain outcomes can be predicted with a high degree of accuracy.

GOALS OF THE SKILLS PROGRAM

The overall goal of the Skills Program is to help each child progress from his entry level in each subprogram to the stage of independent learning in the language arts. This stage has been identified as what is generally acknowledged as sixth grade achievement levels. Some children may reach aspects of this stage in three years or less; others may take the current average of seven years. And some may take more than seven years as 50% of the nation's children now do (excluding the still considerable percentage which represents the early dropouts who presumably never reach that level). The planning team feels confident that the majority (not just half) will attain this level well before seven years and that the number of students who do not currently attain these levels within seven years will be substantially reduced from the inception of the program wherever its integrity and design are reasonably maintained and wherever its conditions are ever approximately met. The team is further confident that the design for an annual incremental increase in product for each of several successive years (seven or more) will materialize under such conditions. Field tests are beginning to provide corroboration for the existence of such an increment for the second and third years in any field test school. Tests will soon indicate whether schools that have rejected major aspects of the design (dropping the mixed K-1-2 classes, for example, and retaining classes segregated by age in one-year increments) suffer measurably in output or not.

Specific goals for the Skills Program have been established within and across basic areas that may be viewed in alternative ways, depending on the emphasis that is needed: (*a*) listening and reading skills contributing to a receptive repertory, and oral and writing skills leading to a productive repertory; (*b*) the listening and speaking programs contributing to development of skills with the oral representations of language symbols, and reading and writing programs contributing to development of skills with the graphic representations of language symbols; (*c*) listening, speaking, reading, and writing as separate strands with criteria for achievement of goals and objectives at all levels; (*d*) correlation of skills with oral representations and skills with graphic representations, including both receptive and productive repertories, in order to accomplish appropriately complex tasks of interchange and communication. The subprograms to accomplish these objectives are seen organizationally as separated strands,[1] but in operation they are not. They are interrelated parts of a total system that will take the child toward the synthesized control which is the primary aim. Again specific student goals are established and criteria set for determining when such goals have been attained. Student objectives are organized toward the goal

---

[1]Callendar, Port, and G. Dykstra, "Peer Tutoring—A Rationale." *Educational Perspectives* XII, 1, 1973.

and precise criteria are established for determining the attainment of the objectives so that the student will know if he is on target for the goal. For example, the child learning to write cursive small letters from film loops knows that his goal is to copy from models all 26 small letters of the alphabet sequenced in any order. He knows that he has reached his target when he can correctly copy in his practice book a series of letters in any order from models provided by his teacher, and do so well enough for a series of readers, or respondents, to respond correctly to every attempt to make each letter in isolation.

A RATIONALE FOR THE LANGUAGE SKILLS PROGRAM

The acquisition of language skills is stressed in the early years of schooling because effective interaction with others and effective learning in school are both assumed to depend on proficiency in these skills. The Skills Program is a performance curriculum, in which the fundamental goal is synthesized language control—the combined mastery of listening, speaking, reading, and writing skills for the purpose of communicating and learning, both in and out of school.

The Language Skills Program is further based upon the need for materials which respond adequately to the assumptions in the foregoing section which lead to individualization and communication. Individual differences and differences of needs as well as the potential for taking advantage of these differences are concepts that have long been recognized. They are important in a pluralistic society, a society that recognizes and values the individual, but we have had no appropriate materials. Communication—perhaps in part a response to the need for relevance—emphasizes purpose and meaning in a social context. It emphasizes the individual in his environment. It emphasizes the use of language, not first of all the forms of language, which are important, certainly, but exclusive emphasis on them constitutes an inadequate educational opportunity. Purpose and function are not to be bypassed in an effective educational system that is to be broadly applied, including application for segments of the population in which the home environment may not make immediately clear the purposefulness of education itself. Language skills materials which adequately incorporate either individualization or communication have not been available. The need to make such materials available is a fundamental reason for the Skills Program.

A great deal has been learned about the importance and the potential of peer teaching in recent years. When a child participates actively in communicating to another something that he has learned, a sense of responsibility, purpose, and self-fulfillment are important outcomes, but at least equally important from a skills-learning standpoint is the gain that accrues to the child who teaches. Helping another learn constitutes a review, but it is review in a situation that appropriates real-life activity with an adult-type purpose to enhance it. It is also a delayed test of the tutor's own learning. Altogether, it is an effective instructional instrument. Evidence already accumulated in the English Project shows far superior gains for children who teach than for comparable children who do not teach. There is, further, for the "tutored" child, convincing evidence to indicate that children *learn* effectively from their peers, in some instances much more readily and under less threatening circumstances than in learning from adults only. In the small teaching-learning groups that are used in the Skills Program there are great potential benefits for each child as he fulfills the role of learner and again as he may fulfill the role of tutor. It seems possible, in effect, to harness the educational process to itself, to allow education to pull itself up by its own bootstraps, in fact. The potential is akin to the discovery of atomic energy. It allows us to build in an almost automatic increment such that we can expect an increase in output annually for many years on the basis of organization. Materials must be appropriate, but the promise is clearly worth the effort.

Teachers must be used more effectively on a professional level. They must not be used primarily to fulfill tasks which can better be done by other means. The teachers' jobs must not be primarily those of simple cuer, test giver and corrector, and keeper of records. The teachers' professional training must prepare for roles of professional guidance, professional management, teaching, and scholarship. Materials that will allow the teacher to do a professional job instead of a caretaker's job are essential.

The incorporation of clearly established goals with even clearer criteria for goal attainment (well beyond the commonly known and used "behavioral objectives") must let every child, not just the teacher, know at every moment, not just at "test times," where he is going. This is an essential part of this systems approach highlighting individualization, and communication with a high density of student interaction.

The need for an educational system in which all elements are integrated cannot be adequately met by materials not specifically designed for this purpose. We must recognize the importance, the interdependence, and the interaction of all elements, and the materials must be flexible enough to fulfill their appropriate function adequately.

The need for this program is considered established. The reasons given seem compelling and provide a basis for undertaking the development work. A major contribution to education, in the state and generally, is a realistic hope.

ARE TESOL CLASSES THE ONLY ANSWER ?

Thomas M. Hale and Eva C. Budar

In 1964 there appeared in the *Modern Language Journal* an article entitled: "The Danger of Assumption Without Proof." The author made a strong plea for more research and experimentation, warning that if we fail to do this, language teaching as we know it today may very well ". . . go the way of the 'reading-by-word-memorization' and the 'have-fun-at-school' vogues (and) we will be in danger of reaping the same public contempt and of being similar targets for humorous absurdities . . ."[1]

Having serious reservations about our TESOL program in the secondary schools of Honolulu, we conducted the research we are reporting here. The results were surprising.

Prior to this study, the information we had concerning the success of our program was limited in scope and highly subjective. For the most part, we depended upon feedback from the few trained TESOL teachers we had working in the schools. In spite of the fact that their opinions and observations may have been reasonably valid, we had to take into consideration the obvious fact that their observations were limited to their particular classroom experiences in their particular schools; in other words, we were aware of what parts of the elephant looked like, but we were unable to see the whole beast. Too many questions remained unanswered, and unless we acquired more reliable and extensive data, no program of any real merit could be developed.

Programs designed to aid the immigrant students attending Hawaii's public schools have existed for the past several years; however, these were individual efforts conducted by regular classroom teachers having no TESOL training. With the recent relaxation of immigration laws resulting in increasing numbers of immigrants entering our schools, the Department of Education, in January 1969, took steps to initiate, on a limited scale, what would be, by the fall of 1970, a statewide TESOL program.

In initiating this program, trained and experienced TESOL teachers were hired and assigned only to those schools having the largest concentration of immigrant students. Because of the relative

---

[1] Beverly Moen Bazan, "The Danger of Assumption Without Proof," *Modern Language Journal*, 48 No. 6 (1964), 337-46.

scarcity of trained TESOL people, we supplemented the program by employing teaching assistants on a part-time basis.

For the most part, emphasis was placed on the audio-lingual approach to language teaching, but the teachers were free to use whatever method they felt achieved the best results. Most of these classes met daily, for from one to three fifty-minute periods.

Because of the difficulty of determining which of all the commercially available materials best suited our needs, we encouraged our teachers to try anything and everything in hopes of eventually finding something suitable for all.

In March, 1970, at the conclusion of approximately a full year of our formal TESOL program, we conducted this study.

Deciding upon a method of program evaluation was not an easy task. It seemed to us impractical to attempt to measure the relative merits of teachers, methods, and materials; furthermore, we were well aware of the fact that, as far as the students were concerned, we had no way of measuring such variables as, for example, the quality of English language instruction received by the immigrant student prior to his arrival in Hawaii, the student's general academic aptitude, the student's second language learning aptitude, or the attitude of the student and his family toward the English language and the culture it represents (in other parts of the United States, measuring these factors might be possible by using tests written in the student's vernacular, but in Honolulu our students represent more than twenty different language communities).

We finally decided that, given a normal distribution, perhaps all of the nonmeasurable items noted above would cancel each other out, and that the only thing we knew for certain was that some students were attending schools with TESOL programs, and some were not; we concluded, therefore, that if we applied the same measuring stick in all situations, then perhaps we could find an answer to a very important question: of all the nonnative speakers of English attending our public schools, *which ones were succeeding* in learning English, and *under what circumstances* were they doing it?

Our measuring instruments, because of our lack of sophistication in language testing techniques, had to be simple. What was important was that we apply the same measuring stick in all instances for the purpose of comparing students who were attending TESOL classes, with those who were not. Our primary goal was not that of accurately determining levels of proficiency, or even of establishing norms, although we were able to do the latter upon completion of the study. Our final decision was to do three things: conduct oral interviews, administer a written test, and take into consideration the students' scholastic averages. In so doing, we hoped to be able to find an answer to the question we have posed.

Oral interview

All students were given an oral interview in which they were required to respond to a series of general questions concerning their background, their family, the language used at home, the language used socially, the kinds of movies preferred (Chinese, Japanese, Filipino, English, etc.), and the amount of English language instruction received in their native country. Depending upon the degree to which the students seemed to understand the examiner's questions, and depending upon the degree to which the examiner understood the students' answers, they were graded on a scale from zero through three with zero indicating that the students have no ability to understand and use the English language orally, and three indicating an acceptable degree of fluency in English.

In an attempt to better standardize the results of the oral interview, the same examiner, the TESOL Program Coordinator, examined *all* of the immigrant students tested. It should also be noted that the oral examiner had no prior knowledge of the results of the students' scores on the Davis Test (see below), nor any prior knowledge of the students' academic standing.

Written test

All students took the "Diagnostic Test for Students of English as a Second Language," developed by Dr. A. L. Davis. This is a one-hundred-fifty-item, multiple-choice test of one's ability to use the major grammatical elements of the English language.

By comparing the results of the oral interview, the Davis Test, and the students' scholastic averages, and taking into consideration the assumption that the goal of the TESOL program is to prepare the immigrant students to function in a regular classroom situation in which the language of instruction is English, we discovered that if a student achieved a score of 2 or better on the oral test, and a score of 100 or better on the Davis Test (raw score), he was generally able to acquire a C or better scholastic average. Therefore, three factors, a score of 2 or better on the oral test, 100 or better on the Davis Test, and a C or better scholastic average, were combined and used as a measuring stick by means of which all of the students were compared in terms of their English language proficiency. This composite score is referred to on the chart as *Criteria I.*

TESOL Research—Secondary Schools—Honolulu District

	I School Population	II NNSE's Tested	III Ratio NNSE/ Nat.	IV NNSE's Enrolled 2 years or more	V 2 Yr. Enrollees Meeting Criteria I*	VI NNSE's Enrolled as of Sept. '69	VII Sept. Enrollees Meeting Criteria I*
1. Kaimuki Interm.	1,926	7	1/275	2	2 (100%)	2	2 (100%)
2. Jarrett Interm.	1,057	4	1/264	0	0	2	2 (100%)
3. Niu Valley Interm.	1,231	9	1/136	2	2 (100%)	2	2 (100%)
4. Kalani High	2,538	19	1/134	9	9 (100%)	5	5 (100%)
5. Stevenson Interm.	1,370	14	1/98	0	0	8	1 (12.5%)
6. Kaimuki High	2,264	33	1/68	23	23 (100%)	3	3 (100%)
7. Kawananakoa Interm.	820	16	1/51	11	7 (64%)	1	1 (100%)
8. Central Interm.	957	22	1/44	4	1 (25%)	8	1 (12.5%)
9. Farrington High	3,055	104	1/29	37	26 (70%)	34	22 (65%)
10. Washington Interm.	1,421	55	1/26	25	14 (56%)	11	7 (64%)
11. Dole Interm.	1,299	56	1/23	8	4 (50%)	24	7 (29%)
12. Kalakaua Interm.	1,626	80	1/20	13	4 (31%)	33	16 (48%)
13. McKinley: TESOL		85		27	22 (81%)	15	7 (47%)
Bilingual	2,393	33	1/20	18	12 (66%)	2	1 (50%)
	21,957	537	1/45	179	126	150	77

Intermediate School = Grades 7 through 9.
High School = Grades 10 through 12.
*Criteria I: a) 2 or better, oral interview.
b) 100 or better, Davis Test.
c) "C" or better, scholastic average.

The scholastic average alone, without the oral interview and the Davis Test, was not considered a sufficiently reliable criterion. For example, many students from the Orient achieve A's in mathematics and in science courses, and thus maintain fairly high scholastic averages, but they score very low in the oral interview and on the Davis Test. On the other hand, students from the Pacific Islands, who often score high in the oral interview, and are somehow managing to get through school, may score very low on the Davis Test because they lack proficiency in reading.

The results of our inquiry are summarized in the table which appears on the preceding page.

EXPLANATION OF THE TABLE

1. Those schools above the broken line are schools which have had NNSEs (Non-Native Speakers of English) in attendance, but have never had a formal program designed to help them. Except for the assistance occasionally offered them by their regular classroom teachers, the students were in a sink-or-swim situation.

2. Those schools below the broken line have had state-supported TESOL programs for one year prior to the time of testing and for the past two to four years have had special programs sponsored by the individual schools.

3. Those schools below the line are located in low socioeconomic areas, and those above the line are located in middle and upper-middle class neighborhoods.

4. Column III shows the ratio of NNSEs to native speakers of English. *(This is probably the most significant information in the table.)*

5. Column IV refers to those NNSEs who have been in-country for two years or more, and Column V indicates how many of these have reached Criteria I.

6. In Column VI are the numbers of NNSEs who, at the time of testing, had been in-country approximately six months. Column VII indicates the numbers of these NNSEs who achieved Criteria I.

7. At Niu Valley Intermediate (No. 3, Columns VI and VII), we have a typical example of what generally happens in those situations in which the NNSEs rapidly achieve proficiency in English in spite of the fact that no TESOL program exists in their school. Here we have two Ilocano speaking brothers who, in six months, have not only met our requirements for Criteria I, but are also "B" students in totally English-speaking classes. The boys are two years apart in age, and

have separate groups of friends, all of whom speak only English The boys told us that at home, although their parents do not speak English, the parents insist that the boys and their sister, a student at the local high school, speak English when speaking to each other. We thus have a situation in which the NNSEs are getting maximum exposure to English, in school and out, and where the parental attitude is a positive one.

8. The situation at Stevenson Intermediate (No. 5, Columns VI and VII), which deviates considerably from what we found in other schools in similar neighborhoods, is an interesting example summarizing what we discovered in all situations in which the NNSEs were failing to achieve proficiency in English.

Of the seven six-month NNSEs who failed to achieve Criteria I, two are Korean girls of the same age, who, at recess, during lunch hour, and outside the school, including the home, speak only Korean. They informed us that they attend only Korean and Japanese movies. Their exposure to English is limited to the classroom.

Four of the NNSEs in this group of seven are Cantonese-speaking girls from Hong Kong, friends, and all of approximately the same age, who also use their native tongue exclusively outside of the classroom.

The seventh student is an Ilocano speaker and the only one in the school. Although he is in a total immersion situation, the boy is an isolate and as such has chosen to withdraw completely rather than attempt to join this new culture in which he now finds himself.

9. At Central Intermediate (No. 8, Columns VI and VII), we have a situation which, for all practical purposes, is identical to that which we have described at Stevenson Intermediate, except that the NNSEs at Central did attend special TESOL classes for two periods daily; nevertheless, only one out of eight managed to achieve our Criteria I standard.

A particularly interesting thing at Central concerns the one student who did meet Criteria I. This student, and his sister who scored poorly on our tests, are Korean children one year apart in age, who first entered Hawaii at the same time, and both of whom speak Korean exclusively at home; the boy, however, is a friendly, outgoing, gregarious type, who loves sports and enjoys school, and who therefore has a strong social need to learn English. His sister, on the contrary, does not like school and her teachers report that she avoids contact with other students in the school.

10. At McKinley High School (No. 13), there are two programs designed for immigrant students: a state-supported TESOL program and a small Federally-funded Japanese bilingual program.

OBSERVATIONS AND COMMENTS

The following observations and comments are largely based upon information acquired during the oral interviews. In spite of the subjectivity of this kind of information, we feel that consideration of this data is important.

1. Those students who attained the highest degree of proficiency in the use of English in the shortest amount of time generally met all of the following criteria:

a) For all practical purposes they were totally immersed in the English languages and culture, were isolated from speakers of their native tongue, in school and out, and therefore had little or no opportunity to use their native language.
b) Outside of the classroom they associated socially primarily with English speakers.
c) The attitude of their parents was such that only English was spoken in the home, or, if the parents were not speakers of English, they insisted that their sons and daughters spoke English to each other.

2. Those students who failed to attain a high degree of proficiency in English, in spite of the fact that some had been in-country for several years, generally fit into the following categories:

a) Their exposure to English was limited to the classroom.
b) They spoke their native language in social situations, and usually had no English-speaking friends.
c) They spoke only their native tongue at home.
d) They preferred movies in their native language as opposed to English-language movies.

3. Those students who reached our Criteria I level generally strongly resented having to attend special classes in TESOL. Their attitude seemed to be that they could benefit more from attending regular classes and should be allowed to do so.

4. There seemed to be little evidence that those who had attended special TESOL classes for one, two, and sometimes three periods daily, had progressed in their acquisition of English any more than those students who had not attended special classes.

5. It appeared that those who spent two to three periods of the six-period school day in special TESOL classes were being more harmed than helped. This might be crucial when the students are getting little or no English language exposure outside of school. It might also be true that by bringing these non-English-speaking students together for extended periods of time in TESOL classes, in effect offered them an added opportunity to use their native language. Granted that the teacher could insist that only English be spoken in the TESOL classroom, but this is generally more easily said than done.

6. Many students expressed an interest in attending special classes designed to help them with their pronunciation difficulties. However, most modified this by stating that they would prefer this help in classes scheduled so that they would not interfere with their classes in the regular curriculum.

7. There was agreement among both the NNSEs interviewed and the TESOL teachers that there is a need for a special class in the area of written composition in English.

8. Some NNSEs, in spite of having been in-country four, five, and sometimes as long as eight years, still scored low in our tests, and were doing unsatisfactorily in their other academic work. Although some of these cases might be attributed to low scholastic aptitude, we strongly suspect a lack of cultural commitment on the part of many of these students, and no apparent need, at least as far as they are concerned, to attain proficiency in the use of English.

9. In the TESOL classes there was a wide range of proficiency, making it nearly impossible to group the students homogeneously. For example, a teacher starting a class with six students in September, all of whom had zero ability in oral production and could thus be taught from Chapter One, Book One, soon found the students differing widely in their ability to handle the language. This, we feel, was due to outside-TESOL-class exposure to the language as well as numerous other factors beyond the control of the teacher in the formal teaching situation.

RECOMMENDATIONS

These recommendations are those we have made to our schools in Honolulu. They are based on the conclusion we have reached that a student's exposure to the English language and culture in *real* situations is primary, and special TESOL courses secondary. We feel that unless the immigrant student makes a commitment to join this new culture in which he now lives, he will never attain a very high degree of proficiency in his use of the English language regardless of how many hours of TESOL courses we make him suffer through. He does not have to make this cultural commitment—he can easily live in Honolulu for the rest of his life speaking any one of a dozen languages—nor can we force him to make such a commitment; but we can do everything within our power to place him in situations which will allow him to do so, if he so wishes. If he decides to join, then at that time we can help him improve his English. If he decides not to join, then he has every right not to. But if we continue to place him in special classes, locking him into his minority group for a large part of his school day, then we are depriving him of the opportunity to make a fair decision.

The recommendations which follow are really very simple, and if carried out will add little or nothing to our budget; yet we are confident they will accomplish our purpose better than anything we have tried so far:

1. Maximize the immigrant student's total in-school exposure to the English language and culture, and minimize English language teaching in formal TESOL classes.

2. Provide the student with the opportunity to internalize the value system of the American culture by exposing him to that culture through numerous field trips. We agree with J. R. Gladstone who wrote: "A child is not Canadian because he speaks English, rather he speaks English because he is Canadian . . . a basic problem [is] getting the non-English speaking child to identify himself with the new value system . . . "[2] These trips need not be elaborate affairs, simply to places representative of the American culture, such as gas stations, supermarkets, neighborhood stores, banks, police and fire stations, walks through different residential areas, or even visits to private homes.

3. Brief the regular classroom teachers, making them aware of certain facts; for example, anyone learning to speak a foreign language after the age of puberty is very likely to have a "foreign accent" which he never may be able to eliminate. Thus the teachers should not be too hasty to recommend that a particular student be assigned to special classes because he "speaks funny." The teachers should also be made aware that only the exceptional student will attain fluency in English in less than two years, regardless of what we do to help him, and thus they should refrain from using the TESOL

---

[2]J. R. Gladstone, "An Experimental Approach to the Teaching of English as a Second Language," *English Language Teaching*, 21, No. 3 (1967), 229-34.

classes as a dumping ground for students whom they fear they can not teach.

4. In the regular school curriculum, enroll the newly-arrived immigrant students in the upper ability level classes, at least for their first semester, rather than placing them with the slow learners. The intention is *not* for the immigrant student to have to compete academically with the brighter students, but rather to expose him to better models, models who would not only tend to use "better" English, but even more important, models who would be more apt to be sensitive to the immigrant student's needs, and who would be less likely to tease and taunt the newcomer.

5. Organize a "buddy" system wherein the more able student, on a one-to-one basis, takes the foreign student in hand, especially during his initial stages in-country. This should include tutoring, showing the student around campus, introducing him to friends, teaching him new games.

6. Assign newly-arrived immigrant students to a minimal academic load during their first semester in-country, and assign them to more courses in nonacademic areas such as music, arts and crafts, and physical education.

7. Assign no immigrant students to daily sessions in a language laboratory. They are literally living in a language laboratory. It is all around them: radio, television, movies, the people on the street and in the stores. Help them to take advantage of it.

8. Beginning TESOL courses should only be for new arrivals. These classes should be restricted to no more than one period daily and, if possible, they should be so scheduled that they do not take the place of regularly assigned classes. The students should be allowed to "graduate" from the TESOL classes as soon as they reach Criteria I. They must have a goal: To get out of the special class as soon as possible and into the mainstream.

9. Offer *elective* courses in pronunciation and composition for those who have reached Criteria I.

10. Explore means by which we can increase the student's exposure to and use of English in situations outside of school (i.e., socially and in the home).

It is possible that the recommendations we have made here are applicable elsewhere. We do not know. The critical factor appears to be one of numbers, and considering the large, concentrated populations of non-English-speaking groups found on the mainland, it may be that the recommendations would be impossible to implement.

To help avoid the pitfalls of attempting to design and implement a program based upon assumptions without proof, we conducted this study. We make no claim to having discovered the ultimate answer to our problem, but we are confident that the conclusions we have reached and the recommendations we have made are more right than wrong.

PART VI: DISCUSSION QUESTIONS

1. How would you characterize the differences between a foreign language program, a second language program, and a bilingual education program? Must these differences be maintained or might a single basic model be extended to cover all three situations?

2. Middle-class, English-speaking children in Montreal, schooled for their early years entirely in French, are reported not to have suffered in educational achievement—a fact noted by both Spolsky and Stern. On the other hand, some minority group children, similarly deprived of their home language and schooled in another language have not always fared as well, e.g., Spanish-speaking, or native American children in the Southwestern United States. Discuss probable reasons for these differences in achievement. Consider the possibility of different roles for the respective mother tongues in the communities, different values represented by the various language systems, and differing motivations and attitudes that may be operating.

3. Why might bilingual education be a more successful method of generating second language learning than more formal and more conventional classroom approaches to foreign language education? (Refer to Oller in Part I and Tucker and Lambert in Part V.)

4. Spolsky notes that some ESL programs have been described as "arrogant linguistic imperialism." Stern notes that in Canada some policies designed to promote bilingualism have been interpreted as attempting to erode the position of certain languages. What are some possible motivations for such arguments? What would you consider to be key ingredients to fair language policies? Discuss this in terms of specific multilingual communities you are familiar with.

5. To what degree do you think school problems of non-English-speaking students are language-centered? What about students of a different dialect background? What other factors need consideration? Discuss these questions in light of the observations made by Dykstra and Nunes on the importance of individualizing instruction.

6. How would you distinguish between bilingualism and biculturalism? Does one necessarily entail the other?

7. "The possibility of maintenance [of a nonstandard dialect] for cultural purposes is presumably available, but it is unlikely to be chosen simply because the nonstandard dialect is generally not regarded as a valuable culture transmitter" (Spolsky, p. 272). What defines a "nonstandard dialect"? Consider linguistic features; the social status of the people who speak it; the circumstances under which it is learned; and any other factors you think are relevant. Do you know of any features of a "standard dialect" which would be considered "nonstandard" in other dialects of English, or at other periods in time? What does this suggest about the nature of standard dialects?

8. If you were asked to draw up a profile of the learner most likely to benefit from a TESOL class or a foreign language course, how would you characterize him? Refer to Macnamara, Kennedy, Gardner, and Hale and Budar.

9. Do you think that the recommendations made by Hale and Budar transfer directly to learner groups in other communities? What differences between the communities might be important?

INDEX